ARIZONA TRAILS
SOUTH REGION

Printed in the United States of America

Cover photos
Clockwise from bottom left: Mexican Border Road, Ajo Mountain Drive, Puerto Blanco Drive

Rear cover photos
From left: El Camino del Diablo Trail, Cipriano Pass Trail

ARIZONA TRAILS
SOUTH REGION

PETER MASSEY
JEANNE WILSON
ANGELA TITUS

ADLER
PUBLISHING

Acknowledgements

Many people and organizations have made major contributions to the research and production of this book.

Cover Design Concept: **Rudy Ramos**
Text Design and Maps: **Deborah Rust Design**
Copyediting and Proofreading: **Alice Levine, Jody Berman, and Sallie Greenwood**

We would also like to thank Alfredo L. Casillas, public information officer at the United States Border Patrol, Yuma, for guidelines on encounters with undocumented aliens; Joanne Scruggs, Interagency Office in Phoenix, for assistance with trails and attractions on BLM land; Paul O'Donoghue for assistance with historical research; Staff at many offices of the U.S. Forest Service also provided us with valuable assistance.

Publisher's Note: Every effort has been taken to ensure that the information in this book is accurate at press time. Please visit our website to advise us of any changes or corrections you find. We also welcome recommendations for new trails or other suggestions to improve the information in this book.

Adler Publishing Company, Inc.
1601 Pacific Coast Highway, Suite 290
Hermosa Beach, CA 90254
Phone: 310-698-0706
Toll-free: 800-660-5107
Fax: 310-698-0709
www.4WDbooks.com

Contents

Before You Go		**7**
South Regional Map		**26**
Trail #1:	Tinajas Altas Pass Trail	30
Trail #2:	Fortuna Mine Trail	37
Trail #3:	El Camino del Diablo Trail	45
Trail #4:	Cipriano Pass Trail	58
Trail #5:	Christmas Pass Trail	63
Trail #6:	Puerto Blanco Drive	69
Trail #7:	Ajo Mountain Drive	75
Trail #8:	Parker Canyon Lake Road	79
Trail #9:	Canelo Hills Trail	85
Trail #10:	Blacktail Ridge Trail	89
Trail #11:	Sunnyside Trail	92
Trail #12:	Mexican Border Road	97
Trail #13:	Harshaw Road	110
Trail #14:	Flux Canyon Trail	115
Trail #15:	Cumero Canyon–Three R Canyon Trail	119
Trail #16:	Temporal Gulch Trail	124
Trail #17:	Carr Canyon Trail	129
Trail #18:	Mule Mountains Trail	131
Trail #19:	Tex Canyon Trail	136
Trail #20:	Pinery Canyon Trail	142
Trail #21:	Hands Pass Trail	148
Trail #22:	Pine Canyon Trail	156
Trail #23:	Barfoot Park Trail	162

Trail #24: Swift Trail   165

Trail #25: Tripp Canyon Road   171

Trail #26: Willow Springs Road   174

Trail #27: Oracle Control Road   181

Trail #28: Catalina Ridge Trail   188

Trail #29: Copper Creek Mining District Trail   192

Trail #30: Sibley Mansion and Bluebird Mine Trail   199

Trail #31: Redington Road   204

Trail #32: Buehman Canyon Trail   210

Trail #33: Jackson Cabin Trail   214

Selected Further Reading   **220**

Before You Go

Why a 4WD Does It Better

The design and engineering of 4WD vehicles provide them with many advantages over normal cars when you head off the paved road:

■ improved distribution of power to all four wheels;

■ a transmission transfer case, which provides low-range gear selection for greater pulling power and for crawling over difficult terrain;

■ high ground clearance;

■ less overhang of the vehicle's body past the wheels, which provides better front and rear clearance when crossing gullies and ridges;

■ large-lug, wide-tread tires;

■ rugged construction (including underbody skid plates on many models).

If you plan to do off-highway touring, all of these considerations are important, whether you are evaluating the capabilities of your current 4WD or are looking to buy one; each is considered in detail in this chapter.

In order to explore the most difficult trails described in this book, you will need a 4WD vehicle that is well rated in each of the above features. If you own a 2WD sport utility vehicle, a lighter car-type SUV, or a 2WD pickup truck, your ability to explore the more difficult trails will depend on conditions and your level of experience.

A word of caution: Whatever type of 4WD vehicle you drive, understand that it is not invincible or indestructible. Nor can it go everywhere. A 4WD has a much higher center of gravity and weighs more than a car, and so has its own consequent limitations.

Experience is the only way to learn what your vehicle can and cannot do. Therefore, if you are inexperienced, we strongly recommend that you start with trails that have lower difficulty ratings. As you develop an understanding of your vehicle and of your own taste for adventure, you can safely tackle the more challenging trails.

One way to beef up your knowledge quickly, while avoiding the costly and sometimes dangerous lessons learned from on-the-road mistakes, is to undertake a 4WD course taught by a professional. Look in the Yellow Pages for courses in your area.

Using This Book

Route Planning

The regional map on pages 26 to 29 provides a convenient overview of the trails in the southern portion of the state. Each 4WD trail is shown, as are major highways and towns, helping you to plan various routes by connecting a series of 4WD trails and paved roads.

As you plan your overall route, you will probably want to utilize as many 4WD trails as possible. However, check the difficulty rating and time required for each trail before finalizing your plans. You don't want to be stuck 50 miles from the highway—at sunset and without camping gear, since your trip was supposed to be over hours ago—when you discover that your vehicle can't handle a certain difficult passage.

Difficulty Ratings

We utilize a point system to provide a guide rating the difficulty of each trail. Any such system is subjective, and your experience of the trails will vary depending on your skill and the road conditions at the time. Indeed, particularly in Arizona, any amount of rain makes the trails much more difficult, if not completely impassable.

We have rated the 4WD trails on a scale of 1 to 10—1 being passable for a normal passenger vehicle in good conditions and 10 requiring a heavily modified vehicle and an experienced driver who expects to encounter vehicle damage. Because this book is designed for owners of unmodified 4WD vehicles—who we assume do not want to damage their vehicles—most of the trails are rated 5 or lower. A few trails are included that rate as high as 7, while those rated 8 to 10 are beyond the scope of this book.

This is not to say that the moderate-rated trails are easy. We strongly recommend that inexperienced drivers not tackle trails rated at 4 or higher until they have undertaken a number of the lower-rated ones, so that they can gauge their skill level and prepare for the difficulty of the higher-rated trails.

In assessing the trails, we have always assumed good road conditions (dry road surface, good visibility, and so on). The factors influencing our ratings are as follows:

■ obstacles such as rocks, mud, ruts, sand, slickrock, and stream crossings;

■ the stability of the road surface;

■ the width of the road and the vehicle

clearance between trees or rocks;

■ the steepness of the road;

■ the margin for driver error (for example, a very high, open shelf road would be rated more difficult even if it was not very steep and had a stable surface).

The following is a guide to the ratings.

Rating 1: The trail is graded dirt but suitable for a normal passenger vehicle. It usually has gentle grades, is fairly wide, and has very shallow water crossings (if any).

Rating 2: High-clearance vehicles are preferred but not necessary. These trails are dirt roads, but they may have rocks, grades, water crossings, or ruts that make clearance a concern in a normal passenger vehicle. The trails are fairly wide, so that passing is not a concern, and mud is not a concern under normal weather conditions.

Rating 3: High-clearance 4WDs are preferred, but any high-clearance vehicle is acceptable. Expect a rough road surface; mud and sand are possible but will be easily passable. You may encounter rocks up to 6 inches in diameter, a loose road surface, and shelf roads, though these will be wide enough for passing or will have adequate pull-offs.

Rating 4: High-clearance 4WDs are recommended, though most stock SUVs are acceptable. Expect a rough road surface with rocks larger than 6 inches, but there will be a reasonable driving line available. Patches of mud are possible but can be readily negotiated; sand may be deep and require lower tire pressures. There may be stream crossings up to 12 inches deep, substantial sections of single-lane shelf road, moderate grades, and sections of moderately loose road surface.

Rating 5: High-clearance 4WDs are required. These trails have a rough, rutted surface, rocks up to 9 inches, mud and deep sand that may be impassable for inexperienced drivers, and stream crossings up to 18 inches deep. Certain sections may be steep enough to cause traction problems, and you may encounter very narrow shelf roads with steep drop-offs and tight clearance between rocks or trees.

Rating 6: These trails are for experienced four-wheel drivers only. They are potentially dangerous, with large rocks, ruts, or terraces that may need to be negotiated. They may also have stream crossings at least 18 inches deep, involve rapid currents, unstable stream bottoms, or difficult access; steep slopes, loose surfaces, and narrow clearances; and very narrow shelf roads with steep drop-offs and possibly challenging road surfaces.

Rating 7: Skilled, experienced four-wheel drivers only. These trails include very challenging sections with extremely steep grades, loose surfaces, large rocks, deep ruts, and/or tight clearances. Mud or sand may necessitate winching.

Rating 8 and above: Stock vehicles are likely to be damaged and may find the trail impassable. Highly-skilled, experienced four-wheel drivers only.

Scenic Ratings

If rating the degree of difficulty is subjective, rating scenic beauty is guaranteed to lead to arguments. Arizona contains a spectacular variety of scenery—from its grand canyons and towering mountains and buttes to its seemingly endless desert country. We love the wide-open remoteness of many areas of Arizona, but realize they are not to everyone's liking. Nonetheless, we have tried to provide some guide to the relative scenic quality of the various trails. The ratings are based on a scale of 1 to 10.

Remoteness Ratings

Many of the trails in Arizona are in remote country; sometimes the trails are seldom traveled, and the likelihood is low that another vehicle will appear within a reasonable time to assist you if you get stuck or break down. We have included a ranking for remoteness of +0 through +2. Summer temperatures can make a breakdown in the more remote areas a life-threatening experience. Prepare carefully before tackling the higher-rated, more remote trails (see Special Preparations for Remote Travel, page 12). For trails with a high remoteness rating, con-

sider traveling with a second vehicle.

Estimated Driving Times

In calculating driving times, we have not allowed for stops. Your actual driving time may be considerably longer depending on the number and duration of the stops you make. Add more time if you prefer to drive more slowly than good conditions allow.

Current Road Information

All the 4WD trails described in this book may become impassable in poor weather conditions. Storms can alter roads, remove tracks, and create impassable washes. Most of the trails described, even easy 2WD trails, can quickly become impassable even to 4WD vehicles after only a small amount of rain. For each trail, we have provided a phone number for obtaining current information about conditions.

Abbreviations

The route directions for the 4WD trails use a series of abbreviations as follows:

SO	CONTINUE STRAIGHT ON
TL	TURN LEFT
TR	TURN RIGHT
BL	BEAR LEFT
BR	BEAR RIGHT
UT	U-TURN

Using Route Directions

For every trail, we describe and pinpoint (by odometer reading) nearly every significant feature along the route—such as intersections, streams, washes, gates, cattle guards, and so on—and provide directions from these landmarks. Odometer readings will vary from vehicle to vehicle, so you should allow for slight variations. Be aware that trails can quickly change in the desert. A new trail may be cut around a washout, a faint trail can be graded by the county, or a well-used trail may fall into disuse. All these factors will affect the accuracy of the given directions.

If you diverge from the route, zero your trip meter upon your return and continue along the route, making the necessary adjustment to the point-to-point odometer readings. In the directions, we regularly reset the odometer readings—at significant landmarks or popular lookouts and spur trails—so that you won't have to recalculate for too long.

Most of the trails can be started from either end, and the route directions include both directions of travel; reverse directions are printed in green below the main directions. When traveling in reverse, read from the bottom of the table and work up.

Route directions include cross-references whenever two 4WD trails included in this book connect; this allows for an easy change of route or destination.

Each trail includes periodic latitude and longitude readings to facilitate using a global positioning system (GPS) receiver. These readings may also assist you in finding your location on the maps. The GPS coordinates were taken using the NAD 1927 datum and are in the format dd°mm.mm'. When loading coordinates into your GPS receiver, you may wish to include only one decimal place, since in Arizona, the third decimal place equals only about 2 yards and the second less than 20 yards.

Map References

We recommend that you supplement the information in this book with more-detailed maps. For each trail, we list the sheet maps and road atlases that provide the best detail for the area. Typically, the following references are given:

- Bureau of Land Management Maps,
- U.S. Forest Service Maps,
- Arizona Road & Recreation Atlas, 5th ed. (Medford, Oregon: Benchmark Maps, 1998)—Scale 1:400,000,
- *Arizona Atlas & Gazetteer*, 6th ed. (Freeport, Maine: DeLorme Mapping, 2004)—Scale 1:250,000,
- Maptech-Terrain Navigator Topo Maps —Scale 1:100,000 and 1:24,000,
- *Trails Illustrated* Topo Maps; National Geographic Maps—Various scales, but all contain good detail,
- Recreational Map of Arizona (Canon City, Colorado: GTR Mapping, 2006)—

Scale: 1 inch=12.5 miles.

We recommend the *Trails Illustrated* series of maps as the best for navigating these trails. They are reliable, easy to read, and printed on nearly indestructible plastic paper. However, the series does not cover many of the 4WD trails described in this book.

The DeLorme atlas is useful and has the advantage of providing you with maps of the entire state at a reasonable price. While its 4WD trail information doesn't go beyond what we provide, it is useful if you wish to explore the hundreds of side roads.

The *Arizona Road & Recreation Atlas* provides two types of maps for each part of the state. The landscape maps show changes in terrain and elevation while the public lands maps show what organizations control what lands. Aside from the maps, the atlas also provides a good recreation guide with a number of local contacts for different recreation opportunities.

U.S. Forest Service maps lack the topographic detail of the other sheet maps and, in our experience, are also out of date occasionally. They have the advantage of covering a broad area and are useful in identifying land use and travel restrictions. These maps are most useful for the longer trails.

In our opinion, the best single option by far is the Terrain Navigator series of maps published on CD-ROM by Maptech. These CD-ROMs contain an amazing level of detail because they include the entire set of 1,524 U.S. Geological Survey topographical maps of Utah at the 1:24,000 scale and all 59 maps at the 1:100,000 scale. These maps offer many advantages over normal maps:

- GPS coordinates for any location can be found, which can then be loaded into your GPS receiver. Conversely, if you have your GPS coordinates, your location on the map can be pinpointed instantly.
- Towns, rivers, passes, mountains, and many other sites are indexed by name so that they can be located quickly.
- 4WD trails can be marked and profiled for elevation change and distance from point to point.
- Customized maps can be printed out.

Maptech uses eight CD-ROMs to cover the entire state of Arizona, but the CD-ROMs can be purchased individually. The CD-ROMs can be used with a laptop computer and a GPS receiver in your vehicle to monitor your location on the map and navigate directly from the display.

Cheaper CD-ROM topographic maps are published, but none that we know of compare with the Maptech series. DeLorme publishes an alternative series entitled *TopoUSA* that is modestly priced, especially considering that it covers the entire country. However, the level of topographical detail available on-screen bears no comparison to the Maptech series—which comes as no surprise when you find there are only six CD-ROMs in the entire set.

All these maps should be available through good map stores. The Maptech CD-ROMs are available directly from the company (800-627-7236, or on the internet at www.maptech.com).

Backcountry Driving Rules and Permits

Four-wheel driving involves special driving techniques and road rules. This section is an introduction for 4WD beginners.

4WD Road Rules

To help ensure that these trails remain open and available for all four-wheel drivers to enjoy, it is important to minimize your impact on the environment and not be a safety risk to yourself or anyone else. Remember that the 4WD clubs in Arizona fight a constant battle with the U.S. Forest Service (USFS) and the Bureau of Land Management (BLM) to retain the access that currently exists.

The fundamental rule when traversing the 4WD trails described in this book is to use common sense. In addition, special road rules for 4WD trails apply:
■ Vehicles traveling uphill have the right of way.
■ If you are moving more slowly than the vehicle behind you, pull over to let the other

vehicle by.
■ Park out of the way in a safe place. Blocking a track may restrict access for emergency vehicles as well as for other recreationalists. Set the parking brake—don't rely on leaving the transmission in park. Manual transmissions should be left in the lowest gear.

Tread Lightly!

Remember the rules of the Tread Lightly! program:
■ Be informed. Obtain maps, regulations, and other information from the forest service or from other public land agencies. Learn the rules and follow them.
■ Resist the urge to pioneer a new road or trail or to cut across a switchback. Stay on constructed tracks and avoid running over young trees, shrubs, and grasses, damaging or killing them.
■ Stay off soft, wet roads and 4WD trails readily torn up by vehicles. Repairing the damage is expensive, and quite often authorities find it easier to close the road rather than repair it.
■ Travel around meadows, steep hillsides, stream banks, and lake shores that are easily scarred by churning wheels.
■ Stay away from wild animals that are rearing young or suffering from a food shortage. Do not camp close to the water sources of domestic or wild animals.
■ Obey gate closures and regulatory signs.
■ Preserve America's heritage by not disturbing old mining camps, ghost towns, or other historical features. Leave historic sites, Native American rock art, ruins, and artifacts in place and untouched.
■ Carry out all your trash, and even that of others.
■ Stay out of designated wilderness areas. They are closed to all vehicles. It is your responsibility to know where the boundaries are.
■ Get permission to cross private land. Leave livestock alone. Respect landowners' rights.

Report violations of these rules to help keep these 4WD trails open and to ensure that others will have the opportunity to visit these backcountry sites. Many groups are actively seeking to close these public lands to vehicles, thereby denying access to those who are unable, or perhaps merely unwilling, to hike long distances. This magnificent countryside is owned by, and should be available to, all Americans.

Special Preparations for Remote Travel

Due to the remoteness of some areas in Arizona and the very high summer temperatures, you should take some special precautions to ensure that you don't end up in a life-threatening situation:

■ When planning a trip into the desert, always inform someone as to where you are going, your route, and when you expect to return. Stick to your plan.

■ Carry and drink at least one gallon of water per person per day of your trip. (Plastic gallon jugs are handy and portable.)

■ Be sure your vehicle is in good condition with a sound battery, good hoses, spare tire, spare fan belts, necessary tools, and reserve gasoline and oil. Other spare parts and extra radiator water are also valuable. If traveling in pairs, share the common spares and carry a greater variety.

■ Keep an eye on the sky. Flash floods can occur in a wash any time you see thunderheads—even when it's not raining a drop where you are.

■ If you are caught in a dust storm while driving, get off the road and turn off your lights. Turn on the emergency flashers and back into the wind to reduce windshield pitting by sand particles.

■ Test trails on foot before driving through washes and sandy areas. One minute of walking may save hours of hard work getting your vehicle unstuck.

■ If your vehicle breaks down, stay near it. Your emergency supplies are there. Your car has many other items useful in an emergency. Raise your hood and trunk lid to denote "help needed." Remember, a vehicle can be seen for miles, but a person on foot is very difficult to spot from a distance.

■ When you're not moving, use available shade or erect shade from tarps, blankets, or seat covers—anything to reduce the direct rays of the sun.

■ Do not sit or lie directly on the ground. It may be 30 degrees hotter than the air.

■ Leave a disabled vehicle only if you are positive of the route and the distance to help. Leave a note for rescuers that gives the time you left and the direction you are taking.

■ If you must walk, rest for at least 10 minutes out of each hour. If you are not normally physically active, rest up to 30 minutes out of each hour. Find shade, sit down, and prop up your feet. Adjust your shoes and socks, but do not remove your shoes—you may not be able to get them back on swollen feet.

■ If you have water, drink it. Do not ration it.

■ If water is limited, keep your mouth closed. Do not talk, eat, smoke, drink alcohol, or take salt.

■ Keep your clothing on, despite the heat. It helps to keep the body temperature down and reduces your dehydration rate. Cover your head. If you don't have a hat, improvise a head covering.

■ If you are stalled or lost, set signal fires. Set smoky fires in the daytime and bright ones at night. Three fires in a triangle denote "help needed."

■ A roadway is a sign of civilization. If you find a road, stay on it.

■ If hiking in the desert, equip each person, especially children, with a police-type whistle. It makes a distinctive noise with little effort. Three blasts denote "help needed."

■ To avoid poisonous creatures, put your hands or feet only where your eyes can see. One insect to be aware of in western Arizona is the Africanized honeybee. Though indistinguishable from its European counterpart, these bees are far more aggressive and can be a threat. They have been known to give chase of up to a mile and even wait for people who have escaped into the water to come up for air. The best thing to do if attacked is to cover your face and head with clothing and run to the nearest enclosed shelter. Keep an eye on your pet if you notice a number of bees in the area, as many have been killed by Africanized honeybees.

■ Avoid unnecessary contact with wildlife. Some mice in Arizona carry the deadly hantavirus, a pulmonary syndrome fatal in 60 to 70 percent of human cases. Fortunately the disease is very rare—by September 2006, only 49 cases had been reported in Arizona and 453 nation-wide—but caution is still advised. Other rodents may transmit bubonic plague, the same epidemic that killed one-third of Europe's population in the 1300s. Be especially wary near sick animals and keep pets, especially cats, away from wildlife and their fleas. Another creature to watch for is the western black-legged tick, the carrier of Lyme disease. Wearing clothing that covers legs and arms, tucking pants into boots, and using insect repellent are good ways to avoid fleas and ticks.

Special Note on Travel Near the Mexican Border

Arizona's southern border forms part of the international boundary with Mexico. This location can bring with it its own unique set of potential situations that the intrepid traveler may encounter. Every month, thousands of undocumented immigrants attempt to gain unauthorized entry into the United States from Mexico. It is estimated that approximately 70 percent of all border jumpers will be apprehended and returned to Mexico immediately.

What does this mean for you? Any re-mote area traveler who spends any time at all in the deserts near the border is highly likely to encounter undocumented aliens. First and foremost, it should be stressed that the majority of meetings pose ab-solutely no threat to the traveler at all. You are most likely to meet people just like you who want little more than food and water before they move on and leave you alone. However, many people find these meetings worrisome and upsetting, and some even feel threatened.

It is suggested that travelers adopt the following guidelines compiled from advice given by the U.S. Border Patrol:

■ If possible, avoid all contact with sus-pected undocumented alien activity. Do not go out of your way to offer unsolicited assistance.

■ If it is impossible to avoid contact—for example, if you are approached and asked for help—then stop. Remain in your vehicle. Most of the time you will be asked for food and water. Give them what you can safely spare without depleting your own supplies and move on as soon as possible. This is not regarded by the border patrol as aiding and abetting; it is humanitarian aid and you may be saving another human being's life. Many people die each year try-ing to cross the desert.

■ Do not give anyone a lift in your vehi-cle unless you can see it is a life-threatening situation.

■ As soon as is practical, notify the bor-der patrol or sheriff's department of the location, number, and physical condition of the group so that they can be apprehended as soon as possible. Be as specific as you can; GPS coordinates are extremely useful. Again, by doing this you may be saving someone's life.

■ Do not attempt to engage people in conversation and avoid giving exact dis-tances to the nearest town. Many undocu-mented aliens arrive in the United States by paying a "coyote" to bring them safely across the border. They are often deliberate-ly misled and woefully unprepared for the desert conditions they encounter and the distances they will have to travel to safety. Giving exact distances, especially if it is many miles away, is putting yourself and your vehicle at risk. Carjackings are *extremely rare,* but the possibility should not be discounted.

■ Be extremely wary of groups traveling in vehicles, as these are the professionals who smuggle both humans and drugs. However, fewer than 5 percent of encoun-ters are with smugglers; most are with indi-viduals or groups after the "coyotes" have dropped them off.

■ If you are traveling exceptionally remote routes in areas of high activity, consider traveling as part of a large group. Individual vehicles and small groups stand a higher chance of being approached.

■ Always lock your vehicle when you leave it, even for a short period of time, and carry as few valuables as possible.

■ The distance from the border is not the determining factor in how likely you are to have an encounter.

■ Finally, do not let this be a deterrent to exploring the wonderful trails to be found in the South Coast Region. Be alert and aware but not paranoid. Many thousands of recreationalists travel these trails every year with very little danger to themselves or their vehicles.

Obtaining Permits

Backcountry permits, which usually cost a fee, are often required for certain activities on public lands in Arizona, whether the area is a national park, state park, national monument, Indian reservation, or BLM land.

Restrictions may require a permit for all overnight stays, which can include backpacking and 4WD or bicycle camping. Permits may also be required for day use by vehicles, horses, hikers, or bikes in some areas.

When possible, we include information about fees and permit requirements and where permits may be obtained, but these regulations change constantly. If in doubt, check with the most likely governing agency.

Assessing Your Vehicle's Off-Road Ability

Many issues come into play when evaluating your 4WD vehicle, though most of the 4WDs on the market are suitable for even the roughest trails described in this book. Engine power will be adequate in even the least powerful modern vehicle. However, some vehicles are less suited to off-highway driving than others, and some of the newest, carlike sport utility vehicles (SUVs) simply are not designed for off-highway touring. The following information should

allow you to identify the good, the bad, and the ugly.

Differing 4WD Systems

All 4WD systems have one thing in common: The engine provides power to all four wheels rather than to only two, as is typical in most standard cars. However, there are a number of differences in the way power is applied to the wheels.

The other feature that distinguishes nearly all 4WDs from normal passenger vehicles is that the gearboxes have high and low ratios that effectively double the number of gears. The high range is comparable to the range on a passenger car. The low range provides lower speed and more power, which is useful when towing heavy loads, driving up steep hills, or crawling over rocks. When driving downhill, the 4WD's low range increases engine braking.

Various makes and models of SUVs offer different drive systems, but these differences center on two issues: the way power is applied to the other wheels if one or more wheels slip, and the ability to select between 2WD and 4WD.

Normal driving requires that all four wheels be able to turn at different speeds; this allows the vehicle to turn without scrubbing its tires. In a 2WD vehicle, the front wheels (or rear wheels in a front-wheel-drive vehicle) are not powered by the engine and thus are free to turn individually at any speed. The rear wheels, powered by the engine, are only able to turn at different speeds because of the differential, which applies power to the faster-turning wheel.

This standard method of applying traction has certain weaknesses. First, when power is applied to only one set of wheels, the other set cannot help the vehicle gain traction. Second, when one powered wheel loses traction, it spins, but the other powered wheel doesn't turn. This happens because the differential applies all the engine power to the faster-turning wheel and no power to the other wheels, which still have traction. All 4WD systems are designed to overcome these two weaknesses. However, different 4WDs address this common objective in different ways.

Full-Time 4WD. For a vehicle to remain in 4WD all the time without scrubbing the tires, all the wheels must be able to rotate at different speeds. A full-time 4WD system allows this to happen by using three differentials. One is located between the rear wheels, as in a normal passenger car, to allow the rear wheels to rotate at different speeds. The second is located between the front wheels in exactly the same way. The third differential is located between the front and rear wheels to allow different rotational speeds between the front and rear sets of wheels. In nearly all vehicles with full-time 4WD, the center differential operates only in high range. In low range, it is completely locked. This is not a disadvantage because when using low range the additional traction is normally desired and the deterioration of steering response will be less noticeable due to the vehicle traveling at a slower speed.

Part-Time 4WD. A part-time 4WD system does not have the center differential located between the front and rear wheels. Consequently, the front and rear drive shafts are both driven at the same speed and with the same power at all times when in 4WD.

This system provides improved traction because when one or both of the front or rear wheels slips, the engine continues to provide power to the other set. However, because such a system doesn't allow a difference in speed between the front and rear sets of wheels, the tires scrub when turning, placing additional strain on the whole drive system. Therefore, such a system can be used only in slippery conditions; otherwise, the ability to steer the vehicle will deteriorate and the tires will quickly wear out.

Some vehicles, such as Jeeps with Selectrac and Mitsubishi Monteros with Active Trac 4WD offer both full-time and part-time 4WD in high range.

Manual Systems to Switch Between 2WD and 4WD. There are three manual systems for switching between 2WD and 4WD. The most basic requires stopping and getting out of the vehicle to lock the front hubs manually before selecting 4WD. The second requires you to stop, but you change to 4WD by merely throwing a lever inside the vehicle (the hubs lock automatically). The third allows shifting between 2WD and 4WD high range while the vehicle is moving. Any 4WD that does not offer the option of driving in 2WD must have a full-time 4WD system.

Automated Switching Between 2WD and 4WD. Advances in technology are leading to greater automation in the selection of two- or four-wheel drive. When operating in high range, these high-tech systems use sensors to monitor the rotation of each wheel. When any slippage is detected, the vehicle switches the proportion of power from the wheel(s) that is slipping to the wheels that retain grip. The proportion of power supplied to each wheel is therefore infinitely variable as opposed to the original systems where the vehicle was either in two-wheel drive or four-wheel drive.

In recent years, this process has been spurred on by many of the manufacturers of luxury vehicles entering the SUV market—Mercedes, BMW, Cadillac, Lincoln, and Lexus have joined Range Rover in this segment.

Manufacturers of these higher-priced vehicles have led the way in introducing sophisticated computer-controlled 4WD systems. Although each of the manufacturers has its own approach to this issue, all the systems automatically vary the allocation of power between the wheels within milliseconds of the sensors' detecting wheel slippage.

Limiting Wheel Slippage

4WDs employ various systems to limit wheel slippage and transfer power to the wheels that still have traction. These systems may completely lock the differentials, or they may allow limited slippage before transferring power back to the wheels that retain traction.

Lockers completely eliminate the operation of one or more differentials. A locker on the center differential switches between full-time and part-time 4WD. Lockers on the front or rear differentials ensure that power remains equally applied to each set of wheels regardless of whether both have traction. Lockers may be controlled manually by a switch or lever in the vehicle, or they may be automatic.

The Toyota Land Cruiser offers the option of having manual lockers on all three differentials, while other brands such as the Mitsubishi Montero offer manual locks on the center and rear differential. Manual lockers are the most controllable and effective devices for ensuring that power is provided to the wheels with traction. However, because they allow absolutely no slippage, they must be used only on slippery surfaces.

An alternative method for getting power to the wheels that have traction is to allow limited wheel slippage. Systems that work this way may be called limited-slip differentials, posi-traction systems, or in the center differential, viscous couplings. The advantage of these systems is that the limited difference they allow in rotational speed between wheels enables such systems to be used when driving on a dry surface. All full-time 4WD systems allow limited slippage in the center differential.

For off-highway use, a manually locking differential is the best of the above systems, but it is the most expensive. Limited-slip differentials are the cheapest but also the least satisfactory, as they require one wheel to be slipping at two to three mph before power is transferred to the other wheel. For the center differential, the best system combines a locking differential and, to enable full-time use, a viscous coupling.

Tires

The tires that came with your 4WD vehicle may be satisfactory, but many 4WDs are fitted with passenger-car tires. These are unlikely to be the best choice because they are less rugged and more likely to puncture on rocky trails. They are particularly prone to sidewall damage. Passenger vehicle tires also have a less aggressive tread pattern than specialized 4WD tires, providing less traction in mud.

For information on purchasing tires better suited to off-highway conditions, see Special 4WD Equipment on page 21.

Clearance

Road clearances vary considerably among different 4WD vehicles—from less than 7 inches to more than 10 inches. Special vehicles may have far greater clearance. For instance, the Hummer has 16-inch ground clearance. High ground clearance is particularly advantageous on the rockier or more rutted 4WD trails in this book.

When evaluating the ground clearance of your vehicle, you need to take into account the clearance of the body work between the wheels on each side of the vehicle. This is particularly relevant for crawling over larger rocks. Vehicles with sidesteps have significantly lower clearance than those without.

Another factor affecting clearance is the approach and departure angles of your vehicle—that is, the maximum angle the ground can slope without the front of the vehicle hitting the ridge on approach or the rear of the vehicle hitting on departure. Mounting a winch or tow hitch to your vehicle is likely to reduce your approach or departure angle.

If you do a lot of driving on rocky trails, you will inevitably hit the bottom of the vehicle sooner or later. When this happens, you will be far less likely to damage vulnerable areas such as the oil pan and gas tank if your vehicle is fitted with skid plates. Most manufacturers offer skid plates as an option. They are worth every penny.

Maneuverability

When you tackle tight switchbacks, you will quickly appreciate that maneuverability is an important criterion when assessing 4WD vehicles. Where a full-size vehicle may be forced to go back and forth a number of times to get around a sharp turn, a small 4WD might go straight around. This is not only easier, it's safer.

If you have a full-size vehicle, all is not lost. We have traveled many of the trails in this book in a Suburban. That is not to say that some of these trails wouldn't have been easier to negotiate in a smaller vehicle! We have noted in the route descriptions if a trail is not suitable for larger vehicles.

In Summary

Using the criteria above, you can evaluate how well your 4WD will handle off-road touring, and if you haven't yet purchased your vehicle, you can use these criteria to help select one. Choosing the best 4WD system is, at least partly, subjective. It is also a matter of your budget. However, for the type of off-highway driving covered in this book, we make the following recommendations:

■ Select a 4WD system that offers low range and, at a minimum, has some form of limited slip differential on the rear axle.

■ Use light truck, all-terrain tires as the standard tires on your vehicle. For sand and slickrock, these will be the ideal choice. If conditions are likely to be muddy, or traction will be improved by a tread pattern that will give more bite, consider an additional set of mud tires.

■ For maximum clearance, select a vehicle with 16-inch wheels, or at least choose the tallest tires that your vehicle can accommodate. Note that if you install tires with a diameter greater than standard, the odometer will undercalculate the distance you have traveled. Your engine braking and gear ratios will also be affected.

■ If you are going to try the rockier 4WD trails, don't install a sidestep or low hanging front bar. If you have the option, have underbody skid plates mounted.

■ Remember that many of the obstacles you encounter on backcountry trails are more difficult to navigate in a full-size vehicle than in a compact 4WD.

Four-Wheel Driving Techniques

Safe four-wheel driving requires that you observe certain golden rules:

■ Size up the situation in advance.

■ Be careful and take your time.

■ Maintain smooth, steady power and momentum.

■ Engage 4WD and low-range gears before you get into a tight situation.

■ Steer toward high spots, trying to put the wheel over large rocks.

■ Straddle ruts.

■ Use gears and not just the brakes to hold the vehicle when driving downhill. On very steep slopes, chock the wheels if you park your vehicle.

■ Watch for logging and mining trucks and smaller recreational vehicles, such as all-terrain vehicles (ATVs).

■ Wear your seat belt and secure all luggage, especially heavy items such as tool boxes or coolers. Heavy items should be secured by ratchet tie-down straps rather than elastic-type straps, which are not strong enough to hold heavy items if the vehicle rolls.

Arizona's 4WD trails have a number of common obstacles, and the following section provides an introduction to the techniques required to surmount them.

Rocks. Tire selection is important in negotiating rocks. Select a multiple-ply, tough sidewall, light-truck tire with a large-lug tread.

As you approach a rocky stretch, get into 4WD low range to give you maximum slow-speed control. Speed is rarely necessary, since traction on a rocky surface is usually good. Plan ahead and select the line you wish to take. If a rock appears to be larger than the clearance of your vehicle, don't try to straddle it. Check to see that it is not higher than the frame of your vehicle once you get a wheel over it. Put a wheel up on the rock and slowly climb it, then gently drop over the other side using the brake to ensure a smooth landing. Bouncing the car over rocks increases the likelihood of damage, as the body's clearance is reduced by the suspension compressing. Running boards also significantly reduce your clearance in this respect.

It is often helpful to use a "spotter" outside the vehicle to assist you with the best wheel placement.

Slickrock. When you encounter slickrock, first assess the correct direction of the trail. It is easy to lose sight of the trail on slickrock, as there are seldom any developed edges. Often the way is marked with small rock cairns, which are simply rocks stacked high enough to make a landmark.

All-terrain tires with tighter tread are more suited to slickrock than the more open, luggier type tires. As with rocks, a multiple-ply sidewall is important. In dry conditions, slickrock offers pavement-type grip. In rain or snow, you will soon learn how it got its name, and even the best tires may not get an adequate grip. Walk steep sections first; if you are slipping on foot, chances are your vehicle will slip too.

Slickrock is characterized by ledges and long sections of "pavement." Follow the guidelines for travel over rocks. Refrain from speeding over flat-looking sections, as you may hit an unexpected crevice or water pocket, and vehicles bend easier than slickrock! Turns and ledges can be tight, and vehicles with smaller overhangs and better maneuverability are at a distinct advantage—hence the popularity of the compacts in the slickrock mecca of Moab.

On the steepest sections, engage low range and pick a straight line up or down the slope. Do not attempt to traverse a steep slope sideways.

Steep Uphill Grades. Consider walking the trail to ensure that the steep hill before you is passable, especially if it is clear that backtracking is going to be a problem.

Select 4WD low range to ensure that you have adequate power to pull up the hill. If the wheels begin to lose traction, turn the steering wheel gently from side to side to give the wheels a chance to regain traction.

If you lose momentum, but the car is not in danger of sliding, use the foot brake, switch off the ignition, leave the vehicle in gear (if manual transmission) or park (if automatic), engage the parking brake, and get out to examine the situation. See if you can remove any obstacles, and figure out the line you need to take. Reversing a couple of yards and starting again may allow

you to get better traction and momentum.

If, halfway up, you decide a stretch of road is impassably steep, back down the trail. Trying to turn the vehicle around on a steep hill is extremely dangerous; you will very likely cause it to roll over.

Steep Downhill Grades. Again, consider walking the trail to ensure that a steep hill is passable, especially if it is clear that backtracking uphill is going to be a problem.

Select 4WD low range and use first gear to maximize braking assistance from the engine. If the surface is loose and you are losing traction, change up to second or third gear. Do not use the brakes if you can avoid it, but don't let the vehicle's speed get out of control. Feather (lightly pump) the brakes if you slip under braking. For vehicles fitted with ABS, apply even pressure if you start to slip; the ABS helps keep vehicles on line.

Travel very slowly over rock ledges or ruts. Attempt to tackle these diagonally, letting one wheel down at a time.

If the back of the vehicle begins to slide around, gently apply the throttle and correct the steering. If the rear of the vehicle starts to slide sideways, do not apply the brakes.

Mud. Muddy trails are easily damaged, so they should be avoided if possible. But if you must traverse a section of mud, your success will depend heavily on whether you have open-lugged mud tires or chains. Thick mud fills the tighter tread on normal tires, leaving the tire with no more grip than if it were bald. If the muddy stretch is only a few yards long, the momentum of your vehicle may allow you to get through regardless.

If the muddy track is very steep, uphill or downhill, or off camber, do not attempt it. Your vehicle is very likely to skid in such conditions, and you may roll or slip off the edge of the road. Also, check to see that the mud has a reasonably firm base. Tackling deep mud is definitely not recommended unless you have a vehicle-mounted winch—and even then, be cautious, because the winch may not get you out. Finally, check to see that no ruts are too deep for the ground clearance of your vehicle.

When you decide you can get through and have selected the best route, use the following techniques to cross through the mud:

■ Avoid making detours off existing tracks to minimize environmental damage.

■ Select 4WD low range and a suitable gear; momentum is the key to success, so use a high enough gear to build up sufficient speed.

■ Avoid accelerating heavily, so as to minimize wheel spinning and to provide maximum traction.

■ Follow existing wheel ruts, unless they are too deep for the clearance of your vehicle.

■ To correct slides, turn the steering wheel in the direction that the rear wheels are skidding, but don't be too aggressive or you'll overcorrect and lose control again.

■ If the vehicle comes to a stop, don't continue to accelerate, as you will only spin your wheels and dig yourself into a rut. Try backing out and having another go.

■ Be prepared to turn back before reaching the point of no return.

Stream Crossings. By crossing a stream that is too deep, drivers risk far more than water flowing in and ruining the interior of their vehicles. Water sucked into the engine's air intake will seriously damage the engine. Likewise, water that seeps into the air vent on the transmission or differential will mix with the lubricant and may lead to serious problems in due course.

Even worse, if the water is deep or fast flowing, it could easily carry your vehicle downstream, endangering the lives of everyone in the vehicle.

Some 4WD manuals tell you what fording depth the vehicle can negotiate safely. If your vehicle's owner's manual doesn't include this information, your local dealer may be able to assist. If you don't know, then avoid crossing through water that is more than a foot or so deep.

The first rule for crossing a stream is to know what you are getting into. You need to ascertain how deep the water is, whether there are any large rocks or holes, if the bottom is solid enough to avoid bogging down the vehicle, and whether the entry and exit points are negotiable. This may take some time and involve getting wet, but you take a great risk by crossing a stream without first properly assessing the situation.

The secret to water crossings is to keep moving, but not too fast. If you go too fast, you may drown the electrics, causing the vehicle to stall midstream. In shallow water (where the surface of the water is below the bumper), your primary concern is to safely negotiate the bottom of the stream, avoiding any rock damage and maintaining momentum if there is a danger of getting stuck or of slipping on the exit.

In deeper water (between 18 and 30 inches), the objective is to create a small bow wave in front of the moving vehicle. This requires a speed that is approximately walking pace. The bow wave reduces the depth of the water around the engine compartment. If the water's surface reaches your tailpipe, select a gear that will maintain moderate engine revs to avoid water backing up into the exhaust; and do not change gears midstream.

Crossing water deeper than 25 to 30 inches requires more extensive preparation of the vehicle and should be attempted only by experienced drivers.

Sand. As with most off-highway situations, your tires are the key to your ability to cross sand. It is difficult to tell how well a particular tire will handle in sand just by looking at it, so be guided by the manufacturer and your dealer.

The key to driving in soft sand is floatation, which is achieved by a combination of low tire pressure and momentum. Before crossing a stretch of sand, reduce your tire pressure to between 15 and 20 pounds. If necessary, you can safely go to as low as 12 pounds. As you cross, maintain momentum so that your vehicle rides on top of the soft sand without digging in or stalling. This may require plenty of engine power. Avoid using the brakes if possible; removing your foot from the accelerator alone is normally enough to slow or stop. Using the brakes digs the vehicle deep in the sand.

Pump the tires back up as soon as you are out of the sand to avoid damage to the tires and the rims. Pumping back up requires a high-quality air compressor. Even then, it is a slow process.

In the backcountry of Arizona, sandy conditions are commonplace. You will therefore find a good compressor most useful.

Vehicle Recovery Methods

If you do enough four-wheel driving, you are sure to get stuck sooner or later. The following techniques will help you get back on the go. The most suitable method will depend on the equipment available and the situation you are in—whether you are stuck in sand, mud, or snow, or are high-centered or unable to negotiate a hill.

Towing. Use a nylon yank strap of the type discussed in the Special 4WD Equipment section on page 21. This type of strap will stretch 15 to 25 percent, and the elasticity will assist in extracting the vehicle.

Attach the strap only to a frame-mounted tow point. Ensure that the driver of the stuck vehicle is ready, take up all but about six feet of slack, then move the towing vehicle away at a moderate speed (in most circumstances this means using 4WD low range in second gear) so that the elasticity of the strap is employed in the way it is meant to be. Don't take off like a bat out of hell or you risk breaking the strap or damaging a vehicle.

Never join two yank straps together with a shackle. If one strap breaks, the shackle will become a lethal missile aimed at one of the vehicles (and anyone inside). For the same reason, never attach a yank strap to the tow ball on either vehicle.

Jacking. Jacking the vehicle enables you to pack under the wheel (with rocks, dirt, or logs) or use your shovel to remove an obstacle. However, the standard vehicle jack is unlikely to be of as much assistance as a high-lift jack. We highly recommend purchasing a good high-lift jack as a basic accessory if you decide that you are going to do a lot of serious, off-highway four-wheel driving. Remember a high-lift jack is of limited use if your vehicle does not have an appropriate jacking point. Some brush bars have two built-in forward jacking points.

Tire Chains. Tire chains can be of assistance in both mud and snow. Cable-type chains provide much less grip than link-type chains. There are also dedicated mud chains with larger, heavier links than on normal snow chains. It is best to have chains fitted to all four wheels.

Once you are bogged down is not the best time to try to fit the chains; if at all possible, try to predict their need and have them on the tires before trouble arises. An easy way to affix chains is to place two small cubes of wood under the center of the stretched-out chain. When you drive your tires up on the blocks of wood, it is easier to stretch the chains over the tires because the pressure is off.

Winching. Most recreational four-wheel drivers do not have a winch. But if you get serious about four-wheel driving, this is probably the first major accessory you should consider buying.

Under normal circumstances, a winch would be warranted only for the more difficult 4WD trails in this book. Having a winch is certainly comforting when you see a difficult section of road ahead and have to decide whether to risk it or turn back. Also, major obstacles can appear when you least expect them, even on trails that are otherwise easy.

Owning a winch is not a panacea to all your recovery problems. Winching depends on the availability of a good anchor point, and electric winches may not work if they are submerged in a stream. Despite these constraints, no accessory is more useful than a high-quality, powerful winch when you get into a difficult situation.

If you acquire a winch, learn to use it properly; take the time to study your owner's manual. Incorrect operation can be extremely dangerous and may cause damage to the winch or to your anchor points, which are usually trees.

Navigation by the Global Positioning System (GPS)

Although this book is designed so that each trail can be navigated simply by following the detailed directions provided, nothing makes navigation easier than a GPS receiver.

The global positioning system (GPS) consists of a network of 24 satellites, nearly 13,000 miles in space, in six different orbital paths. The satellites are constantly moving at about 8,500 miles per hour, making two complete orbits around the earth every 24 hours.

Each satellite is constantly transmitting data, including its identification number, its operational health, and the date and time. It also transmits its location and the location of every other satellite in the network.

By comparing the time the signal was transmitted to the time it is received, a GPS receiver calculates how far away each satellite is. With a sufficient number of signals, the receiver can then triangulate its location. With three or more satellites, the receiver can determine latitude and longitude coordinates. With four or more, it can calculate altitude. By constantly making these calculations, it can determine speed and direction. To facilitate these calculations, the time data broadcast by GPS is accurate to within 40 billionths of a second.

The U.S. military uses the system to provide positions accurate to within half an inch. When the system was first established, civilian receivers were deliberately fed slightly erroneous information in order to effectively deny military applications to hostile countries or terrorists—a practice called selective availability (SA). However on May 1, 2000, in response to the growing importance of the system for civilian applications, the U.S. government stopped intentionally downgrading GPS data. The

military gave its support to this change once new technology made it possible to selectively degrade the system within any defined geographical area on demand. This new feature of the system has made it safe to have higher-quality signals available for civilian use. Now, instead of the civilian-use signal having a margin of error between 20 and 70 yards, it is only about one-tenth of that.

A GPS receiver offers the four-wheeler numerous benefits:

■ You can track to any point for which you know the longitude and latitude coordinates with no chance of heading in the wrong direction or getting lost. Most receivers provide an extremely easy-to-understand graphic display to keep you on track.

■ It works in all weather conditions.

■ It automatically records your route for easy backtracking.

■ You can record and name any location, so that you can relocate it with ease. This may include your campsite, a fishing spot, or even a silver mine you discover!

■ It displays your position, allowing you to pinpoint your location on a map.

■ By interfacing the GPS receiver directly to a portable computer, you can monitor and record your location as you travel (using the appropriate map software) or print the route you took.

However, remember that GPS units can fail, batteries can go flat, and tree cover and tight canyons can block the signals. Never rely entirely on GPS for navigation. Always carry a compass for backup when you are going to be traveling in very remote areas.

Special 4WD Equipment

Tires

When 4WD touring, you will likely encounter a wide variety of terrain: rocks, mud, talus, slickrock, sand, gravel, dirt, and bitumen. The immense variety of tires on the market includes many specifically targeted at one or another of these types of terrain, as well as tires designed to handle a range of terrain adequately.

Every four-wheel driver seems to have his or her own preference when it comes to tire selection, but most people undertaking the 4WD trails in this book will need tires that can handle all of the above types of terrain adequately.

The first requirement is to select rugged, light-truck tires rather than passenger-vehicle tires. Check the size data on the sidewall: it should have "LT" rather than "P" before the number.

Among light-truck tires, you must choose between tires that are designated "all-terrain" and more-aggressive, wider-tread mud tires. Either type will be adequate, especially on rocks, gravel, talus, or dirt. Although mud tires have an advantage in muddy conditions and soft snow, all-terrain tires perform better on slickrock, in sand, and particularly on ice and paved roads.

When selecting tires, remember that they affect not just traction but also cornering ability, braking distances, fuel consumption, and noise levels. It pays to get good advice before making your decision.

Global Positioning System Receivers

GPS receivers have come down in price considerably in the past few years and are rapidly becoming indispensable navigational tools. Many higher-priced cars now offer integrated GPS receivers, and within the next few years, receivers will become available on most models.

Battery-powered, hand-held units that meet the needs of off-highway driving currently range from less than $100 to a little over $300 and continue to come down in price. Some high-end units feature maps that are incorporated in the display, either from a built-in database or from interchangeable memory cards. Currently, only a few of these maps include 4WD trails.

If you are considering purchasing a GPS unit, keep the following in mind:

■ Price. The very cheapest units are likely outdated and very limited in their display features. Expect to pay from $125 to $300.

■ The number of channels, which indicates the number of satellites that the unit tracks concurrently. Many older units have only one channel that switches from one satellite to another to collect the required information. Modern units have up to 12 channels that are each dedicated to tracking one satellite. This provides greater accuracy, faster start-up (because the unit can acquire the initial data it needs much more rapidly), and better reception under difficult conditions, such as when located in a deep canyon or in dense foliage.

■ The number of routes and the number of sites (or waypoints) per route that can be stored in memory. For off-highway use, it is important to be able to store plenty of waypoints so that you do not have to load coordinates into the machine as frequently. Having plenty of memory also ensures that you can automatically store your present location without fear that the memory is full.

■ Waypoint storage. The better units store up to 500 waypoints and 20 reversible routes of up to 30 waypoints each. Also consider the number of characters a GPS receiver allows you to use to name waypoints. When you try to recall a waypoint, you may have difficulty recognizing names restricted to only a few characters.

■ Automatic route storing. Most units automatically store your route as you go along and enable you to display it in reverse to make backtracking easy.

■ The display. Compare the graphic display of one unit with another. Some are much easier to decipher or offer more alternative displays.

■ The controls. GPS receivers have many functions, and they need to have good, simple controls.

■ Vehicle mounting. To be useful, the unit needs to be placed where it can be read easily by both the driver and the navigator. Check that the unit can be conveniently located in your vehicle. Different units have different shapes and different mounting systems. Be careful to locate the GPS out of the way of the passenger-side airbag.

■ Position-format options. Different

maps use different grids, and you want to be able to display the same format on your GPS unit as on the map you are using, so that cross-referencing is simplified. There are a number of formats for latitude and longitude, as well as the Universal Transverse Mercator (UTM) grid, which is used on some maps.

After you have selected a unit, a number of optional extras are also worth considering:

■ A cigarette lighter electrical adapter. Important because GPS units eat batteries!

■ A vehicle-mounted antenna, which will improve reception under difficult conditions. (The GPS unit can only "see" through the windows of your vehicle; it cannot monitor satellites through a metal roof.) Having a vehicle-mounted antenna also means that you do not have to consider reception when locating the receiver in your vehicle.

■ An in-car mounting system. If you are going to do a lot of touring using the GPS, consider attaching a bracket on the dash rather than relying on a Velcro mount.

■ A computer-link cable. Data from your receiver can be downloaded to your PC; or if you have a laptop computer, you can monitor your route as you go along, using one of a number of inexpensive map software products on the market.

We used a Garmin 45 and a Garmin 45 XL receiver to take the GPS positions included in this book. These Garmin units are now outdated, but both have served us well for the past six years in our travels throughout the United States and around the world and we recommend Garmin GPS products to our readers.

Yank Straps

Yank straps are industrial-strength versions of the flimsy tow straps carried by the local discount store. They are made of heavy nylon, are 20 to 30 feet long and 2 to 3 inches wide, are rated to at least 20,000 pounds, and have looped ends.

Do not use tow straps with metal hooks in the ends (the hooks can become missiles in the event the strap breaks free). Likewise, never join two yank straps together using a shackle.

CB Radios

If you are stuck, injured, or just want to know the conditions up ahead, a citizen's band (CB) radio can be invaluable.

CB radios are relatively inexpensive and do not require an FCC license. Their range is limited, especially in very hilly country, as their transmission patterns basically follow lines of sight. Range can be improved using single sideband (SSB) transmission, an option on more expensive units. Range is even better on vehicle-mounted units that have been professionally fitted to ensure that the antenna and cabling are matched appropriately.

Winches

There are three main options when it comes to winches: manual winches, removable electric winches, and vehicle-mounted electric winches.

If you have a full-size 4WD vehicle—which can weigh in excess of 7,000 pounds when loaded—a manual winch is of limited use without a lot of effort and considerable time. However, a manual winch is a very handy and inexpensive accessory if you have a small 4WD. Typically, manual winches are rated to pull about 5,500 pounds.

Electric winches can be mounted to your vehicle's trailer hitch to enable them to be removed, relocated to the front of your vehicle (if you have a hitch installed), or moved to another vehicle. Although this is a very useful feature, a winch is heavy, so relocating one can be a two-person job. Consider that 5,000-pound-rated winches weigh only about 55 pounds, while 12,000-pound-rated models weigh around 140 pounds. Therefore, the larger models are best permanently front-mounted. Unfortunately, this position limits their ability to winch the vehicle backward.

When choosing between electric winches, be aware that they are rated for their maximum capacity on the first wind of the cable around the drum. As layers of cable wind onto the drum, they increase its diameter and thus decrease the maximum load the winch can handle. This decrease is significant: a winch rated to pull 8,000 pounds on a bare drum may only handle 6,500 pounds on the second layer, 5,750 pounds on the third layer, and 5,000 pounds on the fourth. Electric winches also draw a high level of current and may necessitate upgrading the battery in your 4WD or adding a second battery.

There is a wide range of mounting options—from a simple, body-mounted frame that holds the winch to heavy-duty winch bars that replace the original bumper and incorporate brush bars and mounts for auxiliary lights.

If you buy a winch, either electric or manual, you will also need quite a range of additional equipment so that you can operate it correctly:

■ at least one choker chain with hooks on each end,
■ winch extension straps or cables,
■ shackles,
■ a receiver shackle,
■ a snatch block,
■ a tree protector,
■ gloves.

Grill/Brush Bars and Winch Bars
Brush bars protect the front of the vehicle from scratches and minor bumps; they also provide a solid mount for auxiliary lights and often high-lift jacking points. The level of protection they provide depends on how solid they are and on whether they are securely mounted onto the frame of the vehicle. Lighter models attach in front of the standard bumper, but the more substantial units replace the bumper. Prices range from about $150 to $450.

Winch bars replace the bumper and usually integrate a solid brush bar with a heavy-duty winch mount. Some have the brush bar as an optional extra to the winch bar component. Manufacturers such as Warn, ARB, and TJM offer a wide range of inte-grated winch bars. These are significantly more expensive, starting at about $650.

Remember that installing heavy equipment on the front of the vehicle may necessitate increasing the front suspension rating to cope with the additional weight.

Portable Air Compressors
Most portable air compressors on the market are flimsy models that plug into the cigarette lighter and are sold at the local discount store. These are of very limited use for four-wheel driving. They are very slow to inflate the large tires of a 4WD vehicle; for instance, to reinflate from 15 to 35 pounds typically takes about 10 minutes for each tire. They are also unlikely to be rated for continuous use, which means that they will overheat and cut off before completing the job. If you're lucky, they will start up again when they have cooled down, but this means that you are unlikely to reinflate your tires in less than an hour.

The easiest way to identify a useful air compressor is by the price—good ones cost $200 and over. Many of the quality units feature a Thomas-brand pump and are built to last. Another good unit is sold by ARB. All these pumps draw between 15 and 20 amps and thus should not be plugged into the cigarette lighter socket but attached to the vehicle's battery with clips. The ARB unit can be permanently mounted under the hood. Quick-Air makes a 10-amp compressor that can be plugged into the cigarette lighter socket and performs well.

Auxiliary Driving Lights
There is a vast array of auxiliary lights on the market today, and selecting the best lights for your purpose can be a confusing process.

Auxiliary lights greatly improve visibility in adverse weather conditions. Driving lights provide a strong, moderately wide beam to supplement headlamp high beams, giving improved lighting in the distance and to the sides of the main beam. Fog lamps throw a wide-dispersion, flat beam; and spots provide a high-power, narrow beam to improve lighting range directly in front of the vehicle. Rear-mounted auxiliary lights provide greatly improved visibility for backing up.

For off-highway use, you will need quality lights with strong mounting brackets. Some high-powered off-highway lights are not approved by the U.S. Department of Transportation.

Packing Checklist

Before embarking on any 4WD adventure, whether a lazy Sunday drive on an easy trail or a challenging climb over rugged terrain, be prepared. The following checklist will help you gather the items you need.

Essential

☐ Rain gear
☐ Small shovel or multipurpose ax, pick, shovel, and sledgehammer
☐ Heavy-duty yank strap
☐ Spare tire that matches the other tires on the vehicle
☐ Working jack and base plate for soft ground
☐ Maps
☐ Emergency medical kit, including sun protection and insect repellent
☐ Bottled water
☐ Blankets or space blankets
☐ Parka, gloves, and boots
☐ Spare vehicle key
☐ Jumper leads
☐ Heavy-duty flashlight
☐ Multipurpose tool, such as a Leatherman
☐ Emergency food—high-energy bars or similar

Worth Considering

☐ Global Positioning System (GPS) receiver
☐ Cell phone
☐ A set of light-truck, off-highway tires and matching spare
☐ High-lift jack
☐ Additional tool kit
☐ CB radio
☐ Portable air compressor
☐ Tire gauge
☐ Tire-sealing kit
☐ Tire chains
☐ Handsaw and ax
☐ Binoculars
☐ Firearms
☐ Whistle
☐ Flares
☐ Vehicle fire extinguisher
☐ Gasoline, engine oil, and other vehicle fluids
☐ Portable hand winch
☐ Electric cooler

If Your Credit Cards Aren' t Maxed Out

☐ Electric, vehicle-mounted winch and associated recovery straps, shackles, and snatch blocks
☐ Auxiliary lights
☐ Locking differential(s)

Trails in the South Region

- **S1** Tinajas Atlas Pass Trail *(page 30)*
- **S2** Fortuna Mine Trail *(page 37)*
- **S3** El Camino del Diablo Trail
  (page 45)
- **S4** Cipriano Pass Trail *(page 58)*
- **S5** Christmas Pass Trail *(page 63)*
- **S6** Puerto Blanco Drive *(page 69)*
- **S7** Ajo Mountain Drive *(page 75)*

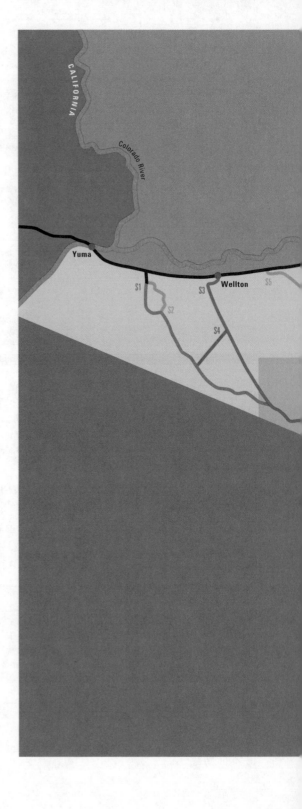

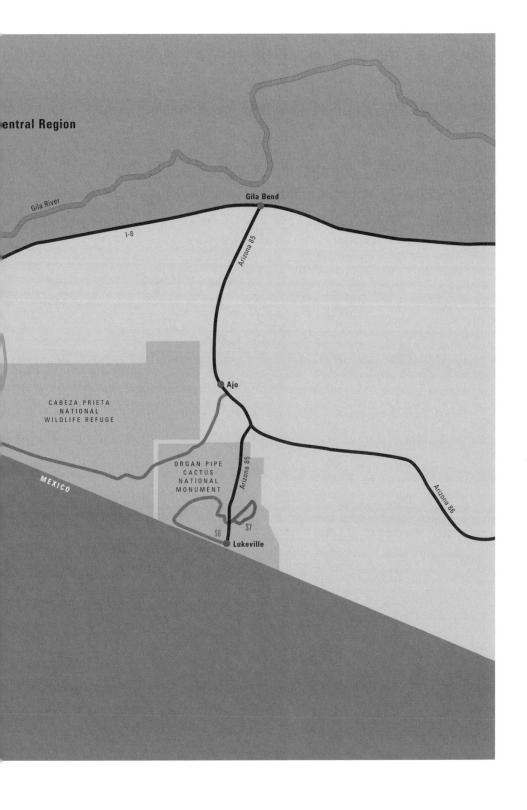

entral Region

Gila River

Gila Bend

I-8

Arizona 85

CABEZA PRIETA
NATIONAL
WILDLIFE REFUGE

Ajo

ORGAN PIPE
CACTUS
NATIONAL
MONUMENT

Arizona 85

Arizona 86

MEXICO

S6

S7

Lukeville

Trails in the South Region

- **S8** Parker Canyon Lake Road *(page 79)*
- **S9** Canelo Hills Trail *(page 85)*
- **S10** Blacktail Ridge Trail *(page 89)*
- **S11** Sunnyside Trail *(page 92)*
- **S12** Mexican Border Road *(page 97)*
- **S13** Harshaw Road *(page 110)*
- **S14** Flux Canyon Trail *(page 115)*
- **S15** Cumero Canyon–Three R Canyon Trail *(page 119)*
- **S16** Temporal Gulch Trail *(page 124)*
- **S17** Carr Canyon Trail *(page 129)*
- **S18** Mule Mountains Trail *(page 131)*
- **S19** Tex Canyon Trail *(page 136)*
- **S20** Pinery Canyon Trail *(page 142)*
- **S21** Hands Pass Trail *(page 148)*
- **S22** Pine Canyon Trail *(page 156)*
- **S23** Barfoot Park Trail *(page 162)*
- **S24** Swift Trail *(page 165)*
- **S25** Tripp Canyon Trail *(page 171)*
- **S26** Willow Springs Road *(page 174)*
- **S27** Oracle Control Road *(page 181)*
- **S28** Catalina Ridge Trail *(page 188)*
- **S29** Copper Creek Mining District Trail *(page 192)*
- **S30** Sibley Mansion and Bluebird Mine Trail *(page 199)*
- **S31** Redington Road *(page 204)*
- **S32** Buehman Canyon Trail *(page 210)*
- **S33** Jackson Cabin Trail *(page 214)*

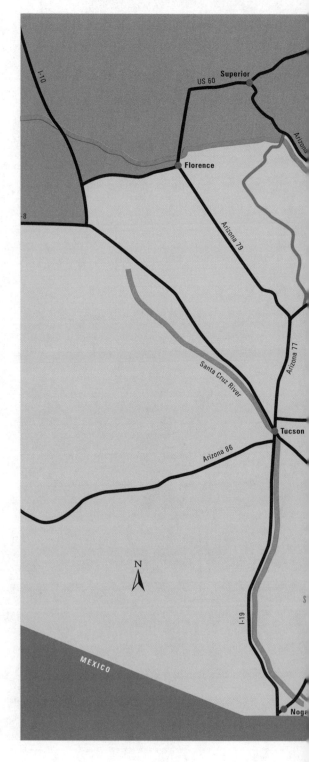

Central Region

Arizona 77

US 70

Gila River

S25

Safford

S30

S24

ammoth

S29

US 191

le

S28

S33

Redington

S32

San Pedro River

S31

Willcox

Arizona 186

S21

I-10

Benson

S22

S20

Arizona 83

Arizona 181

S23

Arizona 90

Arizona 80

Rodeo

Arizona 82

S8

Tombstone

Arizona 80

S9

S14

US 191

S19

Sierra
Vista

S18

S11

Arizona 90

Bisbee

S17

S13

S10

Arizona 92

Douglas

NEW MEXICO

Tinajas Altas Pass Trail

STARTING POINT	I-8, Exit 14 at Foothills Boulevard
FINISHING POINT	South #3: El Camino del Diablo, 30.4 miles south of Wellton
TOTAL MILEAGE	35 miles
UNPAVED MILEAGE	35 miles
DRIVING TIME	2 hours
ELEVATION RANGE	400–1,200 feet
USUALLY OPEN	Year-round
BEST TIME TO TRAVEL	November to March
DIFFICULTY RATING	3
SCENIC RATING	9
REMOTENESS RATING	+2

Special Attractions

■ Remote, less-traveled entrance to the main El Camino del Diablo route.
■ Western end of historic immigrant trail.
■ Tinajas Altas Pass.
■ Access to a network of 4WD trails.

Description

The original El Camino del Diablo had two possible exits that could be taken, depending on the availability of water and the stamina of the traveler. The rugged west route over Tinajas Altas Pass and the waterless Davis Plain to Yuma is described here. For the well-prepared desert four-wheel driver, this western route combined with the main route over to Ajo is possibly the best, most scenic, and most remote of the trails that follow sections of the original El Camino del Diablo. Combining the two routes will almost certainly require a second night's camp and a third day on the trail as well as additional fuel. Although the length is similar to the skipped portion of the main route, the rougher and sandier trail surface is slower going and will use more fuel.

An option for those with less time who still want to sample the remote grandeur of this historic trail is to combine this west route with the faster leg of the main route up to Wellton. This route can be traveled in one day.

As with the main El Camino del Diablo, a permit to enter the Barry M. Goldwater Air Force Range is essential. For permit information and other necessary information regarding travel in this region, refer to South #3: El Camino del Diablo Trail.

The trail begins near the south side of Yuma at exit 14 on I-8. Fuel and water are available along Foothills Boulevard for last-minute replenishment. The trail immediately enters the range, skirting the end of the prohibited area before cutting across to join the route of El Camino del Diablo at the junction with South #2: Fortuna Mine Trail. The trail runs in a straight line along the western face of the Gila Mountains. It parallels Vopoki Ridge, a smaller ridge of mountains in front of the taller Gila Mountains, before meeting the junction of South #4: Cipriano Pass Trail, which is between the Gila Mountains and the Tinajas Altas Mountains.

Navigation gets slightly more confusing as you approach Tinajas Altas Pass—there are several smaller trails, many of which rejoin later, so often there is not one "main" trail. The route can be faint and poorly defined as it crosses the desert pavement. The GPS can be invaluable here to maintain the correct direction. As the trail approaches the range, it becomes rougher and crosses several deep washes. Approaching the gap of the pass, there are several good campsites tucked into the side of the range. This area is one of the prettiest parts of the trail.

Once in the gap of Tinajas Altas Pass, navigation is easier as the trail winds through the steep-sided, light-colored granite walls of the pass, which rise abruptly from the flat desert floor.

The earliest sections of the trail can be very washboardy before quickly turning to soft sand; otherwise the trail is not technically difficult. The BLM map shows most of the tracks in the region and is sufficient to use for navigation. However, it does not show the location of the tanks at the eastern end of the trail: the coordinates for the tanks are GPS: N32°18.70' W114°03.00'

The tanks, which are a string of natural pockets in the rock, run up a narrow cleft in the range. It is a strenuous climb up to the higher tanks.

The trail finishes on South #3: El Camino del Diablo Trail, 30.4 miles from Wellton.

Current Road Information

Luke Air Force Base
Gila Bend Auxiliary Field
Security Forces
Gila Bend, AZ 85337
(928) 683-6220

Bureau of Land Management
Yuma Field Office
2555 Gilda Ridge Rd.
Yuma, AZ 85365
(928) 317-3200

Map References

BLM   Yuma, Tinajas Altas Mtns.
USGS 1:24,000   Fortuna, Fortuna SW,
          Vopoki Ridge, Cipriano Pass, Butler
          Mtns., Tinajas Altas Mtns.
          1:100,000 Yuma, Tinajas Altas Mtns.
Maptech CD-ROM: Southwest Arizona/Yuma
Arizona Atlas & Gazetteer, p. 62

Route Directions

▼ 0.0   From exit 14 on I-8, turn onto Foothills
           Boulevard and proceed south for 1.8
           miles. At the crossroads where the
           paved road turns left, continue straight
           on into the Barry M. Goldwater Air Force
           Range and zero trip meter. A valid range
           permit is essential beyond this point.
           Proceed south on the wide, graded dirt
           road. Road on left is South #2: Fortuna
           Mine Trail.
3.8 ▲   Trail ends at the south end of Foothills

The trail with an ocotillo in the foreground and the Gila Mountains in the background

YUMA INDIANS (QUECHAN)

The Yuma, or Quechans as they prefer to be called, trace their ancestral home to a sacred mountain called Avikwamé near what is now Needles, California. Sometime before Spanish explorers made contact with the tribe in 1540 they moved to the area around the confluence of the Colorado and Gila Rivers in southwest Arizona. Here they controlled the Yuma crossing, an important passage across of the Colorado River.

Conditions in the region were harsh, with temperatures that often reached 120°F. The Yuma lived along the banks of the river, moving to higher lands to avoid the spring floods. Their dwellings varied from open, rectangular structures to Apache-like wickiups. They supplemented their diet of fish and wild plants by farming corn, beans, squash, and grass-

A group of Yuma Indians, circa 1910

es in the silt left over from floods.

In the late 1700s, Spanish missionaries established two settlements near the Yuma crossing. Soldiers from the missions mistreated the Indians, stealing food supplies and Yuman land. On July 17, 1781, Chief Palma and his brother Ygnacio Palma led their people in a revolt. Local settlements were burned to the ground and about 95 priests, settlers, and soldiers were killed. The Yuma rebellion shut down the Spanish route into Alta California that had been created by Juan Bautista de Anza. Spanish soldiers tried to regain the lost land, but the Quechan fought them off and were never subdued.

By the 1840s, Americans began to pass through Quechan territory. At first, the Yuma were able to exploit the situation, charging travelers for passage across the Colorado. However, non-Indian ferry companies soon challenged Quechan control of the crossing. When Yuma Indians attacked a rival ferryman, John C. Morehead, a California lawyer raised a volunteer militia and destroyed Quechan crops and boats. Skirmishes between Indians and travelers became frequent. Those who traversed the Yuma crossing did so with trepidation. Fort Yuma was built in 1850 to quell the situation, but poor supplies and frequent attacks upon the fort caused its abandonment. Not until the following year did a stronger garrison return and secure the crossing.

In 1884, the Yuma Indians were provided a reservation along the Colorado River. Later, the Cocopah Reservation was established for them in 1917. Since then, the Quechan have had to continually battle for land. By the 1950s, the federal government had taken or sold 8,500 acres of Quechan territory. Twenty-five thousand acres of land were returned to the reservation in 1978, but the 1,000 remaining Indians still fight for water rights.

South Trail #1: Tinajas Altas Pass Trail

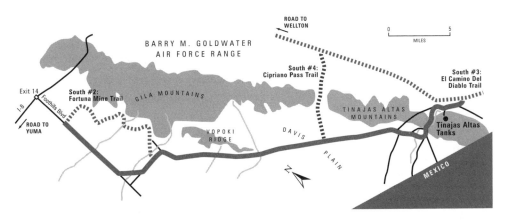

Boulevard on the edge of Yuma.
Continue north for 1.8 miles to reach exit
14 on I-8. Road on right is South #2:
Fortuna Mine Trail.
GPS: N32°37.60′ W114°24.55′

▼ 0.1   SO   Track on left, trail is following alongside telegraph lines.
3.7 ▲   SO   Track on right.

▼ 2.9   SO   Cross through wash.
0.9 ▲   SO   Cross through wash.

▼ 3.0   SO   Cross through wash.
0.8 ▲   SO   Cross through wash.

▼ 3.8   BL   Equally used track on right. Zero trip meter.
0.0 ▲   Continue north toward Yuma following alongside telegraph lines.
GPS: N32°34.06′ W114°24.51′

▼ 0.0   Continue to the southeast.
3.2 ▲   SO   Equally used track on left. Zero trip meter.

▼ 1.1   SO   Track on left and track on right.
2.1 ▲   SO   Track on left and track on right.

▼ 2.5   SO   Cross through wash.
0.7 ▲   SO   Cross through wash.

▼ 3.2   TL   Turn left at T-intersection along the edge of the prohibited area.
0.0 ▲   Continue northwest toward Yuma.
GPS: N32°31.43′ W114°22.94′

▼ 0.0   Continue east toward the Gila Mountains.
1.2 ▲   TR   Turn right at unmarked junction onto well-used sandy trail. Zero trip meter.

▼ 1.2   BR   Track on left is South #2: Fortuna Mine Trail. Junction is marked by marker post A3 and a sign for El Camino del Diablo. Zero trip meter.
0.0 ▲   Continue to the west.
GPS: N32°31.51′ W114°21.61′

▼ 0.0   Continue to the east.
8.4 ▲   BL   Track on right is South #2: Fortuna Mine Trail. Junction is marked by marker post A3 and a sign for El Camino del Diablo. Zero trip meter.

▼ 0.7   BR   Track on left joins South #2: Fortuna Mine Trail. Bear right to the south following along the edge of the prohibited area (on right).
7.7 ▲   BL   Track on right joins South #2: Fortuna Mine Trail. Bear left following along the edge of the prohibited area (on left).
GPS: N32°31.41′ W114°20.82′

▼ 1.5   SO   Cross through wash.
6.9 ▲   SO   Cross through wash.

▼ 1.9   SO   Track on left.
6.5 ▲   SO   Track on right.
           GPS: N32°30.38' W114°20.43'

▼ 2.1   SO   Cross through wash.
6.3 ▲   SO   Cross through wash.

▼ 2.8   SO   Cross through wash.
5.6 ▲   SO   Cross through wash.

▼ 3.3   SO   Faint track on left.
5.1 ▲   SO   Faint track on right.

▼ 4.9   SO   Cross through wash; then small track on left. Vopoki Ridge is to the left.
3.5 ▲   SO   Small track on right; then cross through wash.
           GPS: N32°28.44' W114°18.20'

▼ 6.9   SO   Passing directly beside the southern end of Vopoki Ridge.
1.5 ▲   SO   Trail starts to angle away from Vopoki Ridge.
           GPS: N32°27.11' W114°16.87'

▼ 8.3   SO   Two well-used tracks on right enter prohibited area.
0.1 ▲   BR   Two well-used tracks on left enter prohibited area.
           GPS: N32°26.32' W114°15.73'

▼ 8.4   BR/BL   Track on left at southern end of Vopoki Ridge leads off through sandy clearing. Marker post A4 in clearing. Zero trip meter.
0.0 ▲   Continue northwest along Vopoki Ridge.
           GPS: N32°26.22' W114°15.53'

▼ 0.0   Continue to the southeast. Trail crosses many small washes over this section.
4.9 ▲   BL   Track on right at southern end of Vopoki Ridge leads off through sandy clearing. Marker Post A4 in clearing. Zero trip meter.

▼ 0.1   SO   Cross through wash.
4.8 ▲   SO   Cross through wash.

▼ 0.2   SO   Faint track on left.
4.7 ▲   SO   Faint track on right.

▼ 0.5   SO   Faint track on left, remain on main trail.
4.4 ▲   SO   Faint track on right, remain on main trail.

▼ 0.7   SO   Cross through wash.
4.2 ▲   SO   Cross through wash.

▼ 4.3   SO   Sign on left, entering Tinajas Altas Mountains Area of Critical Environmental Concern. Survey marker on left.
0.6 ▲   SO   Sign on right, leaving Tinajas Altas Mountains Area of Critical Environmental Concern. Survey marker on right.
           GPS: N32°23.98' W114°11.56'

▼ 4.9   SO   Track on left is South #4: Cipriano Pass Trail. Turn is well-used but unmarked apart from wooden marker post A5 immediately after the turn. Zero trip meter at marker post.
0.0 ▲   Continue to the northwest.
           GPS: N32°23.61' W114°11.23'

▼ 0.0   Continue to the southeast. Tinajas Altas Mountains are now on the left.
5.7 ▲   SO   Track on right is South #4: Cipriano Pass Trail. Turn is well-used but unmarked apart from wooden marker post A5 immediately before the turn. Zero trip meter at marker post.

▼ 5.7   SO   Track on left is the northern pass through the Tinajas Altas Mountains. Wooden marker post A6 at the junction. Zero trip meter.
0.0 ▲   Continue to the northwest along the west face of the range.
           GPS: N32°20.33' W114°06.67'

▼ 0.0   Continue to the south. Trail is faint and poorly defined in places.
2.7 ▲   SO   Track on right is the northern pass through the Tinajas Altas Mountains. Wooden marker post A6 at the junction.

Zero trip meter.

▼ 0.1   SO   Track on right and faint track on left.
2.6 ▲   SO   Track on left and faint track on right.
        GPS: N32°20.18′ W114°06.75′

▼ 0.2   BR   Track on left at wooden post.
2.5 ▲   SO   Track on right at wooden post.
        GPS: N32°20.15′ W114°06.74′

▼ 1.4   BR   Faint track on left followed by a fork,
             bear right at fork.
1.3 ▲   BL   Track on right, keep left followed by
             second faint track on right.
        GPS: N32°19.48′ W114°06.24′

▼ 1.5   SO   Faint track on right. Many tire tracks,
             remain on main, most-used trail.
1.2 ▲   SO   Faint track on left. Many tire tracks,
             remain on main, most-used trail.

▼ 2.2   SO   Track on right.
0.5 ▲   BR   Track on left.
        GPS: N32°18.85′ W114°05.84′

▼ 2.6   SO   Track on right.
0.1 ▲   BR   Track on left.
        GPS: N32°18.64′ W114°05.52′

▼ 2.7   SO   Well-used track on right at wooden
             marker A8. Zero trip meter.
0.0 ▲   Continue away from Tinajas Altas
             Pass.
        GPS: N32°18.67′ W114°05.46′

▼ 0.0   Continue toward Tinajas Altas Pass. Trail
             now leads into the range and is more
             defined.
5.1 ▲   SO   Well-used track on left at wooden mark-
             er A8. Zero trip meter. Trail is faint and
             poorly defined in places.

▼ 0.1   SO   Well-used track on right.
5.0 ▲   BR   Well-used track on left.

▼ 0.3   SO   Well-used track on right. Entering gap in
             range.
4.8 ▲   BR   Well-used track on left. Trail leaves gap
             in range.
        GPS: N32°18.76′ W114°05.23′

▼ 0.6   SO   Track on left.
4.5 ▲   SO   Track on right.
        GPS: N32°18.94′ W114°05.04′

▼ 0.7   SO   Cross through wash in pass.
4.4 ▲   SO   Cross through wash in pass.

▼ 0.8   SO   Cristate saguaro on right of trail (fan-
             shaped mutation).
4.3 ▲   SO   Cristate saguaro on left of trail (fan-
             shaped mutation).
        GPS: N32°18.95′ W114°04.77′

▼ 1.1   SO   Cross through wash.
4.0 ▲   SO   Cross through wash.

▼ 1.2   BL   Bear left up wash.
3.9 ▲   BR   Bear right out of wash.
        GPS: N32°18.87′ W114°04.38′

▼ 1.3   SO   Exit wash.
3.8 ▲   SO   Enter wash.

▼ 1.4   SO   Cross through wash.
3.7 ▲   SO   Cross through wash.

▼ 1.5   SO   Faint track on right.
3.6 ▲   SO   Faint track on left.

▼ 1.6   SO   Start to cross wide wash.
3.5 ▲   SO   Exit wash crossing.

▼ 1.7   SO   Exit wash crossing. Many small tracks
             on right and left are dead-ends, some
             lead to pleasant campsites.
3.4 ▲   SO   Start to cross wide wash.

▼ 1.9   SO   Cross through wash.
3.2 ▲   SO   Cross through wash.

▼ 2.2   SO   Cross through wash then well-used track
             on left exits to El Camino del Diablo far-
             ther to the north. Exiting gap in range,
             looking ahead across the Lechuguilla
             Desert to the Cabeza Prieta Mountains.
2.9 ▲   SO   Well-used track on right returns to El
             Camino del Diablo; then cross through
             wash. Many small tracks on right and
             left are dead-ends, some lead to pleas-

ant campsites.
GPS: N32°19.37' W114°03.48'

▼ 2.6   SO   Track on left.
2.5 ▲   SO   Track on right.

▼ 2.7   SO   Track on left.
2.4 ▲   BL   Track on right.
GPS: N32°19.32' W114°03.02'

▼ 3.0   BR   Cross through wash; then bear right along better-used trail, staying close to the range.
2.1 ▲   SO   Track on right; then cross through wash.

▼ 3.1   SO   Well-used track on left. Keep right along range.
2.0 ▲   BL   Well-used track on right. Keep left along range.

▼ 3.3   SO   Track on right goes to Tinajas Altas Tanks, then cross through wash.
1.8 ▲   SO   Cross through wash, then track on left goes to Tinajas Altas Tanks.
GPS: N32°18.81' W114°02.84'

▼ 3.6   SO   Cross through wash; then faint track on right. Main trail is heading away from range.
1.5 ▲   SO   Faint track on left; then cross through wash. Remain on main trail as it runs close to the range.

▼ 3.8   TR   Closed trails ahead and on left.
1.3 ▲   TL   Closed trails ahead and on right.
GPS: N32°18.64' W114°02.44'

▼ 4.2   SO   Track on right.
0.9 ▲   SO   Track on left.

▼ 5.1   Trail ends at South #3: El Camino del Diablo Trail. Turn left to exit to Wellton.
0.0 ▲   Trail commences on South #3: El Camino del Diablo Trail, 30.4 miles south of Wellton. Turn at the BLM sign for Tinajas Altas and proceed west along formed, sandy trail. The trail starts at the southernmost sign for Tinajas Altas. If approaching from Wellton, note that you will have passed two previous signs for Tinajas Altas.
GPS: N32°18.13' W114°01.17'

The trail leads toward the Gila Mountains

Fortuna Mine Trail

STARTING POINT	South #1: Tinajas Altas Pass Trail
FINISHING POINT	Foothills Boulevard
TOTAL MILEAGE	12 miles
UNPAVED MILEAGE	11 miles
DRIVING TIME	1.5 hours
ELEVATION RANGE	400–600 feet
USUALLY OPEN	Year-round
BEST TIME TO TRAVEL	November to March
DIFFICULTY RATING	3
SCENIC RATING	8
REMOTENESS RATING	+0

Special Attractions

- Old Fortuna Mine.
- Varied trail winding in the Gila Mountains.
- Panoramic views over the Barry M. Goldwater Air Force Range.

History

The rich outcrop that became the site of the Fortuna Mine was first discovered by Charles W. Thomas, William H. Holbert, and Laurent Albert in 1894. Two years later the mine was sold to Charles D. Lane, an experienced miner from Angels Camp, California who paid $150,000 for the claim. Lane set about organizing La Fortuna Gold Mining and Milling Company, which built a 20-stamp mill and employed 80 to 100 Mexican and American miners. The main problem the fledgling company had to overcome was the lack of water at the site. A 100-horsepower pump on the Gila River and more than 12 miles of pipeline to bring the water to the mine solved the problem.

The mining camp that sprang up around the mine was by all accounts a rowdy one. Known as Fortuna, it had a hotel, many saloons, and a stage line that linked it with Blaisdell on the Southern Pacific Railroad. Prostitutes and gamblers regularly made the trip down from Yuma, and fights were common. The saloon did a roaring trade, supposedly because the water tasted so bad the

The trail passing below the Fortuna Mine ruins

miners turned to the stronger stuff.

The mine was a rich and productive one, with an average yield per month of $80,000. In 1899 a cyanide treatment plant was constructed to treat the accumulated tailings, yielding a further $5 per ton. A potential problem with the mine was that the vein was erratic and the ore was contained around an intersection of two short veins. In 1900 the productive vein was lost on a fault line, and only a small segment was found with further exploration. However, between 1896 and 1904, more than $2,500,000 in bullion was sent from the Fortuna Mine to the Selby smelter in California's San Francisco Bay area. The major life of the camp was over in 1904.

The Fortuna Mine reopened briefly a couple of times after 1904, producing a further $25,000 worth of gold. In 1954 the mine was included in the Barry M. Goldwater Air Force Range.

Description

The trail commences 8.2 miles from the north end of South #1: Tinajas Altas Pass Trail and wraps back up along the face of the Gila Mountains to the outskirts of Yuma. It is a well-traveled, popular, short day trip from Yuma. The trail crosses along a desert pavement ridge top before dropping down to enter a wash. The wash is stony, rubbly, and slow going. The trail meanders in and around the wash up to the historic Fortuna Mine, which sits in a cove in the range. Red Top Mountain set to the north of the mine is distinguished by its sandy reddish-colored top, which stands out from the other darker gray rocks of the Gila Range.

Two main tracks run into the mine area, and several smaller tracks run all around the mine to the various remains of buildings and mine workings. The mill site is easily recognizable by the large embankment walls slightly elevated directly to the east.

From the Fortuna Mine, the trail crosses the bajada on the western slope of the Gila Mountains. The route this trail takes runs close to the range, running for a couple of miles along a ridge top with a steep drop down to the wide Fortuna Wash. It crosses the desert pavement, traveling as a well-defined two-track. There are panoramic views to the west over the Barry M. Goldwater Air Force Range.

The trail joins a well-used trail that travels north toward Yuma. In the reverse direction, this junction is easy to miss because it is unmarked and there are no distinguishing features to mark the turn. The trail finishes on the outskirts of Yuma, along County 14 Street. Continuing west along this street leads to Foothills Boulevard, immediately south of exit 14 on I-8.

A permit to enter the Barry M. Goldwater Air Force Range is essential in order to travel this trail. For permit information and other necessary information regarding travel in this region, refer to South #3: El Camino del Diablo Trail.

Current Road Information

Luke Air Force Base
Gila Bend Auxiliary Field
Security Forces
Gila Bend, AZ 85337
(928) 683-6220

Bureau of Land Management
Yuma Field Office
2555 E Gila Ridge Road
Yuma, AZ 85365
(928) 317-3200

Map References

BLM   Yuma
USGS 1:24,000   Fortuna Mine, Fortuna
        SW, Fortuna
        1:100,000 Yuma
Maptech CD-ROM: Southwest Arizona/
        Yuma
Arizona Atlas & Gazetteer, p. 62

Route Directions

▼ 0.0   From South #1: Tinajas Altas Pass
           Trail, 8.2 miles from the north end of the
           trail, turn northeast at marker post A3

South Trail #2: Fortuna Mine Trail

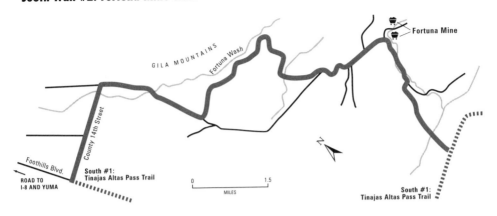

2.6 ▲   and zero trip meter.
Trail ends at the intersection with South #1: Tinajas Altas Pass Trail. Turn right to exit to Yuma, turn left to continue along to Tinajas Altas Pass.
GPS: N32°31.51' W114°21.61'

▼ 0.4   SO   Cross through wide wash.
2.2 ▲   SO   Exit wide wash crossing.

▼ 0.5   SO   Exit wide wash crossing.
2.1 ▲   SO   Cross through wide wash.
GPS: N32°31.90' W114°21.41'

▼ 0.7   SO   Cross through wash.
1.9 ▲   SO   Cross through wash.

▼ 1.0   SO   Cross through wash.
1.6 ▲   SO   Cross through wash.

▼ 1.1   SO   Cross through wash, then trail runs up small ridge. Red Top Mountain ahead.
1.5 ▲   SO   Cross through wash.

▼ 1.5   BR   Bear right and swing down off ridge.
1.1 ▲   BL   Climb up ridge then bear left along ridge top.
GPS: N32°32.62' W114°20.74'

▼ 1.6   BL   Track on right.
1.0 ▲   BR   Track on left.
GPS: N32°32.58' W114°20.64'

▼ 1.7   SO   Cross through wash. Trail now follows the line of the wash, crossing it often for next 0.5 miles.
0.9 ▲   SO   Exit line of wash.

▼ 2.2   SO   Exit wash.
0.4 ▲   SO   Enter wash, trail now follows the line of the wash, crossing it often for the next 0.5 miles.
GPS: N32°32.91' W114°20.18'

▼ 2.3   SO   Small track on left, diggings on right. Start of the diggings of the Fortuna Mine.
0.3 ▲   SO   Small track on right, diggings on left. Leaving the Fortuna Mine.

▼ 2.4   SO   Cross through wash.
0.2 ▲   SO   Cross through wash.

▼ 2.5   SO   Cross through wash.
0.1 ▲   SO   Cross through wash.

▼ 2.6   BL   Two tracks on right lead into main area of Fortuna Mine. Zero trip meter.
0.0 ▲   Continue to the south.
GPS: N32°33.19' W114°20.01'

▼ 0.0   Continue to the northwest.
5.5 ▲   BR   Two tracks on left lead into main area of Fortuna Mine. Zero trip meter.

▼ 0.1   SO   Cross through wash. Small stone ruins

		dotted nearby.
5.4 ▲	SO	Cross through wash. Small stone ruins dotted nearby.

▼ 0.4	SO	Cross through wide wash.
5.1 ▲	SO	Cross through wide wash.

▼ 0.5	SO	Climb up out of wash. Track on right.
5.0 ▲	SO	Track on left, descend to cross through wide wash.
		GPS: N32°33.44' W114°20.42'

▼ 0.6	SO	Track on right.
4.9 ▲	SO	Track on left.

▼ 0.7	SO	Cross through wash; then faint track on left. Remain on main trail.
4.8 ▲	SO	Faint track on right; then cross through wash. Remain on main trail.

▼ 0.8	SO	Two faint tracks on left.
4.7 ▲	SO	Two faint tracks on right.

▼ 1.3	SO	Cross through wide wash.
4.2 ▲	SO	Cross through wide wash.
		GPS: N32°33.80' W114°21.00'

▼ 1.6	SO	Cross through wash.
3.9 ▲	SO	Cross through wash.

▼ 1.7	BR	Track on left. Bear right to the north following the slightly less-used trail that runs closer to the hills. Track looks fainter at the start, but is well defined immediately over the ridge.
3.8 ▲	SO	Track on right is equally used. Continue to the southeast.

▼ 1.8	SO	Cross through small wash.
3.7 ▲	SO	Cross through small wash.

▼ 2.0	SO	Cross through wash.
3.5 ▲	SO	Cross through wash.

▼ 2.1	BL	Faint track on right, remain on main trail.
3.4 ▲	SO	Faint track on left, remain on main trail.

▼ 2.3	SO	Start to cross wide Fortuna Wash.
3.2 ▲	SO	Exit wash.

▼ 2.4	BR	Exit wash and bear right.
3.1 ▲	BL	Bear left and start to cross wide Fortuna Wash.
		GPS: N32°34.66' W114°21.38'

▼ 2.8	SO	Cross through wide wash.
2.7 ▲	SO	Cross through wide wash.
		GPS: N32°34.76' W114°20.98'

▼ 2.9	SO	Track on right.
2.6 ▲	BR	Track on left.
		GPS: N32°34.81' W114°20.98'

▼ 3.4	BL	Smaller track continues straight on. Bear left and continue along ridge.
2.1 ▲	BR	Smaller track on left.
		GPS: N32°35.15' W114°20.75'

▼ 4.1	BL	Smaller track on right drops down into wash.
1.4 ▲	SO	Smaller track on left drops down into wash.
		GPS: N32°35.44' W114°21.37'

▼ 4.7	SO	Track on left.
0.8 ▲	SO	Track on right.

▼ 4.8	BL	Faint track continues straight on.
0.7 ▲	BR	Bear right up ridge top, faint track on left. Beware—abrupt turn with drop straight ahead!
		GPS: N32°35.75' W114°21.94'

▼ 5.0	SO	Cross through wash.
0.5 ▲	SO	Cross through wash.

▼ 5.2	SO	Track on left goes up rise.
0.3 ▲	BL	Track on right goes up rise.
		GPS: N32°35.74' W114°22.39'

▼ 5.5	TR	T-intersection with well-used trail. Turn right and zero trip meter. The junction is unmarked with no noticeable features to mark it.
0.0 ▲		Continue to the east.
		GPS: N32°35.75' W114°22.64'

▼ 0.0		Continue to the north toward Yuma and cross through wash.

3.9 ▲	TL	Cross through wash; then turn left onto well-used trail. The junction is unmarked with no noticeable features to mark it. Zero trip meter.

▼ 0.8	SO	Cross through wash.
3.1 ▲	SO	Cross through wash.
		GPS: N32°36.46' W114°22.51'

▼ 0.9	SO	Small track on left.
3.0 ▲	SO	Small track on right.

▼ 1.1	SO	Cross through wide wash; then track on right.
2.8 ▲	BR	Track on left; then cross through wide wash.
		GPS: N32°36.80' W114°22.39'

▼ 1.3	BL	Faint track on right.
2.6 ▲	SO	Faint track on left.

▼ 1.4	SO	Track on left.
2.5 ▲	BL	Track on right.
		GPS: N32°37.04' W114°22.46'

▼ 1.6	BR	Track on left.
2.3 ▲	SO	Track on right.

▼ 1.8	SO	Leaving Barry M. Goldwater Air Force Range, many small tracks on right and left around boundary, remain on main trail.
2.1 ▲	SO	Entering Barry M. Goldwater Air Force Range, valid permit required beyond this point. Many small tracks on right and left around boundary, remain on main trail.
		GPS: N32°37.39' W114°22.48'

▼ 2.0	BL	Track on right.
1.9 ▲	SO	Track on left.

Ocotillos and saguaros beside the trail and the Tinajas Altas Mountains in the distance

EL CAMINO DEL DIABLO

To many early travelers, El Camino del Diablo (the Devil's Highway) was hell on earth. This 250-mile trail meandered between Sonoita (near the present border between Arizona and Mexico) and Yuma, Arizona. The region was first used by Indians to transport salt and shells back from the Sea of Cortez. These early inhabitants, Pinacatenos and Arenenos, both clans of the Tohono O'odham, eked out an existence in the arid landscape.

The first person known to pioneer a trail across the region was Captain Melchior Diaz, a member of Coronado's expedition who led a party through the desert en route to California in 1540.

It was another Spaniard who first provided some real information on the area and traveled it extensively himself. Between 1698 and 1702, the Jesuit missionary, Padre Eusebio Francisco Kino repeatedly traveled El Camino del Diablo as he carried out his missionary work while pioneering a route to California. Known as "The Padre on Horseback," Kino explored extensively, making the first maps of the region which, most importantly, included many of the major water holes.

Throughout the 1700s, El Camino del Diablo saw a lot of use, mainly by Spanish priests who used it as a shorter route to the missions in California. Although it was a hard route, it was considerably shorter than the alternative land route via Tucson and Gila Bend, which looped to the north, or the long sea route, which

Artist rendering of Padre Eusebio Francisco Kino

passed to the south of Baja California. There was also less risk of being attacked by Apaches. Well-known names who traveled the route in the 1700s include Juan Bautista de Anza (1774–1776) as he searched for the Lost Seven Cities of Gold, Fray Francisco Garcés (1779–1781), and Pedro Fages (1781–1782).

In 1781, the Yuma Indian uprising at the Colorado River crossing meant that fewer travelers were willing to brave the route, and it reverted to a seldom-used trail. It was not until 1849 and the onset of the California Gold Rush that El Camino del Diablo once again saw travelers. It was during this time that El Camino acquired its well-deserved reputation as the most deadly of immigrant roads. "Locally, it is known as El Camino del Diablo, and few names are more appropriate," wrote Capt. D. D. Gaillard in 1896.

The number of deaths that have occurred along this so-called road may never be known. Men trying to connect the vague trail of water holes along the way had their work cut out for them. Shifting sands meant any real trace of a trail was lost and many died of hunger, thirst, and sheer fatigue. It is thought that between 400 and 2,000 people died of thirst along the road and were buried in often unmarked, unremembered graves. There are approximately 50 known graves along the trail, but only a handful are marked in any way.

One of the most obvious graves is that of Dave O'Neill, who is buried on the pass through the hills that bear his name. A prospector near the turn of the twentieth century, he died of exposure and dehydration. His burros made their way into Papago Well without him, prompting a search, and he was buried where his body was found in the pass.

Early travelers had a few options when they reached the natural tanks of Tinajas Altas. Called Agua Escondido, "hidden water" by Padre Kino, the string of nine natural water tanks running up a cleft in the Tinajas Altas Mountains were one of the major water points along the trail. When full, these tinajas could hold 20,000 gallons, but more often than not, the lower tanks were drained dry. The climb up to the higher tanks is a difficult one by anyone's standards. Many people died because they were too weak to make the steep climb up to the higher tanks.

If the tanks were dry, travelers had little choice but to swing to the north following the east side of the Tinajas Altas Mountains to the water and shade along the Gila River. This route was later known as "The Smugglers Trail" after it was resurrected by liquor smugglers during prohibition days. If the tanks had water, stronger and more daring travelers were able to cross through the Tinajas Altas Mountains and proceed more directly to Yuma Crossing.

Other people who passed this way include a wave of Mexican and American boundary surveyors who were formalizing the boundaries of the land acquired by the United States in the 1853–54 Gadsden Purchase. Miners in the 1860s were also rushing to the Colorado River to mine the placer gold discovered there.

The railroad reached Yuma in 1870 and El Camino del Diablo waned. Few were willing to risk their lives crossing the trail when there was the safer option of the railroad available. El Camino was quiet until more recent times, when scientists began to study the desert in depth, and even more recently, the road gained popularity as an exciting and beautiful route for backcountry adventurers.

Other current users of the trail are a steady stream of undocumented immigrants and drug smugglers who take advantage of the extremely remote, unpopulated area to gain access into the United States. The border patrol is active in the region, and there are signs along the Mexican border warning potential border crossers of the dangers of the area they are entering. In spite of this, every year people die of thirst and heat exhaustion as they try to cross the deserts to civilization.

Through the years, travelers have named the features they found along El Camino. Many are named after early travelers; others reflect the physical characteristics of the features they saw. Others are less obvious—Raven Butte, a very dark-colored butte near the eastern end of Cipriano Pass, is not named for its color, but because the ravens in the region were surprisingly trusting and tame.

The Gila Mountains were formerly known as the Sierra de la Gila, when in 1854 Lt. N. Michler reported that they extended north of the Gila River. For a while they were the Gila City Mountains, after the nearby booming settlement of Gila City.

The agave plant, which is plentiful in this desert is called lechuguilla in Spanish, mean-

(Continued from previous page)

ing frill or ruff, a name that reflects the lower shape of the plant. Hence, the Lechuguilla Desert became an obvious name for this region.

The Cabeza Prieta (Spanish for "dark head") is a reflection of the mountain's structure. They were considered to be part of the Tule Mountains to the southeast until the early 1920s when it was thought the gap at Tule Well where El Camino del Diablo passed through was significant enough to divide the range.

Early emigrants learned fast by necessity that in the desert they would find tule plants growing near water and so the name Tule Well developed though no such plant can be found here today. The name Tule is also given to the nearby mountains to the south, which cross the border into Mexico. These mountains were formerly known as the badlands in Spanish—Mesa de Malpais.

Agave plant

El Camino del Diablo was placed on the National Register of Historic Places in 1978. Today, El Camino del Diablo crosses through three distinct land management boundaries. The Barry M. Goldwater Air Force Range occupies most of the western section. The middle section is contained within the Cabeza Prieta National Wildlife Area, and the Organ Pipe Cactus National Monument occupies the eastern end of the trail.

The Barry M. Goldwater Air Force Range is currently public land, which is leased to the military. It was established in 1941 to train World War II pilots and continues in use to this day by the U.S. Air Force and U.S. Marine Corps. It is used for air-to-ground and air-to-air training missions. Ground-based marines also use the 2 million-acre range for ground maneuvers and ground-to-air training exercises. Although it has been accessible to the public for many years under a permit system, the military uses always take precedence, so from time to time the range is closed to the public. Parts of the range are not accessible at anytime.

The Cabeza Prieta National Wildlife Refuge is also overflown by the military, but the area is now designated as wilderness, with vehicle access permitted on designated corridors only.

Today, nearly three hundred years after El Camino acquired its fearsome reputation, people still speak of the trail with awe, wonder, and more than a little trepidation. In many respects, little has changed, and many of the earliest travelers would have little difficulty in recognizing their landmarks today. If you take one of the historic trails in the region, it is an experience that will remain with you long after the sand, dust, and scratches have been cleaned from your vehicle.

▼ 2.1	TL	Turn left onto wide graded dirt road opposite small reservoir.
1.8 ▲	TR	Turn right onto ungraded dirt trail opposite small reservoir. Trail is past the end of the golf course.
		GPS: N32°37.60′ W114°22.58′

▼ 2.9	SO	Road is paved. Road on right is 14E Street. Now traveling on County 14th Street.
1.0 ▲	SO	Road turns to dirt. Road on left is 14E Street.

▼ 3.9		Trail ends at the intersection with Foothills Boulevard. Turn right to exit to I-8. Trail on left is the start of South #1: Tinajas Altas Pass Trail.
0.0 ▲		Trail starts at the intersection of Foothills Boulevard and County 14th Street. Zero trip meter and turn east on County 14th Street. Dirt trail to the south at this point is South #1: Tinajas Altas Pass Trail.
		GPS: N32°37.60′ W114°24.55′

El Camino del Diablo Trail

STARTING POINT	I-8, exit 30 at Wellton
FINISHING POINT	Arizona 85, 2.2 miles south of Ajo
TOTAL MILEAGE	114.1 miles
UNPAVED MILEAGE	110 miles
DRIVING TIME	2 days
ELEVATION RANGE	200–2,000 feet
USUALLY OPEN	Year-round
BEST TIME TO TRAVEL	November to mid-March
DIFFICULTY RATING	4
SCENIC RATING	9
REMOTENESS RATING	+2

Special Attractions

- Extremely long, remote 4WD adventure.
- Historic route used by Indians, Spanish, and gold rush travelers.
- Wide range of spectacular desert scenery.
- Bates Well homestead and site.
- Organ Pipe Cactus National Monument.

An adobe casita at Tule Well

An old, partially dismantled tank standing guard beside the trail

History

El Camino del Diablo (Spanish for The Road of the Devil, although the popular translation is "The Devil's Highway") has long been used by many people crossing the dry Sonoran Desert. Today, this section of El Camino del Diablo does not strictly follow the old paths, as such there were, which meandered south down into Mexico. Different travelers took different routes, and at times the faint trails were obliterated by wind and shifting sand.

At the eastern end of the trail is Bates Well, a former small settlement now contained within Organ Pipe Cactus National Monument. A well was dug here in the 1890s by a man called Bates. Henry Gray was the last rancher at Bates Well before it came under the full control of the national monument. Henry continued ranching after the monument's establishment in 1937. When he died in 1976, ranching ceased, and only the decaying cabins, corrals, and well remain.

The trail ends in Ajo, a historic mining town. The name Ajo seems to derive from the Papago Indians' use of the ores there that produced their red face paint (*au'auho* was their word for paint). Another possible explanation is that the town was named after a lily that grows there, whose root resembles in looks and taste a spring onion. *Ajo* means "garlic" in Spanish.

Though Captain Peter Brady was one of the first to lead mining ventures in the Ajo area after scouting the region for the route of the thirty-second parallel railroad in 1853, his ventures soon ran dry as the copper ore was too costly to process. Basic farming was the main activity of the few folks who remained in old Ajo. The abundant rich ores remained in the ground until the 1910s when leaching processes were developed that allowed the New Cornelia Mine (named by Colonel Greenway) to prosper to boom levels. Several thousand people moved to this growing region. The mine grew so large that the old Ajo town was engulfed by the spreading mine. Phelps-Dodge is still the current owner of the mine, which is classed as an active mine due to a few people being employed mainly for security/safety reasons. No serious mining has occurred since the price of copper dropped in the 1980s, resulting in the town developing an almost ghost town atmosphere compared to its former frantic activity. Now at the turn of the twenty-first century it is becoming an attractive winter retirement setting for many folks, although its growth is restricted by the Indian reservation and the federal lands that surround it.

Description

For the well-prepared adventurer, this route is a two-day excursion through some of the most remote territory in Arizona. Although becoming more well known and increasingly traveled, the trail should not be treated lightly. Advance preparation is required, as a permit to travel the Barry M. Goldwater Air Force Range and the Cabeza Prieta National Wildlife Refuge is essential (see permit information below).

However, once you are ready to go, two unforgettable days of traveling through some of the most spectacular desert scenery in Arizona awaits. You will need a minimum of two days for the trail, longer if you intend to explore some of the other trails in the region.

The trail commences in Wellton, along I-8, 25 miles east of Yuma. Top off the fuel tank and proceed south and briefly west along the Mohawk Canal before swinging south to enter the Barry M. Goldwater Air Force Range. The trail within the range is easygoing, being a wide, graded road for the most part, as it runs down a broad, flat-bottomed valley, with the Gila Mountains to the west and the lower Wellton Hills to the east. The Gila Mountains are composed of light-colored granite and are bare of vegetation on their slopes. As you get closer to them, you can appreciate the weathering of the pock-marked granite. The southern range is called the Tinajas Altas; the Spanish means "high tanks" and refers to the natural water pockets where the sparse rainfall can collect. Two other 4WD trails lead across the range—South #4: Cipriano Pass Trail is the northernmost trail and South #1: Tinajas Altas Pass Trail crosses at the southern end of the range.

Along the wide valley the trail is normally straight and wide enough that two vehicles can pass without pulling over. Remember you are in a military reserve and can expect to see some signs of its presence. There are some sections, however, where the trail twists and is narrower. It may be slightly brushy for wider vehicles and you need to watch for oncoming, fast-moving vehicles. There are many small tracks to the left and right within the range but only the marked or most noticeable ones have been given in the route directions.

After 31 miles the trail leaves the Barry M. Goldwater Air Force Range and enters the Cabeza Prieta National Wildlife Refuge. From here some of the most interesting, scenic, and difficult parts of the route commence.

The area is also rich in wildlife. Some twenty-four species of snakes, including six types of rattlesnake, make the refuge their home, as well as the desert tortoise, horned lizard, bighorn sheep, coyote, kit fox, kangaroo rat, and eleven species of bats. Many species of migrating birds pass through the refuge. The best times of year to view them are February to May and August to November. Bird watchers may see warblers, phoebes, flycatchers, and swallows. Year-round there are red-tailed hawks and Gambel's quails. The refuge is also habitat for the rare and elusive Sonoran pronghorn antelope, an endangered species.

The trail is a narrow single track as it winds its way through the Cabeza Prieta Mountains. The sand can be deep and lower tire pressures may be necessary. This deep sand is where you will start to chew through the fuel. There are also some rocky sections. The trail is a lot narrower and can be brushy along this section, although with a little care it is possible to avoid the worst of it. The scenery within the Cabeza Prieta Mountains is wonderful. The very light-colored granite mountains, winding trail, saguaros, and ocotillos with their brilliant flags of flowers make for interest and photographic opportunities all the way. There are virtually no public access side trails within the Cabeza Prieta, as it travels along a wilderness corridor. Most old vehicle trails are now designated for management vehicles only. Most of them are given to assist the route directions, but smaller, fainter, and overgrown side trails have been omitted.

It is possible to camp anywhere within the range or the Cabeza Prieta as long as you stay within 50 feet of the trail. There are some pleasant sites for one or two vehicles within the Cabeza Prieta Mountains, but larger groups are probably better off selecting the sites at Tule Well or Papago Well. At Tule Well there are four sites, each with a picnic table and BBQ, as well as additional space for more vehicles. However, there is limited shade at these sites. At Tule Well, there is a small adobe casita, built by National Wildlife Refuge workers in 1941. Also at Tule Well is the tank itself—dry on our visit. Next to the adobe casita is the junction with South #5: Christmas Pass Trail, which provides access to I-8.

From Tule Well, the trail runs only a couple of miles from the international border with Mexico. A major highway runs along the border on the Mexican side, Mexican Highway 2, which can often provide the only sign of civilization in two days; it is possible to catch glimpses of trucks on the highway.

As you cross over a gap in the hills, a keen eye will spot one of the many graves along the route. The location of most graves is unknown, and the elements, animals, and people often disturb the markers, making them hard to find.

Fourteen miles after Tule Well, the trail starts to cross the Pinacate Lava Flow. The lava flow originated in Mexico in the region now contained within the Pinacate Natural Reserve. There are approximately 70 volcanic peaks and a large, barren region covered by black cinders. The region is named for the desert stink beetle, or darkling beetle—a beetle that stands on its head and emits a foul odor when threatened; it is commonly found in Mexico. The Aztecs called this beetle *pinacatl* in their Nahuatl language.

The five miles that cross the Pinacate Lava Flow are some of the roughest of the entire trail. They are not difficult, just extremely lumpy and rough. Take it slowly and enjoy the dramatically different scenery.

The Pinta Sands are an area of soft sand dunes on either side of the Pinacate Lava Flow. On the east side of the Pinta Sands are Las Playas ("the beaches"), a deceptive area of deep, fine sand, often referred to as "bulldust." The trail here has worn down so that it is below the level of the surrounding area. In wet weather, it becomes totally impassable, as the powder-fine sand turns to deep goo. The BLM requests that you do not attempt to cross in wet weather or cut new tracks attempting to pass. This section is also the most brushy part of the trail, and minor scratches are inevitable for all vehicles. The worst section is between the Pinacate Lava Flow and the O'Neill Hills.

There is a second suggested area for group camping at Papago Well. There are cleared areas in the creosote bushes, and four picnic tables and BBQs. The border patrol maintains an active presence around here as it is so close to the international border, and you are likely to be awakened at night by their low-flying, unlit helicopters. Another option for groups needing more space is a pleasant area approximately 1.5 miles east of Papago Well, where there is a smooth, flat, relatively open area set among large saguaros on the western edge of Papago Mountain.

After passing through the well-named Cholla Pass, the trail enters the Organ Pipe Cactus National Monument. The old vehicle trail via Pozo Well to join South #6: Puerto Blanco Drive joins on the right, but has been closed to the public since 1998.

A popular spot for lunch is the old homestead and well at Bates Well. There are the old buildings, cabins, and corrals to explore and even a bit of shade. Past Bates Well, the trail is roughly graded and suitable for 2WD vehicles and it is an easy run into Ajo, passing the huge New Cornelia copper mine as you do.

Ajo has limited supplies and a couple of motels and eating places, as well as fuel.

Permit Information

In recent years the permit system has been streamlined, so that one permit now covers access into the Barry M. Goldwater Air Force Range, the Cabeza Prieta National Wildlife Refuge, and Organ Pipe Cactus National Monument. It is essential that you obtain a permit before you go. The permit allows you to cross Organ Pipe Cactus National Monument on the Bates Well Road only. To visit any other areas of the monument, you need to pay a separate park fee.

A separate permit is required for each person traveling over the age of 18 years. Children under 18 do not need a separate permit if accompanied by a permitted adult. Be prepared to provide details of yourself and your vehicle. You will also have to sign a "Hold Harmless" agreement, which informs you of the many dangers you are likely to encounter and absolves the military of any responsibility.

Permits can be obtained in person or via mail. Faxed applications are no longer accepted due to the requirement of an original signature on the permit application. The application takes about 20 minutes in person. You can also telephone to have an application mailed to you, but allow ample time before your proposed trip if applying via mail. There is no charge for the permit, and it is valid from July 1 to June 30 for multiple trips into the area.

Range permits may be obtained from the following places:

Luke Air Force Base
Gila Bend Auxiliary Field
Security Forces
Gila Bend, AZ 85337
(928) 683-6220

Range Management Department
Box 99160
Marine Corps Air Station
Yuma, AZ 85369-9160
(928) 341-3402

Bureau of Land Management
Yuma Field Office
2555 East Gila Ridge Road
Yuma, AZ 85365
(928) 317-3200

Bureau of Land Management
Phoenix Field Office
21605 North 7th Avenue
Phoenix, AZ 85027
(623) 580-5500

Cabeza Prieta National Wildlife Refuge
1611 North 2nd Avenue
Ajo, AZ 85321
(520) 387-6483

Note that these offices all keep limited hours and are not open on weekends.

In addition, before each visit you MUST call 1-877-CAMP-010. This free call is answered 24 hours a day, 7 days a week. Be prepared to give permit numbers for all travelers, vehicle details, proposed route, and dates of entry and exit to the range. This number cannot answer any questions regarding permits, routes, or general inquiries.

Be aware, too, that authorized routes within the range are subject to change, either permanently or temporarily due to military exercises. It is your responsibility to be aware of any changes or restrictions that apply each time you enter the range. A map showing authorized travel routes is available when you get your permit.

Special Considerations

Special considerations for El Camino del Diablo and trails within the Barry M. Goldwater Air Force Range:

The exceptional remoteness of this trail carries with it additional responsibilities for the traveler. As there are no facilities and no water available; you should be totally self-sufficient. The trail is very lightly traveled, so you cannot rely on a passing driver to help you out. It is especially important to carry ample water over and above your anticipated requirements. Parts of the trail cross areas that are impassable when wet—if you have to sit and wait out a wet spell you don't want to be hungry and thirsty.

Consider traveling as part of a group. This reduces the risk of being stranded and enables you to share essential equipment and vehicle spares. Thirsty vehicles may require additional fuel.

You must have a street-registered four-wheel drive vehicle to enter the Cabeza Prieta NWR. ATVs and 2WD vehicles are not permitted on the refuge.

The proximity of the international border with Mexico carries with it additional hazards. The area is a high-traffic area for undocumented aliens crossing from Mexico into the United States. It is likely that you will encounter these people. Refer to the section on the international border for more details. Nine times out of ten, you will just be asked for water and food and then left alone. If you feel uneasy or uncomfortable with this situation, consider traveling as part of a larger group. Lone vehicles and small groups are far more likely to be approached for assistance.

It is also highly recommended that you top up your fuel tank at Wellton.

Current Road Information
Luke Air Force Base
Gila Bend Auxiliary Field
Security Forces
Gila Bend, AZ 85337
(520) 683-6220

Bureau of Land Management
Yuma Field Office
2555 E Gila Ridge Road
Yuma, AZ 85365
(928) 317-3200

Cabeza Prieta National Wildlife Refuge
1611 North 2nd Avenue
Ajo, AZ 85321
(520) 387-6483

Map References
BLM   Yuma, Tinajas Altas Mtns., Cabeza Prieta Mtns., Ajo
USGS 1:24,000   Wellton, Wellton Hills, Raven Butte, Tinajas Altas, Coyote Water, Tule Mtns., Sierra Arida, Paradise Canyon, Monument Bluff, Las Playas, O'Neill Hills, Agua Dulce Mtns., North of Agua Dulce Mtns., Palo Verde Camp, Bates Well, Ajo South
1:100,000 Yuma, Tinajas Altas Mtns., Cabeza Prieta Mtns., Ajo
Maptech CD-ROM: Southwest Arizona/Yuma
Arizona Atlas & Gazetteer, pp. 62, 63, 64, 71, 70
Arizona Road & Recreation Atlas, pp. 44, 50, 51, 78, 84, 85
Recreational Map of Arizona (incomplete)

Route Directions

▼ 0.0   From I-8, exit 30 at Wellton, zero trip meter immediately on the south side of the freeway at the eastbound freeway entrance/exit. Exit ramp and proceed south on the paved road. Immediately cross over the Wellton Canal.

5.1 ▲   Trail ends at exit 30 on I-8 at the settlement of Wellton.
         GPS: N32°39.56' W114°08.49'

▼ 1.3 TR Turn right onto graded dirt road, immediately before the Mohave Canal and levee.

3.8 ▲ TL Turn left onto paved road.

▼ 5.1 TL Zero trip meter and turn left and cross over Mohawk Canal on bridge, then immediately turn left again.

0.0 ▲   Continue along the north bank of the canal.
         GPS: N32°38.13' W114°12.60'

▼ 0.0   Continue toward Barry M. Goldwater Air Force Range.

13.3 ▲ TR Turn right and cross over Mohawk Canal on bridge, then immediately turn right alongside canal. Zero trip meter.

▼ 0.1   SO   Cross over levee bank, tracks on right and left along the top.

13.2 ▲   SO   Cross over levee bank, tracks on right and left along the top.

▼ 1.2   SO   Crossroads, edge of the Barry M. Goldwater Air Force Range. Valid permit essential from this point. Graded road on right and left along the boundary.

12.1 ▲   SO   Crossroads, leaving the Barry M. Goldwater Air Force Range. Graded road on right and left along the boundary.

GPS: N32°37.20' W114°12.57'

▼ 1.5   SO   Cross through fence line.

11.8 ▲   SO   Cross through fence line.

▼ 1.9   SO   Track on right.

11.4 ▲   SO   Track on left.

▼ 2.2   SO   Several tracks on right, remain on main graded trail.

11.1 ▲   SO   Several tracks on left, remain on main graded trail.

▼ 6.3   SO   Track on left and right under small power lines.

7.0 ▲   SO   Track on right and left under small power lines.

GPS: N32°33.36' W114°09.92'

▼ 8.3   SO   Track on right to old military tank.

5.0 ▲   SO   Track on left to old military tank.

▼ 8.4   SO   Track on right to old military tank, second track on right.

4.9 ▲   SO   Track on left, then second track on left to old military tank.

GPS: N32°31.74' W114°08.77'

▼ 9.1   SO   Track on right is marked S23.

4.2 ▲   SO   Track on left is marked S23.

GPS: N32°31.12' W114°08.38'

▼ 9.5   SO   Track on right is marked B3.

3.8 ▲   SO   Track on left is marked B3.

▼ 10.4   SO   Track on right and left is marked B4.

2.9 ▲   SO   Track on left and right is marked B4.

GPS: N32°30.18' W114°07.71'

▼ 10.5   SO   Track on right is marked S24.

2.8 ▲   SO   Track on left is marked S24.

▼ 11.8   SO   Track on right.

1.5 ▲   SO   Track on left.

▼ 11.9   SO   Track on right is marked S57; then second track on right.

1.4 ▲   SO   Track on left, then second track on left is marked S57.

GPS: N32°29.00' W114°06.84'

▼ 12.0   SO   Track on right.

1.3 ▲   SO   Track on left.

▼ 13.3   SO   Tracks on left and right are marked B5. The track on right is South #4: Cipriano Pass Trail. Zero trip meter.

0.0 ▲   Continue to the northwest.

GPS: N32°27.87' W114°06.27'

▼ 0.0   Continue to southeast. Raven Butte is visible to the south in front of the Tinajas Altas Mountains.

2.8 ▲   SO   Tracks on left and right are marked B5. The track on left is South #4: Cipriano Pass Trail. Zero trip meter.

▼ 0.6   SO   Track on right.

2.2 ▲   SO   Track on left.

▼ 2.5   SO   Track on right is marked B5.

0.3 ▲   SO   Track on left is marked B5.

GPS: N32°25.80' W114°05.18'

▼ 2.7   SO   Track on right is marked S32.

0.1 ▲   SO   Track on left is marked S32.

▼ 2.8   SO   El Camino del Diablo information board on right. Zero trip meter.

0.0 ▲   Continue to the northwest.

GPS: N32°25.50' W114°05.01'

▼ 0.0   Continue to the southeast.

6.6 ▲   SO   El Camino del Diablo information board on left. Zero trip meter.

▼ 0.6   SO   Tracks on right and left are marked

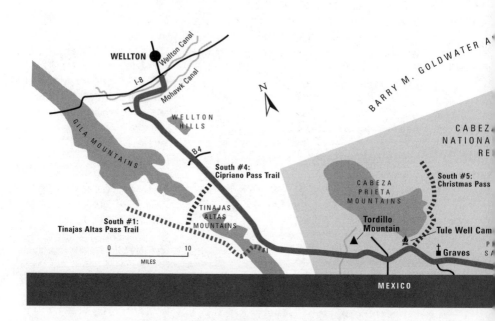

S33.

6.0 ▲   SO Tracks on right and left are marked
         S33.
         GPS: N32°25.00' W114°04.74'

▼ 0.7   SO Faint track on right.
5.9 ▲   SO Faint track on left.

▼ 2.6   SO Track on right and sign for the Tinajas
         Altas Mountains, Area of Critical
         Environmental Concern.
4.0 ▲   SO Track on left and sign for the Tinajas
         Altas Mountains, Area of Critical
         Environmental Concern.
         GPS: N32°23.33' W114°03.95'

▼ 5.4   SO Track on right.
1.2 ▲   SO Track on left.

▼ 5.8   SO Well-used track on right.
0.8 ▲   BR Well-used track on left.
         GPS: N32°20.51' W114°02.94'

▼ 6.6   BL Track on right is signed to Tinajas
         Altas. This joins South #1: Tinajas
         Altas Pass Trail via a maze of small
         trails. Zero trip meter at sign.
0.0 ▲   Continue on El Camino del Diablo.
         GPS: N32°19.83' W114°02.94'

▼ 0.0   Continue on El Camino del Diablo.
2.6 ▲   SO Track on left is signed to Tinajas
         Altas. This joins South #1: Tinajas
         Altas Pass Trail via a maze of small
         trails. Zero trip meter at sign.

▼ 0.4   TL T-intersection, track on right.
2.2 ▲   BR Turn right following better-used grad-
         ed trail. Track continues straight on.
         GPS: N32°19.50' W114°02.81'

▼ 0.6   SO Track on left is marked S34.
2.0 ▲   SO Track on right is marked S34.

▼ 2.1   SO Track on left is marked S35.
0.5 ▲   SO Track on right is marked S35.

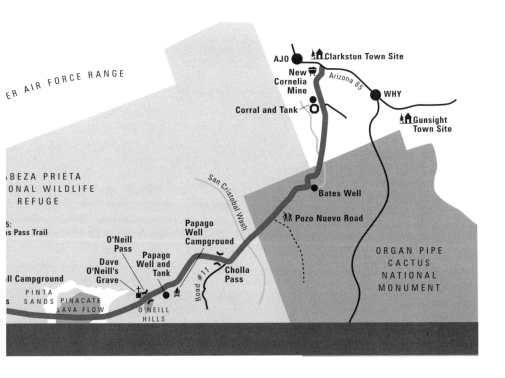

▼ 2.6   SO   Track on right through the bare area is South #1: Tinajas Altas Pass Trail (west route of El Camino del Diablo). Leaving the Area of Critical Environmental Concern. Zero trip meter.

0.0 ▲   Continue toward Wellton.

     GPS: N32°18.13′ W114°01.17′

▼ 0.0   Continue east, toward Tordillo Mountain.

3.5 ▲   SO   Track on left through the bare area is South #1: Tinajas Altas Pass Trail (west route of El Camino del Diablo). Entering the Area of Critical Environmental Concern. Zero trip meter.

▼ 1.6   SO   Faint track on right.

1.9 ▲   SO   Faint track on left.

▼ 3.5   SO   Exiting the military area and entering the Cabeza Prieta National Wildlife Refuge; permit required. Zero trip meter at boundary.

0.0 ▲   Continue into the Barry M. Goldwater Air Force Range.

     GPS: N32°16.92′ W113°57.64′

▼ 0.0   Continue into the Cabeza Prieta NWR.

13.1 ▲   SO   Exiting the Cabeza Prieta National Wildlife Refuge and entering the Barry M. Goldwater Air Force Range; permit required. Zero trip meter at boundary.

▼ 4.3   SO   Management vehicle tracks on right and left. Tordillo Mountain is on left.

8.8 ▲   SO   Management vehicle tracks on right and left. Tordillo Mountain is on right.

     GPS: N32°15.39′ W113°53.32′

▼ 4.6   SO   Cross through wash and ascend short ridge.

8.5 ▲ SO Descend short ridge and cross through wash.
GPS: N32°15.30′ W113°52.97′

▼ 7.0 SO Track on left is numbered 54.
6.1 ▲ SO Track on right is numbered 54.
GPS: N32°14.77′ W113°50.66′

▼ 8.2 SO Cross through wash.
4.9 ▲ SO Cross through wash.

▼ 9.9 SO Track on right and track on left is for management vehicles only.
3.2 ▲ SO Track on right and track on left is for management vehicles only.
GPS: N32°13.22′ W113°48.17′

▼ 10.0 SO Old trail on left is for management vehicles only.
3.1 ▲ SO Old trail on right is for management vehicles only.

▼ 10.1 SO Cross through wash.
3.0 ▲ SO Cross through wash.

▼ 11.0 SO Cross through wash.
2.1 ▲ SO Cross through wash.

▼ 11.3 SO Track on left is for management vehicles only.
1.8 ▲ SO Track on right is for management vehicles only.

▼ 11.4 SO Cross through wash.
1.7 ▲ SO Cross through wash.

▼ 12.6 SO Cross through wash.
0.5 ▲ SO Cross through wash.

▼ 12.9 SO Cross through wash.
0.2 ▲ SO Cross through wash.

▼ 13.1 BR Tule Well camping area. Major track to the left is South #5: Christmas Pass Trail to I-8. There is a small adobe casita at the junction. The hillock behind the casita has a stone plaque recording the dedication of the Cabeza Prieta Refuge in 1941. Zero trip meter.

0.0 ▲ Continue toward the Barry M. Goldwater Air Force Range.
GPS: N32°13.56′ W113°44.92′

▼ 0.0 Continue along El Camino del Diablo.
24.1 ▲ BL Tule Well camping area. Major track on right is South #5: Christmas Pass Trail to I-8. There is a small adobe casita at the junction. The hillock behind the casita has a stone plaque recording the dedication of the Cabeza Prieta Refuge in 1941. Zero trip meter.

▼ 0.1 SO Cross through wash.
24.0 ▲ SO Cross through wash.

▼ 0.3 SO Cross through wash.
23.8 ▲ SO Cross through wash.

▼ 0.7 SO Cross through wash.
23.4 ▲ SO Cross through wash.

▼ 0.9 SO Cross through wash.
23.2 ▲ SO Cross through wash.

▼ 1.0 SO Track on right, #18, is for management vehicles only.
23.1 ▲ SO Track on left, #18, is for management vehicles only.

▼ 2.1 BL Route marker for Papago Well and Ajo on left. Track on right and track on left are for management vehicles only.
22.0 ▲ BR Track on right and track on left are for management vehicles only.

▼ 3.1 SO Cross through wash.
21.0 ▲ SO Cross through wash.

▼ 3.2 SO Cross through wash.
20.9 ▲ SO Cross through wash.

▼ 3.3 SO Grave on left, just after the wash crossing.
20.8 ▲ SO Grave on right, just before wash crossing.
GPS: N32°11.34′ W113°42.60′

▼ 3.7 SO Grave on left, little remains to mark

the spot except some white stones.

20.4 ▲ SO Grave on right, little remains to mark the spot except some white stones.
GPS: N32°11.12′ W113°42.45′

▼ 4.0 SO Cross through wash.
20.1 ▲ SO Cross through wash.

▼ 4.3 SO Cross through wash.
19.8 ▲ SO Cross through wash.

▼ 5.0 SO Cross through wash.
19.1 ▲ SO Cross through wash.

▼ 5.1 SO Cross through wash.
19.0 ▲ SO Cross through wash.

▼ 6.4 SO Cross through wash. Leaving the Cabeza Prieta Mountains and starting to cross the Tule Desert.
17.7 ▲ SO Cross through wash. Leaving the Tule Desert and entering the Cabeza Prieta Mountains.

▼ 7.2 SO Cross through wash.
16.9 ▲ SO Cross through wash.

▼ 7.6 SO Cross through wash.
16.5 ▲ SO Cross through wash.

▼ 8.8 SO Cross through wash.
15.3 ▲ SO Cross through wash.

▼ 14.0 SO Starting to cross the Pinacate Lava Flow.
10.1 ▲ SO Leaving the lava flow to cross the Pinta Sands.

▼ 16.8 SO Turnout on right and cairn on hillock.
7.3 ▲ SO Turnout on left and cairn on hillock.
GPS: N32°06.56′ W113°30.12′

▼ 19.3 SO Leaving the Pinacate Lava Flow, re-entering the Pinta Sands.
4.8 ▲ SO Leaving the Pinta Sands to cross the Pinacate Lava Flow.

▼ 22.7 SO Tracks on right and left.
1.4 ▲ SO Tracks on right and left.
GPS: N32°05.48′ W113°24.20′

▼ 24.1 SO Route marker pointing back for Tule Well, Tule Tank, and Tinajas Altas. Zero trip meter.
0.0 ▲ Continue toward the Pinacate Lava Flow.
GPS: N32°05.27′ W113°22.83′

▼ 0.0 Continue toward the O'Neill Hills.
5.6 ▲ SO Route marker for Tule Well, Tule Tank, and Tinajas Altas. Zero trip meter.

▼ 1.6 SO Grave of Dave O'Neill on left of the trail, marked by a cross and a pile of stones. Trail is passing through O'Neill Pass.
4.0 ▲ SO Grave of Dave O'Neill on right of the trail, marked by a cross and a pile of stones. Trail is passing through O'Neill Pass.
GPS: N32°05.83′ W113°21.23′

▼ 4.8 SO Cross through wash.
0.8 ▲ SO Cross through wash.

▼ 5.5 SO Route marker pointing back for Tule Well, Tule Tank, and Tinajas Altas.
0.1 ▲ SO Route marker for Tule Well, Tule Tank, and Tinajas Altas.

▼ 5.6 SO Papago Well and tank on right. Zero trip meter.
0.0 ▲ Continue toward the O'Neill Hills.
GPS: N32°05.95′ W113°17.16′

▼ 0.0 Continue toward the Organ Pipe Cactus National Monument.
8.4 ▲ SO Papago Well and tank on left. Zero trip meter.

▼ 0.1 SO Papago Well Camp on right.
8.3 ▲ SO Papago Well Camp on left.
GPS: N32°05.98′ W113°16.99′

▼ 8.4 SO Well-used track, #11, on right is for management vehicles only. Zero trip meter.
0.0 ▲ Continue toward Papago Well.
GPS: N32°06.17′ W113°09.95′

▼ 0.0   Continue toward the Organ Pipe Cactus National Monument following the sign to Ajo.

4.9 ▲   BR   Well-used track, #11, on the left is for management vehicles only. Zero trip meter.

▼ 4.9   SO   Track on right is for management vehicles only; then cattle guard. Leaving Cabeza Prieta NWR and entering Organ Pipe Cactus National monument. Track on left after cattle guard. Zero trip meter.

0.0 ▲   Continue into the Cabeza Prieta National Wildlife Refuge.

GPS: N32°07.83′ W113°05.09′

▼ 0.0   Continue straight on into the Organ Pipe Cactus NM.

8.4 ▲   SO   Track on right; then exit Organ Pipe Cactus National Monument over cattle guard and enter the Cabeza Prieta NWR. Track on left is for management vehicles. A valid range permit is essential beyond this point. Zero trip meter.

▼ 2.5   SO   Track on right is the Pozo Nuevo Road, which is closed to vehicles.

5.9 ▲   SO   Track on left is the Pozo Nuevo Road, which is closed to vehicles.

GPS: N32°08.73′ W113°02.58′

▼ 7.2   SO   Cross through wash.
1.2 ▲   SO   Cross through wash.

▼ 8.1   SO   Cattle guard.
0.3 ▲   SO   Cattle guard.

▼ 8.4   SO   Bates Well on right. Zero trip meter.

0.0 ▲   Continue through the Organ Pipe Cactus National Monument. The route is now a formed trail.

GPS: N32°10.20′ W112°57.05′

▼ 0.0   Continue on toward Ajo. The road is now roughly graded.

3.8 ▲   SO   Bates Well on left. Zero trip meter.

▼ 1.6   SO   Track on left is closed to vehicles and goes a short distance to two mines.

2.2 ▲   SO   Track on right is closed to vehicles and goes a short distance to two mines.

▼ 3.8   SO   Exiting Organ Pipe Cactus National Monument over cattle guard. Track on right before cattle guard and track on left after cattle guard. Zero trip meter.

0.0 ▲   Continue into the Organ Pipe Cactus National Monument.

GPS: N32°12.02′ W112°54.28′

▼ 0.0   Continue toward Ajo.

11.9 ▲   SO   Track on right; then enter Organ Pipe Cactus National Monument over cattle guard; then track on left. Zero trip meter.

▼ 0.2   SO   Two entrances to track on left.
11.7 ▲   SO   Two entrances to track on right.

▼ 0.7   SO   Track on left; then cross through wash; then track on right.
11.2 ▲   SO   Track on left; then cross through wash; then track on right.

▼ 1.2   SO   Cross through wash.
10.7 ▲   SO   Cross through wash.

▼ 1.6   SO   Cross through wash.
10.3 ▲   SO   Cross through wash.

▼ 3.0   SO   Major graded road on left; continue straight on and cross through wash; then small tracks on left and right.

8.9 ▲   BL   Small tracks on left and right, then cross through wash; then major graded road to the right.

GPS: N32°14.42′ W112°52.83′

▼ 3.7   SO   Cross through wash, then faint track on right.

8.2 ▲   SO   Faint track on left, then cross through wash.

▼ 3.8   SO   Smaller track on right.
8.1 ▲   BR   Smaller track on left; remain on main

graded road.

▼ 5.1   SO Cross through wash.
6.8 ▲ SO Cross through wash.

▼ 5.2   SO Track on right.
6.7 ▲ SO Track on left.

▼ 5.3   SO Track on right.
6.6 ▲ SO Track on left.

▼ 5.6   SO Track on right.
6.3 ▲ SO Track on left.

▼ 5.8   SO Two tracks on right.
6.1 ▲ SO Two tracks on left.

▼ 6.4   SO Cross through wash; then track on right.
5.5 ▲ SO Track on left; then cross through wash.

▼ 7.0   SO Track on right; then tank and corral on right.
4.9 ▲ SO Tank and corral on left; then track on left.
        GPS: N32°17.81′ W112°51.52′

▼ 7.3   SO Cross through wash.
4.6 ▲ SO Cross through wash.

▼ 7.5   SO Tracks on right and left.
4.4 ▲ SO Tracks on right and left.

▼ 7.6   SO Track on left.
4.3 ▲ SO Track on right.

▼ 8.0   SO Cross through wash.
3.9 ▲ SO Cross through wash.

▼ 8.2   SO Cross through wash.
3.7 ▲ SO Cross through wash.

▼ 9.1   SO Track on left.
2.8 ▲ SO Track on right.

▼ 9.6   SO Cross through wash.
2.3 ▲ SO Cross through wash.

▼ 9.7   SO Track on right; Black Mountain is on the right. The New Cornelia Mine is directly ahead.
2.2 ▲ SO Track on left; Black Mountain is on the left.

▼ 9.8   SO Track on right is private.
2.1 ▲ SO Track on left is private.

▼ 10.0 SO Cross through wash.
1.9 ▲ SO Cross through wash.

▼ 10.1 SO Graded road on left and right is ScenicLoop Road. Continue straight on remaining on Bates Well Road. Street signs mark both junctions. Many smaller roads on right and left, remain on main graded road.
1.8 ▲ SO Graded road on left and right is Scenic Loop Road. Continue straight on remaining on Bates Well Road. Street signs mark both junctions.
        GPS: N32°20.37′ W112°50.93′

▼ 11.9   Trail ends at the junction with Arizona 85, Ajo Highway. Turn left for Ajo, turn right for Lukeville and Why.
0.0 ▲   Trail commences at the junction with Arizona 85, 2.2 miles south of Ajo. Turn southwest on the wide graded Darby Well Road running past the south side of the tailings of the New Cornelia Mine. Zero trip meter and cross cattle guard. Many smaller roads to the right and left for the next 1.8 miles, remain on the main graded road.
        Note: It is highly recommended that you top off your tank at Ajo
        GPS: N32°21.34′ W112°49.59′

Cipriano Pass Trail

STARTING POINT	South #3: El Camino del Diablo Trail, 18.4 miles south of Wellton
FINISHING POINT	South #1: Tinajas Altas Pass Trail, 21.5 miles south of Yuma
TOTAL MILEAGE	7.0 miles
UNPAVED MILEAGE	7.0 miles
DRIVING TIME	1 hour
ELEVATION RANGE	800–1,200 feet
USUALLY OPEN	Year-round
BEST TIME TO TRAVEL	November to March
DIFFICULTY RATING	2
SCENIC RATING	8
REMOTENESS RATING	+1

Special Attractions

■ Alternative crossing through the spectacular Tinajas Altas Mountains.
■ Remote, lightly traveled trail.
■ Enables a shorter loop route between the east and west routes of El Camino del Diablo for those with less time.

Description

This trail, although a scenic trail in its own right, provides an easy cut across the Tinajas Altas Mountains that is farther to the north than the more popular Tinajas Altas Pass. By combining the earlier parts of El Camino del Diablo's east and west route with Cipriano Pass, those people who prefer not to camp, or who have less time available, can still sample parts of the historic route.

The trail cuts through the gap in the ranges passing between the Tinajas Altas Mountains to the south and the Gila Mountains to the north. On the east side, it passes close to the dark lava-capped Raven Butte, similar in appearance to the Cabeza Prieta Peak that gives the wildlife refuge its name. It follows close to the actual Cipriano Pass, which is slightly to the south of

this trail and does not have a vehicle route along its entire length. The trail is well defined, but can be confusing as there are numerous small tracks to the right and left along its length. Only the larger, more noticeable trails are mentioned in the route directions. If in doubt remain on the most-used trail.

The trail is smooth and well-used for the most part; where it enters the gap it is somewhat narrower. There are some pleasant backcountry campsites scattered around in the gap and around the base of the mountains on both sides of the pass. The trail is particularly attractive in spring, when the green of the vegetation contrasts well with the pale-colored granite range. The trail finishes on South #1: Tinajas Altas Pass Trail (the west route of El Camino del Diablo), 21.5 miles south of Foothills Boulevard on the edge of Yuma.

The trail is wholly contained within the air force range. You must have a valid permit to enter the Barry M. Goldwater Air Force Range to travel this trail. For permit information and special considerations regarding this area, refer to South #3: El Camino del Diablo Trail.

Current Road Information

Luke Air Force Base
Gila Bend Auxiliary Field
Security Forces
Gila Bend, AZ 85337
(520) 683-6220

Bureau of Land Management
Yuma Field Office
2555 E Gila Ridge Road
Yuma, AZ 85365
(928) 317-3200

Map References

BLM   Tinajas Altas Mtns.
USGS 1:24,000 Raven Butte, Cipriano Pass
1:100,000 Tinajas Altas Mts.
Arizona Atlas & Gazetteer, p. 62

The trail heading across Lechuguilla Desert

Route Directions

▼ 0.0　　Trail starts 18.4 miles south of Wellton on South #3: El Camino del Diablo Trail. Turn south on well-used, graded sandy trail and zero trip meter. There is a wooden marker post B5 at the junction, but no sign.

3.5 ▲　　Trail finishes on South #3: El Camino del Diablo Trail, 18.4 miles south of Wellton at marker post B5. Turn left for Wellton and I-8, turn right to continue along El Camino del Diablo.
　　　　GPS: N32°27.88′ W114°06.27′

▼ 2.3　SO　Track on right is marked S27.
1.2 ▲　SO　Track on left is marked S27.
　　　　GPS: N32°26.42′ W114°07.88′

▼ 2.5　SO　Faint track on right.
1.0 ▲　SO　Faint track on left.

▼ 2.9　SO　Track on right.
0.6 ▲　SO　Track on left.

▼ 3.5　BL　Track on left; then trail forks; bear left past sign for Tinajas Altas Mountains, Area of Critical Environmental Concern. Zero trip meter.

0.0 ▲　　Continue toward El Camino del Diablo.
　　　　GPS: N32°25.89′ W114°08.80′

▼ 0.0　　Continue past sign, followed by faint track on right.

3.5 ▲　BL　Faint track on left; then larger track leading back to the left at sign for

A sandy section of the trail at the southern end of the Gila Mountains

South Trail #4: Cipriano Pass Trail

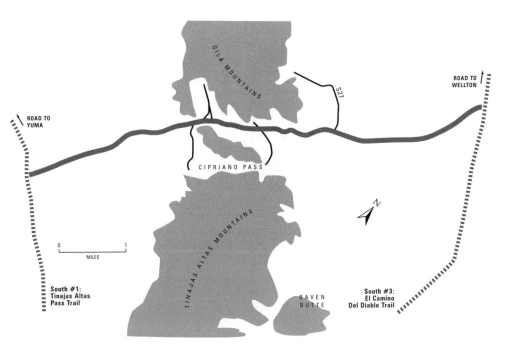

Tinajas Altas Mountains (facing other way), leaving Area of Critical Environmental Concern. Pass sign then bear left at fork after sign. Zero trip meter.

▼ 0.3   SO   Track on left and track on right.
3.2 ▲   SO   Track on left and track on right.

▼ 0.6   SO   Track on right and two tracks on left.
2.9 ▲   SO   Two tracks on right and track on left.

▼ 0.7   BL   Well-used track on right, followed by second entrance to same track in clearing.
2.8 ▲   SO   Well-used track on left in clearing, followed by second entrance on left.
    GPS: N32°25.60' W114°09.50'

▼ 0.8   BL   Well-used track on right.
2.7 ▲   BR   Well-used track on left.
    GPS: N32°25.55' W114°09.56'

▼ 0.9   SO   Trail is leaving gap between the Gila Mountains and Tinajas Altas Mountains.
2.6 ▲   SO   Trail is entering gap between the Gila Mountains and Tinajas Altas Mountains.

▼ 1.0   BR   Trail forks at small hillock.
2.5 ▲   SO   Track on right at small hillock.

▼ 3.5   Trail ends at the junction South #1: Tinajas Altas Pass Trail, at marker post A5. Turn right for Yuma, turn left to continue southeast on South #1: Tinajas Altas Pass Trail.
0.0 ▲   Trail commences on South #1: Tinajas Altas Pass Trail, 21.5 miles from the north end. Turn northeast on formed trail, which leaves through a bare area at marker post A5 and zero trip meter.
    GPS: N32°23.61' W114°11.22'

The blossom of the saguaro (pronounced "sah-waro") cactus is the state flower of Arizona. Some saguaros reach heights of 50 feet, making them the largest cacti in the United States. A saguaro has a tall, thick column-like stem, 18 to 24 inches in diameter, with several large "arms" curving upward. Smooth waxy skin is covered with spines. Saguaros begin life nearby a "nurse" tree or shrub (perhaps a palo verde or mesquite), which provides a moist, shaded habitat. Ironically, the nurse plant will die when the growing saguaro out-rivals and kills it off. Saguaros can increase their weight by up to a ton by absorbing water—and lots of it. But the cactus shrinks as it consumes the reservoir of water during drought. A combination of its slow growth and capacity to store large quantities of water enables the saguaro to flower every year, regardless of rainfall. The plant produces creamy white flowers during cool desert nights in May and June. The

flowers close by noon the next day, never to reopen. Many petals form around a tube (about four inches long) lined with a mass of yellow stamens. In the bottom of this

tube, sweet nectar accumulates. The somewhat skunky-smelling elixir, together with the colors of the flower, serves to attract birds, bats, and insects, which pollinate the saguaro flower. After fertilization, green ovular fruits begin to form immediately. Just prior to the rainy season the ripened fruit will split apart to reveal a pulpy crimson flesh, which all desert creatures seem to relish. Several kinds of birds make their homes in the saguaro cactus by chiseling out holes in the trunk.

Christmas Pass Trail

STARTING POINT	I-8, exit 42 (Tacna)
FINISHING POINT	South #3: El Camino del Diablo Trail near Tule Well
TOTAL MILEAGE	44.1 miles
UNPAVED MILEAGE	44.1 miles
DRIVING TIME	3.5 hours
ELEVATION RANGE	300–1,200 feet
USUALLY OPEN	Year-round
BEST TIME TO TRAVEL	November to March
DIFFICULTY RATING	3
SCENIC RATING	8
REMOTENESS RATING	+2

Special Attractions

- Alternative entry point to El Camino del Diablo.
- Remote desert experience.
- Rugged and beautiful Cabeza Prieta Mountains.

Description

The Christmas Pass Trail sweeps down, following the line of the Mohawk Mountains, crossing the wide, flat, sandy Mohawk Valley to join South #3: El Camino del Diablo Trail at Tule Well. The route is an easy one and it makes a popular entry point to El Camino. The trail travels almost entirely within the Barry M. Goldwater Air Force Range and the Cabeza Prieta National Wildlife Refuge. A permit is essential for both these areas. Refer to South #3: El Camino del Diablo Trail for details. In addition, only 4WD vehicles are permitted in the wildlife refuge.

Fuel is available in Tacna, and it is wise to have your tank full before commencing this route. The trail initially follows along the wide, flat Mohawk Valley along the western edge of the Mohawk Sand Dunes, which have built up against the Mohawk Mountains. These structures, more ridge than dunes, are lightly vegetated. To the west are the Copper Mountains.

As you continue south, the gap of Cipriano Pass is visible to the west immediately north of the black-colored Raven Butte. The

Crossing the Cabeza Prieta Mountains

Looking towards the Drift Hills near Christmas Pass

trail passes the Point of the Pintas, the northern end of the Sierra Pinta, or "Painted Range," before entering the Cabeza Prieta National Wildlife Refuge. The trail becomes narrower, sandy, and less-used. It follows the channel of the Mohawk Wash, and the dense vegetation along the channel makes the trail narrow and brushy in places. Watch for oncoming vehicles that may be moving fast in the soft sand.

Christmas Pass camp area is reached as the trail starts to enter the Cabeza Prieta Mountains. This is one of the suggested group camping areas for El Camino del Diablo. There are no facilities, but it is a pleasant, flat granitic area tucked into the north side of the Drift Hills. Christmas Pass itself is a narrow shelf caught between the hillside and a wash. Some rough concrete has been poured to stop the trail from washing out, but this section is still the roughest part. It is also the prettiest as it winds through the small peaks and ridges of the Cabeza Prieta Mountains.

The trail ends at Tule Well on South #3: El Camino del Diablo Trail. There is a small adobe casita built at Tule Well and a camping area with picnic tables and BBQs tucked among the creosote bushes. From here, the quickest way out of El Camino is to turn right and exit via Wellton along the smoother trail through the Barry M. Goldwater Air Force Range.

Current Road Information

Luke Air Force Base
Gila Bend Auxiliary Field
Security Forces
Gila Bend, AZ 85337
(520) 683-6220

Bureau of Land Management
Yuma Field Office
2555 E Gila Ridge Road
Yuma, AZ 85365
(928) 317-3200

Cabeza Prieta National Wildlife Refuge
1611 North 2nd Avenue
Ajo, AZ 85321
(520) 387-6483

Map References

BLM   Dateland, Cabeza Prieta Mtns.
USGS 1:24,000   Tacna, Mohawk, Mohawk
         SE, Mohawk Mtns. SW, Point of the
         Pintas, Christmas Pass, Sierra Arida
         1:100,000   Dateland, Cabeza Prieta Mtns.
Maptech CD-ROM: Southwest Arizona/Yuma
Arizona Atlas & Gazetteer, pp. 62-63
Arizona Road & Recreation Atlas, pp. 45, 51, 79, 85

Route Directions

▼ 0.0   From exit 42 (Tacna) on I-8, proceed to
           the south side of the freeway and turn
           east. Turn is immediately south of the
           eastbound freeway entrance onto a
           wide graded dirt road that runs along-
           side the freeway. Zero trip meter.
5.7 ▲   Trail ends on the southside of I-8 at
           exit 42 (Tacna).
           GPS: N32°41.48' W113°57.15'

▼ 0.5   SO Track on right.
5.2 ▲   SO Track on left.

▼ 0.6   SO Track on right.
5.1 ▲   SO Track on left.

▼ 0.7   SO Track on right.
5.0 ▲   SO Track on left.

▼ 1.0   SO Track on right.
4.7 ▲   SO Track on left.

▼ 2.0   SO Graded road on left and graded road on
           right.
3.7 ▲   SO Graded road on left and graded road on
           right.

▼ 3.4   SO Cross through wash.
2.3 ▲   SO Cross through wash.

▼ 3.5   SO Graded road on left goes into private
           property.
2.2 ▲   SO Gaded road on right goes into private
           property.

▼ 3.7   SO Cross the abandoned runway of Colfred
           Airfield.

A bird's nest craddled in a saguaro cactus

South Trail #5: Christmas Pass Trail

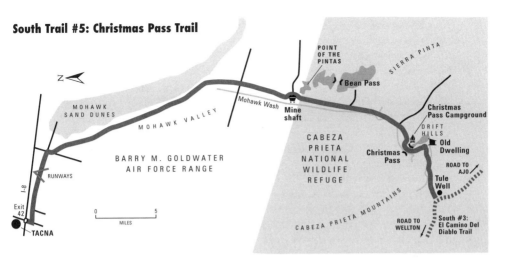

2.0 ▲   SO   Cross second runway.
      GPS: N32°41.63′ W113°53.15′

▼ 4.1   SO   Cross second runway.
1.6 ▲   SO   Cross the abandoned runway of
      Colfred Airfield.

▼ 5.7   TR   Intersection. Turn right and enter the
      Barry M. Goldwater Air Force Range
      past the sign on smaller graded dirt
      road. Marker post F1 at junction. Zero
      trip meter.
0.0 ▲   Continue west toward Tacna.
      GPS: N32°41.62′ W113°50.95′

▼ 0.0   Continue to the south into the permit
      area.
16.7 ▲   TL   Intersection at marker post F1. Turn
      left exiting the Barry M. Goldwater Air
      Force Range onto wide, graded dirt
      road. Zero trip meter.

▼ 16.7   SO   Crossroads at marker post F3. Zero
      trip meter.
0.0 ▲   Continue to the north.
      GPS: N32°29.53′ W113°40.81′

▼ 0.0   Continue south toward the Cabeza
      Prieta NWR.
5.1 ▲   SO   Crossroads at marker post F3. Zero
      trip meter.

▼ 4.8   SO   Track on left at wooden marker post

F4. Small mine shaft on the small
hillock opposite and a flat area suitable
for camping. Point of the Pintas is on
the left.

0.3 ▲   SO   Track on right at wooden marker post
      F4. Small mine shaft on the small
      hillock opposite and a flat area suitable
      for camping. Point of the Pintas is on
      the right.
      GPS: N32°25.39′ W113°40.07′

▼ 5.1   SO   Enter the Cabeza Prieta National
      Wildlife Refuge. Only 4WD vehicles are
      permitted past this point. Zero trip
      meter at sign.
0.0 ▲   Continue into the Barry M. Goldwater
      Air Force Range.
      GPS: N32°25.09′ W113°40.17′

▼ 0.0   Continue into the Cabeza Prieta NWR.
8.2 ▲   SO   Enter the Barry M. Goldwater Air
      Force Range.

▼ 2.0   SO   Bean Pass visible to the left.
6.2 ▲   SO   Bean Pass visible to the right.

▼ 3.9   SO   Management track on left. Trail is fol-
      lowing the line of Mohawk Wash.
4.3 ▲   SO   Management track on right.
      GPS: N32°21.52′ W113°39.91′

▼ 5.5   SO   Cross through wash.
2.7 ▲   SO   Cross through wash.

GPS: N32º20.06′ W113º39.62′

▼ 8.1   SO Management track on left.
0.1 ▲ SO Management track on right.

▼ 8.2   BL Bear left out of the main channel. Vehicle marks continue on ahead, but the trail dead-ends in approximately 100 yards. This turn is easy to miss. Zero trip meter.
0.0 ▲   Continue to the north.
      GPS: N32º17.65′ W113º40.02′

▼ 0.0   Continue toward Tule Well.
2.0 ▲ SO Enter the wash channel. Vehicle marks go to the left but the trail dead-ends in approximately 100 yards. Zero trip meter.

▼ 1.9   SO Faint tracks on left at base of Drift Hills. Entering the gap in the range.
0.1 ▲ BL Keep left and remain on main trail, exiting the gap in the range.

▼ 2.0   SO Christmas Pass Camp on left marked by a sign. Zero trip meter at sign.
0.0 ▲   Continue through the NWR.
      GPS: N32º16.65′ W113º41.53′

▼ 0.0   Continue toward Tule Well.
6.4 ▲ SO Christmas Pass Camp on right marked by a sign. Zero trip meter.

▼ 0.1   BL Trail swings left in front of wash and crosses Christmas Pass.
6.3 ▲ BR Trail follows down alongside wash and swings right to cross Christmas Pass.
      GPS: N32º16.64′ W113º41.60′

▼ 1.1   SO Cross through small wash.
5.3 ▲ SO Cross through small wash.

▼ 1.6   SO Cross through wash.
4.8 ▲ SO Cross through wash.

▼ 1.8   SO Remains of old dwelling on left, then cross through small wash.

4.6 ▲ SO Cross through small wash, remains of old dwelling on right.
      GPS: N32º15.34′ W113º40.94′

▼ 1.9   SO Cross through wash.
4.5 ▲ SO Cross through wash.

▼ 2.0   BR Management track on left.
4.4 ▲ BL Management track on right.

▼ 2.6   SO Cross through wash.
3.8 ▲ SO Cross through wash.

▼ 2.8   SO Cross through wash.
3.6 ▲ SO Cross through wash.

▼ 3.2   SO Cross through wash.
3.2 ▲ SO Cross through wash.

▼ 3.3   SO Cross through wash.
3.1 ▲ SO Cross through wash.

▼ 3.9   SO Cross through wash.
2.5 ▲ SO Cross through wash.

▼ 4.3   SO Cross through wash.
2.1 ▲ SO Cross through wash.

▼ 5.4   SO Cross through wash.
1.0 ▲ SO Cross through wash.

▼ 6.1   SO Cross through wide wash.
0.3 ▲ SO Cross through wide wash.
      GPS: N32º13.76′ W113º44.70′

▼ 6.4   Trail ends at Tule Well at the junction with South #3: El Camino del Diablo Trail. Turn left to travel El Camino to Ajo, turn right for the quicker exit out via Wellton.
0.0 ▲   Trail commences at Tule Well on South #3: El Camino del Diablo Trail. Turn northeast past the small adobe building onto well-used, formed trail and zero trip meter.
      GPS: N32º13.56′ W113º44.92′

Puerto Blanco Drive

STARTING POINT   Arizona 85, at the
Organ Pipe Cactus National Monument
Visitor Center
FINISHING POINT   Arizona 85, near
Lukeville
TOTAL MILEAGE   35.6 miles
UNPAVED MILEAGE   35.4 miles
DRIVING TIME   3 hours
ELEVATION RANGE   1,100–2,000 feet
USUALLY OPEN   Year-round
BEST TIME TO TRAVEL   Fall to spring
DIFFICULTY RATING   1
SCENIC RATING   8
REMOTENESS RATING   +1

Special Attractions

■ Easy drive wholly contained within the
Organ Pipe Cactus National Monument.
■ The green oasis of Quitobaquito Springs.
■ Access to backcountry hiking trails and
picnic areas.

History

The region of the Organ Pipe Cactus National Monument has human history stretching back to archaic times more than 9,000 years ago when Hohokam Indians used the warm waters of Quitobaquito Springs. There is evidence of a foot trail running north from the springs up through the Bates Mountains and south to the Gulf of California.

In 1699 a Jesuit missionary, Padre Eusebio Francisco Kino crossed the Tohono O'odham lands to the east and passed through what is now the monument, continuing on to cross El Camino del Diablo.

Later inhabitants included many miners, who have left their mark and their mines in the hillsides. One mine that can easily be seen beside the trail is the Golden Bell Mine, which include the diggings of Charlie Bell who mined there in the 1930s. He did find some gold and silver, but it was low-grade

ore. Other mines, such as the Dripping Springs Mine and the Milton Mine, can be reached by backcountry hiking. The oldest and most productive mine in the monument is the Victoria Mine, which operated for nearly 100 years, having a total production of $125,000. However, compared to the staggering figures produced by mines in other regions of Arizona, the Victoria Mine's overall yield is relatively poor.

The Puerto Blanco Range was also referred to as the Dripping Springs Range after the springs close to the northern end of the range. The later name of Puerto Blanco (Spanish for "white port") comes from two white rocks used as a marker for a pass through this rugged region.

The Quitobaquito Hills and Quitobaquito Springs have been a savior to many travelers, including the earliest of the Spanish expeditions. In 1540 Melchior Diaz, a member of Coronado's expedition, passed by the springs on his expedition to find a route to the Colorado River mouth. Padre Kino was known to have visited many villages in the Sonora Desert and would have appreciated these springs in his travels around El Camino del Diablo.

The Papago Indians referred to the springs as Alivaipai. The name Quitobaquito appears to be a corruption of the Papago term *ko to bac,* meaning a watering place. Another suggestion is that they are named after an old Mexican town called Quito Bac.

Today, these springs still provide water for other travelers on dangerous trails: The region is heavily trafficked by undocumented immigrants attempting to enter the United States.

Description

This is the longer of the two backcountry drives entirely within Organ Pipe Cactus National Monument. It is a good graded, gravel road that winds around the Puerto Blanco Mountains before running along the international border with Mexico to finish in Lukeville. Although the loop is fairly well traveled in the cooler months, it is still a re-

The U.S.–Mexico border

mote area, and you should take proper precautions for desert travel, including carrying plenty of water.

If you intend to drive the entire length of the trail, you must travel counterclockwise starting at the visitor center. The majority of the trail is one-way with the two-way section stretching from Lukeville to the junction of the Pozo Nuevo Road. Although shown on park maps as a vehicle trail, the Pozo Nuevo Road, which connects Puerto Blanco Drive to El Camino del Diablo, has been closed to vehicle travel since 1998. Increasing use by undocumented aliens traveling at night, mainly in 2WD vehicles, had the National Park Service concerned about resource damage along the rough trail. There are currently no plans to reopen the trail for public vehicle access.

The first part of the trail is beautiful as it winds to the north of the Puerto Blanco Mountains and to the south of the Bates Mountains. The volcanic Pinkley Peak is a dominant feature on the early part of the drive; the peak rises to 3,145 feet and was named for Frank Pinkley, the earliest superintendent of Casa Grande National Monument in Coolidge, AZ.

Views farther around the loop stretch down the Valley of the Ajo, a broad flat valley running between the Bates Mountains and the Ajo Mountains. The most prominent peak in the Bates Mountains is Kino Peak, which is named for Padre Eusebio Francisco Kino.

One unexpected feature along the Puerto Blanco Drive is the desert oasis of Quitobaquito Springs. These warm springs are surrounded by a small marshland oasis with mature trees. It attracts many species of birds and is home to a rare species of freshwater fish, the Quitobaquito Springs pupfish. Quitobaquito Springs are located 0.4 miles down a spur trail from the main drive, followed by a short walk to the spring-fed ponds. There is a parking lot and a pit toilet directly adjacent to the international border with Mexico. Note that the wire fence immediately south of the parking lot is the international boundary, although it is not well marked. The border is patrolled, and it is il-

Chainfruit cholla, ocotillos, and organ pipe cacti with the Little Continental Divide in the background

legal to cross into Mexico, even briefly, at any point other than at an authorized border crossing point. The National Park Service recommends that you do not leave your vehicle unattended here or at any other point along the border due to numerous break-ins.

From Quitobaquito Springs, the trail follows mainly along the international border. The major Mexican Highway 2 is on the far side of the border, and there are many side trails that lead south to the border, which are used by illegal border crossers in both directions. These trails are not authorized trails within the monument.

A second major side trail leads 4 miles to Senita Basin where you can see the senita cacti and the elephant tree, two species found mainly in Mexico.

The trail ends just north of Lukeville, named after Charles Luke, and the border crossing point into Mexico.

Note that no dogs or bicycles are allowed on the hiking trails and vehicle camping is not permitted along the drive. The route directions only detail major wash crossings; there are many smaller ones along the drive.

Current Road Information

Organ Pipe Cactus National Monument
10 Organ Pipe Drive
Ajo, AZ 85321
(520) 387-6849

Map References

BLM Lukeville, Ajo
USGS 1:24,000   Lukeville, Tillotson Peak, Kino Peak, West of Lukeville, Quitobaquito Springs
1:100,000 Lukeville, Ajo
Maptech CD-ROM: Southwest Arizona/Yuma
Trails Illustrated, Organ Pipe Cactus National Monument
Arizona Atlas & Gazetteer, p. 70
Arizona Road & Recreation Atlas, pp. 51, 52, 85, 86
Recreational Map of Arizona
Other: Organ Pipe Cactus Park Map (free leaflet handed out by park service)

Flowering ocotillos with Pinkley Peak in the background

South Trail #6: Puerto Blanco Drive

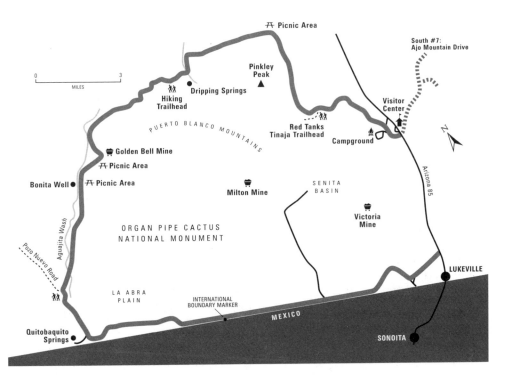

Route Directions

GPS: N31°59.09' W112°50.23'

▼ 0.0   From the visitor center at Organ Pipe Cactus National Monument, continue south through the parking lot, then turn west on the paved road at the sign for Puerto Blanco Drive and zero trip meter.
    GPS: N31°57.27' W112°48.02'

▼ 0.1   BR   Paved road on left goes to campground. Follow signs for North Puerto Blanco Drive.

▼ 0.2   SO   Paved road on left is for authorized vehicles only. Information board on the left. Road is now graded dirt.

▼ 0.5   SO   Service road on right.

▼ 1.5   SO   Cross through wash.

▼ 2.5   SO   Cross through wash.

▼ 3.4   SO   Cross through wash.

▼ 3.7   SO   Red Tanks Tinaja primitive hiking trail leads off to the left.

▼ 3.8   SO   Parking area for hiking trailhead on left.

▼ 4.1   SO   Cross through wash.

▼ 4.4   SO   Cross through wash.

▼ 6.9   SO   Cross through wash.
    GPS: N32°01.67' W112°50.09'

▼ 7.1   SO   Picnic table in shade of ironwood on right at marker post #6. Zero trip meter.
    GPS: N32°01.72' W112°50.27'

▼ 0.0   Continue around loop and cross through wash.

▼ 0.9   SO   Cross through wash.

▼ 1.2   SO   Cross through wash.

▼ 1.4   SO   Cross through wash.

▼ 1.8   SO   Cross through wash.

▼ 3.2   SO   Cross through wash.
    GPS: N32°02.15' W112°53.23'

▼ 4.0   SO   Little Continental Divide. All arroyos to the north drain into the Gila River, those to the south drain to the Rio Sonoyta in Mexico.
GPS: N32°01.85' W112°53.80'

▼ 4.3   SO   Dripping Springs Mine primitive hiking trail and parking area on left. Zero trip meter.
GPS: N32°01.86' W112°54.15'

▼ 0.0   Continue around the loop.
▼ 0.2   SO   Cross through wash.
▼ 0.7   SO   Cross through wash. Views to the right over the plain and wash area to the Bates Mountains and Kino Peak.
▼ 1.5   SO   Cross through wash.
▼ 4.0   SO   Cross through wash.
▼ 4.4   SO   Cross through wash.
▼ 4.8   SO   Golden Bell Mine on left. Picnic tables with limited shade under a palo verde.
GPS: N32°00.98' W112°57.34'

▼ 5.5   SO   Cross through wash.
▼ 6.1   SO   Bonita Well and corral on right. Pit toilets on right, picnic tables, shade ramada, and old hut on left. Zero trip meter.
GPS: N32°00.56' W112°58.45'

▼ 0.0   Continue around loop.
▼ 0.2   SO   Cross through wash.
▼ 0.4   SO   Short trail on right leads to cristate saguaro—abnormal fan-shaped growth.
GPS: N32°00.20' W112°58.67'

▼ 3.0   SO   Cross through Aguajita Wash.
▼ 3.6   TL   Track on right is the Pozo Nuevo Road, closed to vehicles. Start of two-way section. Zero trip meter.
GPS: N31°58.04' W113°00.70'

▼ 0.0   Continue south along two-way road.
1.7 ▲ UT Track straight on is the Pozo Nuevo Road, closed to vehicles. The road to the right is no-entry for vehicles traveling in this direction. Turn around and retrace your steps to Lukeville.

▼ 0.3   SO   Cross through wash.
1.4 ▲ SO Cross through wash.

▼ 1.5   SO   Cross through wash.
0.2 ▲ SO Cross through wash.

▼ 1.7   TL   Track straight on goes 0.4 miles to Quitobaquito Springs. Zero trip meter.
0.0 ▲   Continue away from the international border.
GPS: N31°56.53' W113°00.66'

▼ 0.0   Continue along the international border.
8.1 ▲ TR Track on left goes 0.4 miles to Quitobaquito Springs. Zero trip meter.

▼ 0.9   SO   Cross through wash.
7.2 ▲ SO Cross through wash.

▼ 1.0   SO   Cross through wash.
7.1 ▲ SO Cross through wash.

▼ 2.0   SO   Cross through wash.
6.1 ▲ SO Cross through wash.

▼ 2.3   SO   Cross through wash.
5.8 ▲ SO Cross through wash.

▼ 3.6   SO   Cross through wash.
4.5 ▲ SO Cross through wash.

▼ 3.7   SO   Cross through wash, the trail is now running alongside the international border.
4.4 ▲ SO Cross through wash, the trail now leaves the international border.

▼ 4.9   SO   International boundary marker on right of trail.
3.2 ▲ SO International boundary marker on left of trail.
GPS: N31°55.01' W112°56.20'

▼ 6.1   SO   Cross through wash.
2.0 ▲ SO Cross through wash.

▼ 6.2   SO   Cross through wash.
1.9 ▲ SO Cross through wash.

▼ 8.1	SO	Track on left leads 4 miles to Senita Basin. Zero trip meter.
0.0 ▲		Continue toward Quitobaquito Springs.
		GPS: N31°54.03' W112°52.99'

▼ 0.0		Continue toward Lukeville.
4.7 ▲	SO	Track on right leads 4 miles to Senita Basin. Zero trip meter.

▼ 3.4	SO	Track on right is for authorized vehicles only.
1.3 ▲	SO	Track on left is for authorized vehicles only.

▼ 3.5	SO	Track on right is for authorized vehicles only.
1.2 ▲	BR	Track on left is for authorized vehicles only.

▼ 4.3	SO	Information board on left.
0.4 ▲	SO	Information board on right.
		GPS: N31°53.52' W112°49.15'

▼ 4.7		Trail ends at the junction with the Arizona 85, 1 mile north of Lukeville. Turn right for Lukeville, turn left for Ajo.
0.0 ▲		Trail starts on Arizona 85, 1 mile north of Lukeville and 4 miles south of the park visitor center. Turn west on graded dirt road at the sign for Puerto Blanco Drive South and zero trip meter. The first section of the trail follows mainly along the international border with Mexico.
		GPS: N31°53.62' W112°48.72'

Ajo Mountain Drive

STARTING POINT	Arizona 85, at Organ Pipe Cactus National Monument Visitor Center
FINISHING POINT	Arizona 85, at Organ Pipe Cactus National Monument Visitor Center
TOTAL MILEAGE	18.9 miles
UNPAVED MILEAGE	17.2 miles
DRIVING TIME	1.5 hours
ELEVATION RANGE	1,700–2,800 feet
USUALLY OPEN	Year-round
BEST TIME TO TRAVEL	Fall to Spring
DIFFICULTY RATING	1
SCENIC RATING	9
REMOTENESS RATING:	+0

Special Attractions

- Organ pipe cactus and varied Sonoran Desert scenery and vegetation.
- Easy drive contained within the Organ Pipe Cactus National Monument.
- Access to hiking trails within the monument.
- Large natural arch at Arch Canyon.
- Quiet picnic sites.

History

The Organ Pipe Cactus National Monument region has a long history of human habitation from Indians to miners to today's tourists. Spanish explorers and missionaries were some of the most frequent travelers who named many of the features you see today.

On the return section of the trail, as you head south on the eastern side of the Diablo Mountains, you are looking southwest at Diaz Spire and Diaz Peak. These are named in remembrance of Melchior Diaz who, as a member of Coronado's expedition, found a route west to the mouth of the Colorado River. On his return journey Diaz died after fending off a hound that was threatening their sheep. Apparently his own long lance caught in the ground as he charged the hound. The lance pierced Diaz in the kidney resulting in his death shortly after, despite efforts by his men to save him.

Description

This graded gravel road is one of only two backcountry roads within Organ Pipe Cactus National Monument. It is a loop that travels through prolific and varied Sonoran Desert vegetation before climbing around the face of the Diablo Mountains on the edge of the Ajo Range. The drive is a one-way loop that commences 1.9 miles from the start of the trail.

As the trail drops out of the range, there are wide ranging views over the Sonoyta Valley down into Sonora, Mexico. The vegetation is as spectacular as the rugged Ajo Range: There are giant saguaros and ocotillos, creosote bushes, palo verdes, ironwoods, mesquites, jojobas, and Mexican jumping beans. The Ajo Range was formed approximately 2 million years ago as volcanoes dumped thick layers of lava and ash over the landscape. Faulting and erosion continued to shape the landscape into the jagged peaks and deep canyons characteristic of the region.

The trail passes several picnic areas that make great places to stop for a while and soak up the desert scenery. All of them have a picnic table and a couple have shade ramadas. Several hiking trails leave from along the drive. One of the best leaves the picnic area and travels up Arch Canyon. There are two arches that can be seen from the trail. The lower larger one measures approximately 120 by 30 feet. The other is a smaller 10 by 6 feet. No dogs or bicycles are allowed on the hiking trails.

It is necessary to pay the national monument entrance fee before driving on any of the backcountry roads within the monument. The road is graded gravel for its entire length and is suitable for passenger vehicles. Short sections are paved, typically some of the wash crossings and a longer section as the trail climbs into the Ajo Range.

In the summer months, keep an eye on the weather; thunderstorms can move in quickly. Do not attempt to enter a flooded, fast-moving wash bed; wait for the water to subside before attempting to cross.

The view from the Diablo Canyon picnic area

Some wonderful organ pipe cacti along the trail

Current Road Information
Organ Pipe Cactus National Monument
10 Organ Pipe Drive
Ajo, AZ 85321
(520) 387-6849

Map References
BLM Lukeville, Ajo
USGS 1:24,000 Lukeville, Diaz Peak, Mt.
Ajo
1:100,000 Lukeville, Ajo
Maptech CD-ROM: Southwest Arizona/
Yuma
Trails Illustrated, Organ Pipe Cactus Na-
tional Monument
Arizona Atlas & Gazetteer, p. 70
Arizona Road & Recreation Atlas, pp. 52, 86
Recreational Map of Arizona
Other: Organ Pipe Cactus Park Map (free
leaflet handed out by park service)

Route Directions

▼ 0.0   From Arizona 85, turn east on graded
gravel road at sign for Ajo Mountain
Drive. The turn is opposite the exit
from the visitor center. Zero trip meter.
GPS: N31°57.22′ W112°47.94′

▼ 0.3 SO Information board on right.
▼ 0.9 SO Cross through wash on concrete ford.
▼ 1.8 SO Cross through wash on concrete ford.
▼ 1.9 SO Graded road on right is the end of the
one-way loop. Zero trip meter.
GPS: N31°58.24′ W112°46.44′

▼ 0.0   Continue around the start of the loop.
▼ 0.2 SO Cross through wash on concrete ford.
▼ 0.9 SO Cross through wash.
▼ 3.4 SO Diablo Canyon picnic area on left. Picnic
table and shade ramada. Zero trip meter.
GPS: N32°00.36′ W112°43.99′

South Trail #7: Ajo Mountain Drive

▼ 0.0   Continue around the loop.
▼ 0.1   SO   Road is paved as it starts to climb into the Ajo Range.
▼ 0.4   SO   Birdseye Point on left. Picnic table.
           GPS: N32°00.63′ W112°43.87′

▼ 0.6   SO   Cross through wash on concrete ford.
▼ 1.4   SO   Road turns back to graded dirt.
           GPS: N32°01.17′ W112°43.41′

▼ 1.5   SO   Road returns to paved; then cross through wash.
▼ 1.7   SO   Road turns back to graded dirt.
▼ 2.0   SO   Cross through wash on concrete ford.
▼ 2.4   SO   Cross through wash on paved ford.
▼ 2.8   SO   Cross through wash on concrete ford. First glimpse of natural arch high up to the right.
           GPS: N32°02.21′ W112°43.24′

▼ 3.2   BR   Picnic table on left and parking area and hiking trail up Arch Canyon. The natural arch can clearly be seen high on the cliff.
▼ 3.6   SO   Cross through paved ford.
▼ 3.9   SO   Small arch on rise to the right.
           GPS: N32°01.68′ W112°42.79′

▼ 4.5   SO   Road is paved.
▼ 4.7   SO   Road returns to dirt.

▼ 4.9   SO   Estes Canyon picnic area and pit toilets on right. Two picnic tables and shade ramada. Zero trip meter. Estes Canyon-Bull Pasture Primitive Hiking Trail leaves to the left, a 4-mile round trip.
           GPS: N32°00.97′ W112°42.67′

▼ 0.0   Continue around loop and cross through wash.
▼ 0.5   SO   Cross through wash.
▼ 1.7   SO   Turn out on the left overlooks Diaz Spire, the leftmost of the two rocky peaks.
           GPS: N31°59.63′ W112°42.42′

▼ 5.1   SO   The Cactus Trail—a short hiking trail leads off to the right. Cross through wash on concrete ford.
           GPS: N31°57.78′ W112°45.20′

▼ 5.6   SO   Teddy Bear Pass Trail leads off to the left at marker post 21. Zero trip meter.
           GPS: N31°57.68′ W112°45.66′

▼ 0.0   Continue around the loop.
▼ 0.7   SO   Cross through wash on concrete ford.
▼ 1.2   TL   End of loop. Turn left and retrace your steps for 1.9 miles back to Arizona 85.
           GPS: N31°58.24′ W112°46.44′

Parker Canyon Lake Road

STARTING POINT	Arizona 82 in Sonoita
FINISHING POINT	South #12: Mexican Border Road
TOTAL MILEAGE	31.6 miles
UNPAVED MILEAGE	8.7 miles
DRIVING TIME	2 hours
ELEVATION RANGE	4,800–5,800 feet
USUALLY OPEN	Year-round
BEST TIME TO TRAVEL	Year-round
DIFFICULTY RATING	1
SCENIC RATING	7
REMOTENESS RATING	+0

Special Attractions
- Parker Canyon Lake.
- Easy road linking Sonoita with South #12: Mexican Border Road.

History
The original settlement of Sonoita (which, in the Papago language, means a place suited for growing corn) was located just south of Patagonia. The present-day town that bears the same name, but is somewhat north of that site, developed in 1882 as a result of the railroad that was built between Benson and Nogales.

Although the Gadsden Treaty came into effect in 1854, the Mexican military continued to protect the settlers in this region against the Apache as best they could until

Parker Canyon Lake

1856. Many settlers, uneasy with the constant raids, gave up trying to live within this Apache region. Fort Crittenden and Fort Buchanan, both military posts, were located approximately 2 miles southeast of the heart of today's Sonoita. Named after the then president of the United States, Fort Buchanan was established in 1857 by the First United States Dragoons in an attempt to protect the settlers.

By the 1860s a few people were gaining the confidence to settle. Then in 1861, the stand-off between Lt. Geroge N. Bascom and the Apache Chief Cochise at Apache Pass resulted in about six deaths on both sides. In retaliation, Cochise started what was to be ten years of warfare. Worse still, with the outbreak of the Civil War, Fort Buchanan was abandoned and nearby settlers were left to fend for themselves. Many fought to survive as the Apache raided their crops and cattle, and many gave in, moving to more peaceful territories. When troops were available after the Civil War, Fort Crittenden was built in 1867 just a half mile closer to today's Sonoita. The earlier Fort Buchanan adobe buildings were in ruins, having been burnt under orders before being abandoned. Settlers returned, and mining gained importance with many new prospects being worked. Fort Crittenden, which was also referred to as Camp Crittenden, was short lived and abandoned in the early 1870s.

Parker Canyon, which runs from the Huachuca Mountains southwest into Mexico, is named after a family that relocated from Phoenix to escape over-crowding.

Description

Although much of this road is paved, it is still a very pleasant backcountry drive, suitable for all types of vehicles in dry weather. It also offers options to those wanting to drive sections of South #12: Mexican Border Road as a loop road from either Sierra Vista or Nogales. Combining the Parker Canyon Lake Road with the Mexican Border Road allows for a more leisurely drive.

The trail leaves the small, predominantly ranching town of Sonoita to travel along the paved road, Arizona 82, south toward the Coronado National Forest. Sonoita is the last chance to purchase fuel. None is available at Parker Canyon Lake. Only the major intersections have been given in the route directions for this section of the trail; smaller mainly private entrances have been omitted from the directions.

The trail passes both ends of South #9: Canelo Hills Trail, a very pretty, more rugged alternative to the paved section of this trail. Just off the trail is the Black Oak Cemetery, first used by pioneer families in 1900 and still in use today.

Parker Canyon Lake, constructed in 1966 by the Arizona Game and Fish Department, offers fishing for trout. However, over the years people have illegally introduced northern pike and other species into the lake. The pike are having a particularly detrimental effect as they feed almost exclusively on other fish, upsetting the ecological balance and potentially having an adverse effect on the quality of trout fishing.

Parker Canyon Lake has a national forest campground—Lakeview USFS Campground—along the shore of the lake. A second area is suitable for RVs. A fee is required for camping. A small store, bait shop, and boat launching facilities are the only other amenities.

Past the lake, the road starts to climb away, following a graded gravel road. The entrances to South #10: Blacktail Ridge Trail and South #11: Sunnyside Trail are passed, and then the trail winds down through open landscape to finish at the intersection with South #12: Mexican Border Road.

Current Road Information

Coronado National Forest
Sierra Vista Ranger District
5990 South Hwy 92
Hereford, AZ 85615
(520) 378-0311

A ridge and an off-camber section that requires care to avoid scratching your vehicle

South Trail #8: Parker Canyon Lake Road

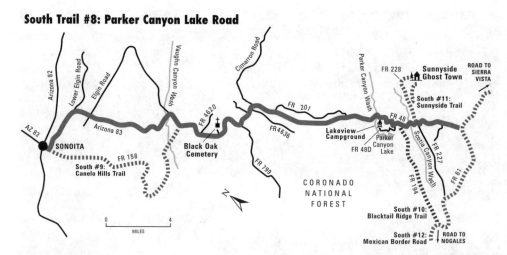

Map References

BLM   Fort Huachuca, Nogales
USFS   Coronado National Forest: Nogales
    and Sierra Vista Ranger Districts
USGS   1:24,000   Sonoita, Elgin, O'Donnell
    Canyon, Pyeatt Ranch, Huachuca
    Peak
    1:100,000 Fort Huachuca, Nogales
Maptech CD-ROM: Southeastern Arizona/
    Tucson
Arizona Atlas & Gazetteer, p. 73
Arizona Road & Recreation Atlas, p. 54, 88
Recreational Map of Arizona

Route Directions

▼ 0.0   From Arizona 82 in Sonoita, zero trip
         meter and turn south on the paved
         Arizona 83 at the sign for Parker
         Canyon Lake and zero trip meter.
4.0 ▲   Trail ends at the intersection with
         Arizona 82 in Sonoita.
         GPS: N31°40.74' W110°39.31'

▼ 0.4 BL South #9: Canelo Hills Trail is straight
         ahead. Bear left, remaining on the
         main paved road.
3.6 ▲ BR South #9: Canelo Hills Trail is on the
         left. Bear right, remaining on major
         paved road to Sonoita.
         GPS: N31°40.40' W110°39.31'

▼ 2.8 BR Bear right remaining on Arizona 83.
         Lower Elgin Road is on the left.

1.2 ▲ BL Bear left remaining on Arizona 83.
         Lower Elgin Road is on the right.
         GPS: N31°40.41' W110°36.65'

▼ 4.0 SO Paved road on left is Elgin Road.
         Graded dirt road on right is Wagon
         Wheel Road. Zero trip meter.
0.0 ▲   Continue to the north.
         GPS: N31°39.54' W110°36.26'

▼ 0.0   Continue to the south.
6.6 ▲ SO Paved road on right is Elgin Road.
         Graded dirt road on left is Wagon
         Wheel Road. Zero trip meter.

▼ 3.5 BL Graded road straight on and to the
         right. Remain on paved road following
         sign for Parker Canyon Lake.
3.1 ▲ BR Graded road straight on and to the left.
         Remain on paved road.
         GPS: N31°36.51' W110°35.18'

▼ 4.0 BR Graded road on left, remain on paved
         road.
2.6 ▲ BL Graded road on right, remain on
         paved road.

▼ 4.4 BL Graded road ahead, remain on paved
         road.
2.2 ▲ BR Graded road on left, remain on paved
         road.
         GPS: N31°36.05' W110°34.68'

▼ 5.4 SO Cross through Vaughn Canyon Wash
         on concrete ford.

1.2 ▲   SO   Cross through Vaughn Canyon Wash on concrete ford.

▼ 5.6   BR   Graded road on left, remain on paved road.

1.0 ▲   BL   Graded road ahead, remain on paved road.

▼ 6.6   SO   Graded road on right is South #9: Canelo Hills Trail, sign-posted as Vaughn Loop Road. Zero trip meter.

0.0 ▲   Continue to the northeast.
       GPS: N31°35.14′ W110°33.74′

▼ 0.0   Continue to the southeast.

2.6 ▲   SO   Graded road on left is South #9: Canelo Hills Trail, sign-posted as Vaughn Loop Road. Zero trip meter.

▼ 1.3   SO   Entering Coronado National Forest. There is no sign at the boundary.

1.3 ▲   SO   Leaving Coronado National Forest. There is no sign at the boundary.

▼ 1.5   SO   Track on left is FR 4620 and track on right.

1.1 ▲   SO   Track on right is FR 4620 and track on left.

▼ 2.1   SO   Track on left is FR 4619A, track on right is FR 4619B.

0.5 ▲   SO   Track on right is FR 4619A, track on left is FR 4619B.
       GPS: N31°33.57′ W110°33.18′

▼ 2.3   SO   Cattle guard.
0.3 ▲   SO   Cattle guard.

▼ 2.6   SO   Track on right and left is FR 4622. Sign for Black Oak Cemetery on left. Left goes 0.2 miles to cemetery. Zero trip meter.

0.0 ▲   Continue to the northwest.
       GPS: N31°33.21′ W110°32.95′

▼ 0.0   Continue to the southeast.

3.5 ▲   SO   Track on right and left is FR 4622. Sign for Black Oak Cemetery on right. Right goes 0.2 miles to cemetery. Zero trip meter.

▼ 0.4   SO   Track on left is FR 5630; then track on right.

3.1 ▲   SO   Track on left; then track on right is FR 5630.

▼ 1.3   SO   Ranch road on left; then track on right.
2.2 ▲   SO   Track on left; then ranch road on right.

▼ 2.1   TL   Remain on paved Arizona 83. Graded dirt road FR 799 continues ahead. Follow sign to Parker Canyon Lake.

1.4 ▲   TR   Remain on paved Arizona 83. Graded dirt road FR 799 on left.
       GPS: N31°32.57′ W110°31.74′

▼ 2.7   SO   Track on right is FR 4892.
0.8 ▲   SO   Track on left is FR 4892.

▼ 3.0   SO   Graded road on left is Membrillo Lane.
0.5 ▲   SO   Graded road on right is Membrillo Lane.
       GPS: N31°32.54′ W110°30.87′

▼ 3.2   SO   Graded road on right is FR 4636.
0.3 ▲   SO   Graded road on left is FR 4636.

▼ 3.5   SO   Paved road on left is Cimarron Road to Fort Huachuca. Zero trip meter.

0.0 ▲   Continue to the southwest.
       GPS: N31°32.61′ W110°30.38′

▼ 0.0   Continue to the southeast.

9.8 ▲   SO   Paved road on right is Cimarron Road to Fort Huachuca. Zero trip meter.

▼ 1.4   SO   Graded road on left and right.
8.4 ▲   SO   Graded road on left and right.

▼ 3.4   SO   Track on right.
6.4 ▲   SO   Track on left.

▼ 6.2   SO   Cattle guard, road turns to graded gravel.

3.6 ▲   SO   Cattle guard, road turns to paved.
       GPS: N31°27.97′ W110°27.77′

▼ 6.3   SO   FR 201 on left opposite mile marker 7.
3.5 ▲   SO   FR 201 on right opposite mile marker 7.

▼ 6.4   SO   Entering Cochise County.
3.4 ▲   SO   Entering Santa Cruz County.

▼ 6.6   SO   Track on left and track on right.
3.2 ▲   SO   Track on right and track on left.

▼ 6.8   SO   Track on right.
3.0 ▲   SO   Track on left.

▼ 6.9   SO   Cross through wash on concrete ford.
2.9 ▲   SO   Cross through wash on concrete ford.

▼ 7.2   SO   Track on left.
2.6 ▲   SO   Track on right.

▼ 7.9   SO   Two tracks on right; then cross through Parker Canyon Wash on concrete ford.
1.9 ▲   SO   Cross through Parker Canyon Wash on concrete ford; then two tracks on left.
      GPS: N31°26.68′ W110°26.76′

▼ 8.6   SO   Track on left.
1.2 ▲   SO   Track on right.

▼ 8.7   SO   Track on right.
1.1 ▲   SO   Track on left.

▼ 9.3   SO   Entering private property, then cross through wash on concrete ford.
0.5 ▲   SO   Cross through wash on concrete ford, leaving private property.

▼ 9.8   TL   Turn left on FR 48 following the sign for Sierra Vista and Nogales. Ahead is FR 48D, which goes 0.5 miles to Parker Canyon Lake. Zero trip meter.
0.0 ▲   Continue to the northeast.
      GPS: N31°25.74′ W110°26.40′

▼ 0.0   Continue to the southeast.
0.6 ▲   TR   Turn right at T-intersection following sign for Sonoita and Tucson. Road on left is FR 48D, which goes 0.5 miles to Parker Canyon Lake. Zero trip meter.

▼ 0.1   SO   Road into houses on right.
0.5 ▲   SO   Road into houses on left.

▼ 0.6   SO   South #10: Blacktail Ridge Trail, FR

194, graded gravel road, marked South Lake Road on right; then cattle guard. Zero trip meter.
0.0 ▲   Continue to the north.
      GPS: N31°25.48′ W110°26.15′

▼ 0.0   Continue to the south.
1.5 ▲   SO   Cattle guard; then South #10: Blacktail Ridge Trail, FR 194, graded gravel road, marked South Lake Road on left. Zero trip meter.

▼ 0.1   SO   Track on right.
1.4 ▲   SO   Track on left.

▼ 0.2   SO   Track on left.
1.3 ▲   SO   Track on right.

▼ 0.6   SO   Track on right; then cross through wash.
0.9 ▲   SO   Cross through wash; then track on left.

▼ 0.7   SO   Track on left and track on right.
0.8 ▲   SO   Track on left and track on right.

▼ 0.8   SO   Cross through Scotia Canyon Wash; then track on left.
0.7 ▲   SO   Track on right; then cross through Scotia Canyon Wash.
      GPS: N31°25.12′ W110°25.72′

▼ 1.3   SO   Cattle guard.
0.2 ▲   SO   Cattle guard.

▼ 1.5   SO   Graded road on left is South #11: Sunnyside Trail, FR 228. Zero trip meter at signpost. Track on right.
0.0 ▲   Continue to the northwest toward Sonoita.
      GPS: N31°24.83′ W110°25.52′

▼ 0.0   Continue to the southeast to Coronado National Memorial.
3.0 ▲   SO   Graded road on right is South #11: Sunnyside Trail, FR 228. Zero trip meter at signpost. Track on left.

▼ 0.1   SO   Graded road on right is FR 227 to Lochiel and Nogales.

2.9 ▲	SO	Graded road on left is FR 227 to Lochiel and Nogales.
		GPS: N31°24.68' W110°25.45'

▼ 0.5	SO	Private property on right, grave at intersection.
2.5 ▲	SO	Private property on left, grave at intersection.
		GPS: N31°24.48' W110°25.25'

▼ 0.6	SO	Cattle guard; then cross through Sunnyside Canyon. Track on left up wash.
2.4 ▲	SO	Cross through Sunnyside Canyon. Track on right up wash; then cattle guard.

▼ 1.3	SO	Track on left.
1.7 ▲	SO	Track on right.

▼ 1.9	SO	Track on right and left; then cattle guard.
1.1 ▲	SO	Cattle guard; then track on right and left.
		GPS: N31°23.62' W110°24.69'

▼ 2.1	SO	Track on right.
0.9 ▲	SO	Track on left.

▼ 2.8	SO	Track on right.
0.2 ▲	SO	Track on left.

▼ 3.0		Trail ends at intersection with South #12: Mexican Border Road, FR 61. Continue straight on for Sierra Vista and Coronado National Memorial, turn right for Nogales.
0.0 ▲		Trail starts on South #12: Mexican Border Road, FR 61, 8.4 miles west of Montezuma Pass. Zero trip meter and turn northwest on graded dirt road, FR 48, signposted to Sonoita and Parker Canyon Lake.
		GPS: N31°22.79' W110°24.13'

Canelo Hills Trail

STARTING POINT	Arizona 83 in Sonoita
FINISHING POINT	South #8: Parker Canyon Lake Road, 0.7 miles south of mile marker 21
TOTAL MILEAGE	14.7 miles
UNPAVED MILEAGE	12.7 miles
DRIVING TIME	2.5 hours
ELEVATION RANGE	4,900–5,600 feet
USUALLY OPEN	Year-round
BEST TIME TO TRAVEL	October to June
DIFFICULTY RATING	4
SCENIC RATING	7
REMOTENESS RATING	+0

Special Attractions

- Small winding trail through the Canelo Hills.
- Views of the Santa Rita and Whetstone Mountains.
- Many pleasant backcountry campsites.
- Trail is popular with horse riders and mountain bikers.

Description

This short winding trail passes through the northern edge of the Canelo Hills (Spanish for "cinnamon-colored") in the Coronado National Forest south of Sonoita. Private property has altered the route of the trail from that shown on the various maps of the region. The trail detailed here is longer and harder to navigate than the straight trail depicted on the forest map.

It leaves from the edge of Sonoita, initially traveling along a paved and then a graded road into the forest. It undulates through grasslands dotted with low shrubs, giving views to the Whetstone Mountains and the Santa Rita Mountains. After 4.2 miles, the graded road ends at private property, and the route turns onto a small formed trail. This section is eroded in places, with many moguls as it climbs in and out of O'Leary Creek. It is muddy when wet

South Trail #9: Canelo Hills Trail

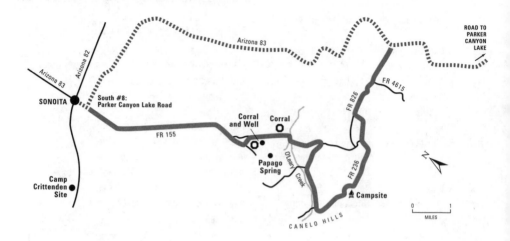

as the ruts testify.

The section that travels within O'Leary Canyon is the roughest along the trail with a couple of short rocky sections. It is also moderately brushy for wider vehicles.

The final section of the trail is again graded dirt road as it leads through open national forest to rejoin South #8: Parker Canyon Lake Road.

Current Road Information

Coronado National Forest
Sierra Vista Ranger District
5990 South Hwy 92
Hereford, AZ 85615
(520) 378-0311

Map References

BLM Fort Huachuca
USFS Coronado National Forest: Nogales and Sierra Vista Ranger Districts
USGS 1:24,000 Sonoita, Mt. Hughes, O'Donnell Canyon
1:100,000 Fort Huachuca
Maptech CD-ROM: Southeast Arizona/ Tucson
Arizona Atlas & Gazetteer, p. 73
Arizona Road & Recreation Atlas, pp. 54, 88
Recreational Map of Arizona

Route Directions

▼ 0.0   From Sonoita, turn south on Arizona 83 at the sign for Parker Canyon Lake. Proceed 0.4 miles to where South #8: Parker Canyon Lake Road (Arizona 83) bears left to Parker Canyon Lake and continue straight ahead on Papago Spring Road. Zero trip meter at intersection. Remain on paved twisty road, ignoring turns to right and left.

3.2 ▲   Trail ends at the intersection of Papago Spring Road and South #8: Parker Canyon Lake Road (Arizona 83). Continue straight on to Sonoita, turn right to travel to Parker Canyon Lake.
            GPS: N31°40.40′ W110°39.31′

▼ 2.0   SO   Road turns to gravel at primitive road sign.
1.2 ▲   SO   Road is now paved.

▼ 2.6   SO   Cattle guard.
0.6 ▲   SO   Cattle guard.

▼ 3.2   BL   Bear left remaining on the major graded road, FR 158. Track on right is FR 636 to Papago Spring. Many pleasant campsites along that trail. Zero trip

		meter.
0.0 ▲		Continue to the northwest.
		GPS: N31°37.68′ W110°37.86′

▼ 0.0		Continue to the southeast and cross cattle guard.
1.0 ▲	SO	Cattle guard; then track on left is FR 636 to Papago Spring. Many pleasant campsites along that trail. Zero trip meter.

▼ 0.1	SO	Track on right.
0.9 ▲	SO	Track on left.

▼ 0.9	SO	Cross through wash.

0.1 ▲	SO	Cross through wash.

▼ 1.0	TR	Turn right onto small, formed trail at marker for FR 158. Graded road continues into private property. Zero trip meter.
0.0 ▲		Continue to the west.
		GPS: N31°37.26′ W110°38.02′

▼ 0.0		Continue to the south.
2.8 ▲	TL	Join larger graded road and turn left. Private property on the right. Zero trip meter.

▼ 0.3	SO	Track on right.

Looking across the trail to the Santa Rita Mountains

2.5 ▲ SO Track on left.

▼ 0.4 TL Track straight on.
2.4 ▲ TR Track on left.
GPS: N31°36.90′ W110°38.01′

▼ 0.5 SO Pass through fence line, corral on right, then pass through second fence line.
2.3 ▲ SO Pass through fence line, corral on left, then pass through second fence line.

▼ 0.7 SO Track on left goes into private property.
2.1 ▲ SO Track on right goes into private property.

▼ 0.9 SO Track on left and well on right; then cross through wash.
1.9 ▲ SO Cross through wash; then track on right and well on left.
GPS: N31°36.72′ W110°37.57′

▼ 1.0 SO Cross through wash.
1.8 ▲ SO Cross through wash.

▼ 1.1 SO Cross through wide wash.
1.7 ▲ SO Cross through wide wash.

▼ 1.2 SO Cross through wash.
1.6 ▲ SO Cross through wash.
GPS: N31°36.47′ W110°37.45′.

▼ 1.5 SO Faint track on left at corral.
1.3 ▲ SO Faint track on right at corral.
GPS: N31°36.33′ W110°37.28′

▼ 1.6 SO Pass through wire gate.
1.2 ▲ SO Pass through wire gate.

▼ 1.8 SO Cross through wash.
1.0 ▲ SO Cross through wash.

▼ 1.9 SO Cross through two washes.
0.9 ▲ SO Cross through two washes.

▼ 2.2 SO Off-camber section around a fallen tree will test the side tilt angle of your vehicle.
0.6 ▲ SO Off-camber section around a fallen tree will test the side tilt angle of your vehicle.

▼ 2.8 TR Pass through wire gate, then turn right onto small unmarked track. Zero trip meter. Ahead goes to private property.
0.0 ▲ Continue to the northeast.
GPS: N31°35.40′ W110°36.84′

▼ 0.0 Continue to the west.
0.9 ▲ TL T-intersection. Turn left and pass through wire gate. Zero trip meter. Track on right goes to private property.

▼ 0.3 SO Cross through wash.
0.6 ▲ SO Cross through wash.

▼ 0.7 SO Pass through wire gate.
0.2 ▲ SO Pass through wire gate.
GPS: N31°35.46′ W110°37.55′

▼ 0.9 TL Turn left onto small trail and zero trip meter. Trail goes into the trees and can be a little hard to spot as it goes slightly back on itself.
0.0 ▲ Continue to the southeast.
GPS: N31°35.53′ W110°37.65′

▼ 0.0 Continue to the southwest.
3.9 ▲ TR Turn right at T-intersection and zero trip meter.

▼ 0.3 SO Cross through wash.
3.6 ▲ SO Cross through wash.

▼ 0.4 SO Cross through rocky wash.
3.5 ▲ SO Cross through rocky wash.

▼ 0.6 SO Cross through wash.
3.3 ▲ SO Cross through wash.

▼ 0.9 SO Dam on right.
3.0 ▲ SO Dam on left.
GPS: N31°34.88′ W110°38.17′

▼ 1.1 SO Cross through wash.
2.8 ▲ SO Cross through wash.

▼ 1.2 TL T-intersection, small track on right.
2.7 ▲ TR Track on left.
GPS: N31°34.79′ W110°38.36′

▼ 1.5	SO	Track on right.
2.4 ▲	SO	Track on left.

▼ 1.8	SO	Cross through wash.
2.1 ▲	SO	Cross through wash.

▼ 1.9	SO	Old dam on left.
2.0 ▲	SO	Old dam on right.

▼ 2.2	SO	Gate.
1.7 ▲	SO	Gate.

▼ 2.4	SO	Track on left, campsite on right.
1.5 ▲	SO	Track on right, campsite on left.

GPS: N31°34.40' W110°37.52'

▼ 2.7	BL	Track on right to tanks.
1.2 ▲	BR	Track on left to tanks.

▼ 3.1	SO	Track on right to campsite.
0.8 ▲	BR	Track on left to campsite.

▼ 3.6	SO	Track on right to campsite.
0.3 ▲	SO	Track on left to campsite.

▼ 3.7	SO	Pass through wire gate at primitive road sign.
0.2 ▲	SO	Pass through wire gate at primitive road sign.

GPS: N31°34.49' W110°36.27'

▼ 3.9	SO	Join graded dirt road at marker for FR 236. Zero trip meter.
0.0 ▲		Continue to the south.

GPS: N31°34.65' W110°36.24'

▼ 0.0		Continue to the north.
2.9 ▲	TL	On right-hand bend, turn left onto FR 236, formed dirt trail and zero trip meter. There is a sign for FR 236.

▼ 0.3	SO	Track on right is private.
2.6 ▲	SO	Track on left is private.

▼ 0.9	TR	Turn right onto FR 826 at sign. FR 826 also continues straight ahead.
2.0 ▲	TL	Turn left at T-intersection onto graded FR 158 at sign. FR 826 is on the right.

GPS: N31°35.13' W110°35.70'

▼ 1.5	SO	Cattle guard.
1.4 ▲	SO	Cattle guard.

▼ 1.6	SO	Cross through wash.
1.3 ▲	SO	Cross through wash.

▼ 1.9	SO	FR 4615 on right. Exiting Coronado National Forest.
1.0 ▲	SO	FR 4615 on left. Entering Coronado National Forest.

▼ 2.1	SO	Cattle guard.
0.8 ▲	SO	Cattle guard.

▼ 2.9		Trail ends at the T-intersection with the paved South #8: Parker Canyon Lake Road. Turn right for Parker Lake, turn left for Sonoita.
0.0 ▲		From South #8: Parker Canyon Lake Road, 0.7 miles south of mile marker 21, turn west on the graded dirt Vaughn Loop Road, FR 826. Zero trip meter and cross cattle guard.

GPS: N31°35.14' W110°33.74'

Blacktail Ridge Trail

STARTING POINT	South #12: Mexican Border Road, 7.4 miles west of the intersection with South #8: Parker Canyon Lake Road
FINISHING POINT	South #8: Parker Canyon Lake Road, 0.6 miles south of Parker Canyon Lake turnoff
TOTAL MILEAGE	6.4 miles
UNPAVED MILEAGE	6.4 miles
DRIVING TIME	45 minutes
ELEVATION RANGE	5,000–5,700 feet
USUALLY OPEN	Year-round
BEST TIME TO TRAVEL	October to May
DIFFICULTY RATING	2
SCENIC RATING	7
REMOTENESS RATING	+0

Special Attractions

- Easy trail running over grasslands.
- Panoramic views of the Huachuca Mountains and south into Mexico.
- Alternative access to Parker Canyon Lake.

Description

This easy, formed trail runs in a straight line along a wide ridge connecting South #12: Mexican Border Road with South #8: Parker Canyon Lake Road. It follows FR 4016 and FR 194, shown on the Coronado National Forest Map. (FR 4016 is shown on the map but not labeled.)

The trail is open and offers good views down into Bodie Canyon on the east. Farther up, the trail follows alongside Jones Canyon on the west.

The whole trail is very exposed with little shade. For those wishing to camp, the north end, near the junction of the Arizona Trail, is the best option. However, nicer spots can be found along the Parker Canyon Lake Road and in the national forest campground at Parker Canyon Lake.

The open views make it easy to spot many raptors. In addition, javelina and desert pronghorn antelope may be seen in the grasslands.

Current Road Information

Coronado National Forest
Sierra Vista Ranger District
5990 South Hwy 92
Hereford, AZ 85615
(520) 378-0311

Map References

BLM   Nogales
USFS Coronado National Forest: Nogales and Sierra Vista Ranger Districts
USGS 1:24,000 Campini Mesa, Huachuca Peak
      1:100,000 Nogales
Maptech CD-ROM: Southeast Arizona/ Tucson
Arizona Atlas & Gazetteer, p. 73
Arizona Road & Recreation Atlas, pp. 54, 88
Recreational Map of Arizona

Crossing grasslands toward Mexico

Route Directions

▼ 0.0   From South #12: Mexican Border Road, 7.4 miles west of the intersection with South #8: Parker Canyon Lake Road, zero trip meter and turn east on small formed trail, FR 4016. Initally the trail crosses grasslands.

2.7 ▲   Trail ends at the T-intersection with South #12: Mexican Border Road. Turn right to continue to Lochiel, turn left to continue toward Sierra Vista.

GPS: N31°20.91' W110°29.67'

▼ 0.2   SO Track on left.
2.5 ▲   SO Track on right.

▼ 0.7   SO Track on right and track on left.
2.0 ▲   SO Track on right and track on left.

▼ 0.9   SO Cattle guard.
1.8 ▲   SO Cattle guard.

▼ 1.8   SO Track on left; then track on right.
0.9 ▲   SO Track on left; then track on right.

▼ 2.0   BL Track on right.
0.7 ▲   SO Track on left.

GPS: N31°22.54' W110°28.57'

▼ 2.3   SO Track on right. Several tracks on left and right, remain on main trail.
0.4 ▲   SO Track on left. Several tracks on left and right, remain on main trail.

▼ 2.7   SO Track on left is FR 194. Continue straight ahead also on FR 194. Zero trip meter.
0.0 ▲   Continue to the southwest.

GPS: N31°22.98' W110°28.16'

▼ 0.0   Continue to the northeast.
3.2 ▲   BL Track on right is the continuation of FR 194. Bear left onto FR 4016 and zero trip meter.

▼ 0.1   SO Cattle guard.
3.1 ▲   SO Cattle guard.

▼ 1.7   BR Track on left is FR 4771. Bear right and

South Trail #10: Blacktail Ridge Trail

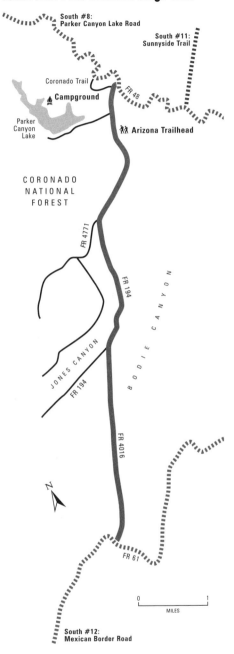

cross cattle guard, then track on left.

1.5 ▲   BL Track on right, cattle guard, then track on right is FR 4771. Bear left remaining on unmarked FR 194.

GPS: N31°24.26' W110°27.42'

▼ 2.4   SO   Track on right through fence line.
0.8 ▲   SO   Track on left through fence line.

▼ 2.9   SO   Campsite on left, no shade but views of Parker Canyon Lake.
0.3 ▲   SO   Campsite on right, no shade but views of Parker Canyon Lake.

▼ 3.1   SO   Track on left, then Arizona Trail parking on left and right. The Arizona Trail on the left and right is for horses and hikers only.
0.1 ▲   SO   The Arizona Trail on the left and right is for horses and hikers only. Trailhead parking on left and right, then track on right.
         GPS: N31°25.16′ W110°26.47′

▼ 3.2   SO   Cattle guard. Zero trip meter.
0.0 ▲   Continue to the southwest.
         GPS: N31°25.20′ W110°26.44′

▼ 0.0   Continue to the northeast.
0.5 ▲   SO   Cattle guard. Zero trip meter.

▼ 0.1   SO   Service road on left.
0.4 ▲   SO   Service road on right.

▼ 0.2   SO   Cattle guard.
0.3 ▲   SO   Cattle guard.

▼ 0.4   SO   Graded road on left called Coronado Trail.
0.1 ▲   SO   Graded road on right called Coronado Trail.

▼ 0.5   Trail ends at the intersection with South #8: Parker Canyon Lake Road. Turn left for Parker Canyon Lake, turn right to return to South #12: Mexican Border Road.
0.0 ▲   0.6 miles south of Parker Canyon Lake turn west from South #8: Parker Canyon Lake Road immediately before a cattle guard. Zero trip meter and continue west on South Lake Road, FR 194.
         GPS: N31°25.48′ W110°26.15′

Sunnyside Trail

STARTING POINT	South #8: Parker Canyon Lake Road, 2.1 miles south of Parker Canyon Lake
FINISHING POINT	Sunnyside
TOTAL MILEAGE	8.4 miles (round-trip)
UNPAVED MILEAGE	8.4 miles (round-trip)
DRIVING TIME	45 minutes (one-way)
ELEVATION RANGE	5,700–6,000
USUALLY OPEN	Year-round
BEST TIME TO TRAVEL	October to May
DIFFICULTY RATING	2
SCENIC RATING	8
REMOTENESS RATING	+0

Special Attractions

■ Remains of Sunnyside ghost town.
■ Sunnyside Cemetery.
■ Hiking trail access to Miller Peak Wilderness and the Copper Glance Mine.
■ Views into Sunnyside Canyon and the Huachuca Mountains.

History

Sunnyside, now a ghost town, was established in the 1890s as a religious community led by Samuel Donnelly, an ex-alcoholic, originally from Scotland. Donnelly, who was a former boxer and sailor, found salvation and sobriety at a Salvation Army meeting in San Francisco. The community of 50 families was a sort of socialist cooperative, with members working at whatever their talents allowed and pooling their money. The members spent their time singing hymns, reading the Bible, and mining the nearby Copper Glance Mine. Other income for the hard-working community came from cutting hay for the military post of Fort Huachuca, running a sawmill, and working on the railroad. There were no stores in Sunnyside. None were needed as the residents pooled everything and cooked and ate in communal areas. The women cooked together and did the laundry in large tubs. Slackers were not tolerated. Anyone who wouldn't work was asked to leave.

Communal living seemed to work very well for the settlement. Visitors would often remark how happy everyone appeared to be, and there was none of the violence, hard drinking, or prostitution often associated with mining camps of the era. Indeed, the community practiced what it preached and often gave food, supplies, and money to people in need.

Samuel Donnelly died in 1901, but the Donnelites, as they were known, remained on. The little town, which was the only settlement in Arizona known to be wholly religious, got a post office on July 16, 1914. It finally closed after 20 years when the mines were exhausted. The Donnelites dispersed after giving the mine to their creditors.

To the north of Sunnyside is Fort Huachuca, a cavalry post founded in 1877 that played a prominent role in subduing the last significant Indian group ranging outside of reservations in the United States. The group, the Chiricahua Apache, were led by Geronimo and ranged across into Mexico pursued by the cavalry. The post was also the headquarters of the "Buffalo Soldiers," the name given by Native Americans to black soldiers. The post was the headquarters for the army's four all-black regiments: 9th and 10th Cavalry Regiments, and the 24th and 25th Infantry Regiments. The fort survives today as an active military installation.

Some of the structures still located at Sunnyside

GERONIMO (GOYATHLAY)

Geronimo, born in 1829, was actually named Goyathlay. The origin of the name "Geronimo" is unknown, although some say that it comes from a mispronounciation of his name by Mexican soldiers. Others say that the name is a corruption of St. Jerome, the saint that soldiers called out for when Geronimo came barreling toward them. Geronimo is recognized as the leader of the last organized resistance in Native American history.

Geronimo first tasted war and revenge in 1858 when Mexican soldiers slaughtered women and children of the Bedonkohe Apache. Geronimo's wife, Alope, and his three children died beneath the Mexican sword. He committed himself to avenging these deaths. The Mexicans were not the only ones to witness Geronimo's fighting prowess. When Mangas Coloradas was captured through treachery, Geronimo joined Cochise to battle the Americans.

By the 1870s, most of the Apache bands had been settled in reservations. Geronimo joined his fellow Apache, but found the conditions deplorable. He resisted with a group of followers, escaping from the San Carlos Reservation in 1878. They joined Apache in Mexico, but grew tired of fighting and returned to the reservation in 1880. When a religious gathering was suppressed, and the Indian shaman Nakaidoklini was killed, Geronimo escaped once again with his supporters. The following spring Geronimo came back, killed the chief of police, and led hundreds of Apaches out of the San Carlos Reservation. Led by Geronimo, the band raided American and Mexican settlements. In response, General George Crook was called to apprehend the rampaging Apaches. Using Apache scouts, he did just that. The Apache were returned to San Carlos. Rumor circulated that the rebels were going to be executed, so they fled once again. Crook was right on their heels. Tirelessly, the army pursued the renegades, and Geronimo was forced to surrender. While being escorted back to the reservation, Geronimo and 30 followers again escaped

Geronimo

Crook's grasp, severely embarrassing the army. Even though Crook was not at fault, he was replaced by General Nelson Miles, who then sent 5,000 soldiers out after the Apache. On September 4, 1886, in Skeleton Canyon, Miles caught up with Geronimo and he surrendered for the last time.

Geronimo and his followers were sent to internment camps in Florida. Once there, they were forced to give up their way of life and were made to don European dress and cut their long hair. Life was difficult, and the men had to perform hard labor. Those who survived the camps were transferred to Fort Sill in present-day Oklahoma. Geronimo was reunited with one of his wives (he married two others after Alope's death) and he supported his family by farming, ranching, and selling pictures of himself. He became a celebrity and was at Teddy Roosevelt's inaugural parade and the St. Louis World's Fair. Yet he was still a prisoner of war. He longed to go back to his homeland, but he never did. Pneumonia took him on February 17, 1909.

South Trail #11: Sunnyside Trail

Description

This short trail follows alongside Sunnyside Canyon, traveling on a roughly graded dirt road. The trail gradually climbs, giving excellent views over the Huachuca Mountains. At a T-intersection, the trail makes the loop around to the Sunnyside town site. A sign-posted track on the left leads to the wilderness boundary, and the start of a hiking trail that leads to the remains of the Copper Glance Mine, which was worked successfully by the Donnelites for many years. Sunnyside is a short distance past the mine. The town site is now privately owned and posted. However, it is possible to get a good view of the remains of the two substantial wooden houses that remain, some smaller buildings, and water tanks. The original schoolhouse collapsed a few years ago, and most of the remaining buildings are in a precarious state.

After viewing the wooden buildings, retrace your steps nearly to the start of the trail and visit the Sunnyside Cemetery. The trail to the cemetery is small with many turns and it is easy to get confused. The most reliable way of finding it is to enter the coordinates for the spur to the cemetery into your GPS and use the GoTo feature to help you navigate.

The cemetery has undergone restoration work over the years but looks a little dilapidated these days. The small plot is enclosed by a sagging wire fence. Most of the graves are marked with plaques. The trail peters out immediately after the cemetery.

Current Road Information

Coronado National Forest
Sierra Vista Ranger District
5990 South Hwy 92
Hereford, AZ 85615
(520) 378-0311

Map References

BLM Nogales
USFS Coronado National Forest: Nogales and Sierra Vista Ranger Districts
USGS 1:24,000 Huachuca Peak
1:100,000 Nogales
Maptech CD-ROM: Southeast Arizona/ Tucson
Arizona Atlas & Gazetteer, p. 73
Arizona Road & Recreation Atlas, pp. 54, 88
Recreational Map of Arizona

Route Directions

▼ 0.0   From South #8: Parker Canyon Lake Road, 2.1 miles south of Parker Canyon Lake, zero trip meter and turn northeast on graded dirt road, sign-posted to Sunnyside Canyon, FR 228.
GPS: N31°24.83′ W110°25.52′

Sunnyside Cemetery

▼ 0.1 SO Cattle guard.
▼ 0.5 SO Large camping area on right.
▼ 0.9 BL Track on right is the start of spur trail to Sunnyside Cemetery. Zero trip meter.
        GPS: N31°25.48′ W110°24.98′

Spur to Sunnyside Cemetery

▼ 0.0 BR At the fork in the trail pointing toward Sunnyside, take the right fork (northeast) and zero trip meter.
        GPS: N31°25.48′ W110°24.98′

▼ 0.3 SO Track on right.
▼ 0.5 SO Track on right.
        GPS: N31°25.54′ W110°24.69′

▼ 0.6 SO Gate; then track on right.
        GPS: N31°25.63′ W110°24.65′

▼ 0.8 BR Bear right, track on left, then cross through wash and bear right again, track on left.
        GPS: N31°25.77′ W110°24.53′

▼ 0.85 TR Turn right at top of bank in open area.
        GPS: N31°25.75′ W110°24.47′

▼ 0.9 BL Turn left, well-used track on right.
        GPS: N31°25.67′ W110°24.46′

▼ 1.0 BR Enter trees, well-used track on left, bear right. Then small track on right.
        GPS: N31°25.64′ W110°24.45′

▼ 1.2 UT Sunnyside Cemetery on left, enclosed by wire fence. Retrace your steps to the start of the spur trail.
        GPS: N31°25.53′ W110°24.53′

Continuation of Trail

▼ 0.0 Zero trip meter and continue to the north.

▼ 0.8 SO Track on left.
▼ 1.2 SO Cattle guard.
        GPS: N31°26.41′ W110°24.29′

▼ 1.5 SO Cross through wash.
▼ 1.6 TR T-intersection. FR 228 to Fort Gate #7 on left, FR 204 to Sunnyside Canyon and Copper Glance on right.
        GPS: N31°26.50′ W110°24.13′

▼ 1.8 SO At sign for Sunnyside Canyon and Copper Glance, continue straight on. Left goes 0.7 miles to the boundary of the Miller Peak Wilderness and the start of Sunnyside Canyon hiking trail which goes approximately 3.5 miles to the Copper Glance Mine. Zero trip meter.
        GPS: N31°26.28′ W110°24.12′

▼ 0.0 Continue to the south.
▼ 0.2 Cross through creek, then trail ends at a gate. Sunnyside ghost town is just beyond the gate. No camping is permitted. The town site is on private property, hike for 0.1 miles down the wash to view the buildings from public land.
        GPS: N31°26.13′ W110°24.19′

Mexican Border Road

STARTING POINT	Arizona 92, 0.8 miles past mile marker 334
FINISHING POINT	Arizona 82, 4.1 miles north of Nogales
TOTAL MILEAGE	50.4 miles
UNPAVED MILEAGE	43.6 miles
DRIVING TIME	5 hours
ELEVATION RANGE	3,600–6,600 feet
USUALLY OPEN	Year-round
BEST TIME TO TRAVEL	November to June
DIFFICULTY RATING	1
SCENIC RATING	10
REMOTENESS RATING	+0

Special Attractions
- Old border crossing town of Lochiel.
- Washington Camp and Duquesne ghost towns.
- Montezuma Pass and the Coronado National Memorial.
- Sweeping views of mountains and grasslands in the United States and Mexico.

History
The Spanish padres criss-crossed the route of this trail on many of their missions. Two of the best known of these early European travelers were Padre Eusebio Francisco Kino and Fray Marcos de Niza (who is believed to be the earliest European to pass this way back in 1539). The development of this route started at the western end and over time forged its way to the east.

Further Spanish exploration in the 1760s extended the trail east. In the 1860s miners forged a trail through to Washington Camp as they pressed onward searching for the next lucky strike. The trail then lengthened again, pushing farther east to more mines at Luttrell, later known as Lochiel, and on to Sunnyside, which was a timber supply point for the mines at Washington Camp and Duquesne. The final section of the trail was cut through by the Civilian Conservation Corps in 1933 and went east over Montezuma Pass. Early travelers reported abundant wildlife throughout this region including Mexican wolves, bears, wild horses, and panthers.

Thomas Shane and his associate Mr. Capen brought life back to Washington Camp with the discovery of the Bonanza Mine in the early 1880s. Claims changed hands often, until the Duquesne Company took hold of many of the mining claims in the late 1880s, and the boom was on. The Duquesne and Washington Camps were less than a mile apart with more than 70 mines active and nearly 2,000 residents between the

An old house in Duquesne ghost town

DANGER! PELIGRO!
ABANDONED AND INACTIVE
MINES ARE DEATH TRAPS!
DON'T GET TRAPPED!
STAY OUT!

STAY ALIVE!
DANGERS AWAIT INSIDE AND

An abandoned mine along the trail

two. Washington Camp built a smelter for use by both camps and was the site of the school. The towns flourished and survived into the early 1900s but by 1920, the lights of the towns all but went out. A brief mining resurgence in the early 1940s brought a momentary flicker back to the virtual ghost town. A number of houses have remained occupied over the years as nature has reclaimed the dozens of mine shafts.

Duquesne's most famous resident was probably George Westinghouse of household appliance fame. He amazed his neighbors by having hot and cold running water in his bathroom long before it was commonplace. At the turn of the twenty-first century the camps took on a new boom in the form of real estate. Many of the mining remains of the two camps were bulldozed and the landscape was "tamed." Though Duquesne and Washington Camps may rise again as residential

settlements, it appears their days as mining camps are over.

Lochiel, situated right on the Mexican border, was named after the first settlers' village back in Scotland. The Camerons were partners in securing the nearby San Rafael de la Zanja Land Grant in 1888 from its original owner, Manuel Bustello, who purchased it from the Mexican government in 1825. Records are confused, but Lochiel appears to be the same place as two other settlements known as Luttrell and La Noria. Luttrell housed the Holland Company Smelter and associated workers' cottages. In the 1890s the U.S.-Mexican border was resurveyed as the earlier survey was deemed inaccurate. The new border split the settlement down the middle, and neighbors suddenly found themselves living in different countries.

The green pastures of the San Rafael de la

Ore-loading hopper at the Kansas Mine

Zanja Land Grant, which refers to "the ditch," or water basin, of the Santa Cruz River, have been good grazing lands over the centuries. Settlers' cattle attracted Apache Indians who came to kill them and Texas rustlers who stole them and escaped with guns blazing into Mexico. The rustlers at least were deterred when settlers rounded up some of the offenders and publicly hung them in Tombstone. Other cattle rustlers came north from Mexico. One notorious name was Francisco Pancho Villa, seen as somewhat of a Mexican freedom fighter and rebel. Much of his funds were gained by rounding up the community's cattle and returning south to sell off the booty. More recently, these same rolling pastures were featured in the making of such movies as, *Tom Horn, Monte Walsh,* and *Oklahoma.*

Lochiel finally controlled its "visitors" with the construction of an official U.S. Customs House. But in time this was seen as an unnecessary expense in a remote region and the border crossing performed its last passport stamp in 1986. The border fence has also faded with time, with massive cottonwoods falling across it and sections of the fence gaping open.

The Coronado National Memorial commemorates Francisco Vasquez de Coronado and his 1549 expedition in search of the fabled Cíbola and the Seven Cities of Gold. From Compostela, located 750 miles south on Mexico's western coast, Coronado led an ambitious expedition up through what are now Arizona and New Mexico. With a contingent of 339 soldiers, 4 Franciscan priests, 1,100 Indians and 1,500 livestock, the expedition made slow progress.

The original suggestion put forward was for an international memorial for Coronado, but the Mexican government declined to participate. Their reasons were fair: The Spanish conquistadors were often regarded as looters, taking what they wanted by force when trading was not an option. So the monument remains on the U.S. side.

Description
This long and greatly varied trail travels through some spectacular scenery in southern Arizona, at times running less than a mile north of the border with Mexico. Although the trail can be completed in five hours, it is best to allow a full day to appreciate the many things of interest along the way.

The trail leaves from Arizona 92 south of Sierra Vista and immediately travels through ranchland as a paved road. It enters the Coronado National Memorial where there are picnic areas, an informative visitor center, and the start of several hiking trails within the memorial.

From the visitor center, the trail switchbacks up Montezuma Canyon to Montezuma Pass at the southern end of the Huachuca Mountains and one of the best views along the trail. From here there are broad, panoramic views west into the San Rafael Valley, the Sierra Madre Mountains in Sonora, Mexico, the Patagonia Mountains to the northwest, and the Huachuca Mountains immediately to the north. A short trail leads out from the parking area to the shade ramada at the edge of Coronado Peak, south of the pass. Other trails lead north into the Huachuca Mountains.

From the pass, the trail switchbacks down the south side of the Huachuca Mountains along a wide shelf road, before running parallel to the Mexican border for several miles through a mixture of open grassland and ranchland. You are likely to encounter the U.S. Border Patrol in their distinctive white and green vehicles along the border fence, as well as possibly surprising groups of undocumented aliens from Mexico. (Refer to the Border Patrol section, p. 12 for information on safety and how to handle unexpected encounters.) Many small tracks lead south from the main trail toward the border, these are mainly pushed through by border crossers (in both directions) and when one is closed, another one opens. The route directions have tried to account for the majority of better-used tracks to aid in navigation, but due to constantly changing situations, some may not be accurate. However, the main graded trail is easy to follow and there is little chance of becoming lost.

GADSDEN PURCHASE—1854

In the early 1850s, at the far west of the United States, California was booming. California's success was the result of the 1849 gold rush and the sudden charge of immigrants looking to cash in. California was growing, creating the need for a line of communication between the East and the West. Citizens and railroad companies were pressuring Washington to create a link. Surveyors pointed out that the Gila Trail, which ran through Arizona, would be an excellent road on which to lay track. However, the land on which the U.S. wanted to build was in the hands of Mexico. President Franklin Pierce wanted to make a deal with Mexican president Antonio Lopez de Santa Anna. The good news for the United States was that Mexico was in a severe financial crunch. Pierce sent James Gadsden to Mexico City to work out a deal.

Gadsden had five different proposals for acquiring the needed land, each one with a different price. Santa Anna needed money to supply his army and was in no hurry to get into another war with the United States. He did not buckle under, however. Gadsden was made aware that he would only get enough land to make the railroad and Mexico did not want to give up access to Baja California. A compromise was achieved and the purchase was signed on December 30, 1853. The treaty was not ratified until June 24, 1854, after the Mexican minister, Juan Nepomunceno Almonte, tinkered with the borders just a little bit more. Before the Gadsden Purchase, the border of the United States was along the Gila River. For $10 million the United States bought 9,000 square miles and the foundation for a railroad. The Gadsden Purchase set the present boundary between Arizona and Mexico. Without it, all of the trails in this book would lie in a different country.

These sweeping grasslands are home to a variety of wildlife: Pronghorn antelopes, javelinas, mule deer, and coyotes are the animals most often sighted. Cattle also graze in the area.

The trail passes the southern end of South #8: Parker Canyon Lake Road and South #10: Blacktail Ridge Trail, before continuing through an open landscape toward the small settlement of Lochiel. A handful of people still call Lochiel home, but the customs house and border crossing are no longer active. This is one place where you cannot just pop around to the neighbor's house to borrow a cup of sugar; it is illegal to cross the international border other than at a recognized crossing point. The township is worth the short detour to see the customs house.

The next point of interest along the trail is the old mining camp of Duquesne. The route directions detour from the main graded road at this point to loop past the original settlement of Duquesne, which stands on privately owned land. Currently, Duquesne is in the process of being converted into a residential subdivision, so the future of the remaining houses from the original settlement is uncertain. Currently there are two substantial, old timber and stone houses that would have been considered opulent in their day; the ruins of two adobe houses and various other timber buildings remain as well. The ruins are posted as private property, but are easily viewed from the road. The trail rejoins the main FR 61 at Washington Camp, once a thriving mining camp, now a community of year-round houses and holiday homes. Little remains of the original mining camp.

The trail then climbs toward an unnamed pass in the Patagonia Mountains, passing the wooden hopper of the Kansas Mine still clinging to the side of the hillside immediately west of the southern end of South #13: Harshaw Road. Below the trail in Washington Gulch are the remains of the Pride Mine.

From the pass, the trail descends along a wide shelf road through the Patagonia Mountains, one of the prettiest sections of this long trail. This final section through Sycamore Canyon and the surrounding low hills of the

Patagonia Mountains has the best campsites along the trail, even though they are well used.

The trail ends on Arizona 82, a few miles north of Nogales.

Current Road Information
Coronado National Forest
Sierra Vista Ranger District
5990 South Hwy 92
Hereford, AZ 85615
(520) 378-0311

Map References
BLM Nogales
USFS Coronado National Forest: Nogales and Sierra Vista Ranger Districts
USGS 1:24,000 Nicksville, Bob Thompson Peak, Montezuma Pass, Miller Peak, Huachuca Peak, Campini Mesa, Lochiel, Duquesne, Harshaw, Cumero Canyon, Kino Springs
1:100,000 Nogales
Maptech CD-ROM: Southeast Arizona/ Tucson
Arizona Atlas & Gazetteer, pp. 74, 73
Arizona Road & Recreation Atlas, pp. 54, 88
Recreational Map of Arizona

Route Directions

▼ 0.0   From Arizona 92, 13 miles south of Sierra Vista, 0.8 miles south of mile marker 334, zero trip meter and turn south on paved road sign-posted to Coronado National Memorial. The road is marked as S. Coronado Memorial Drive. There is a forest sign after the turn, giving distances along the route. The road is also called FR 61. Remain on the paved road.

4.6 ▲   Trail ends at the T-intersection with Arizona 92. Turn left for Sierra Vista, turn right for Bisbee.
    GPS: N31°22.78′ W110°12.39′

▼ 2.9 SO Cattle guard, entering Coronado National Memorial.
1.7 ▲ SO Cattle guard, leaving Coronado National Memorial.
    GPS: N31°20.91′ W110°13.44′

▼ 4.6 SO Coronado National Memorial Visitor Center on right, zero trip meter.
0.0 ▲   Continue to the northeast.
    GPS: N31°20.76′ W110°15.16′

▼ 0.0   Continue to the southwest.
3.2 ▲ SO Coronado National Memorial Visitor Center on left, zero trip meter.

▼ 0.1 SO Picnic area and start of Joe's Canyon hiking trail on left.
3.1 ▲ SO Picnic area and start of Joe's Canyon hiking trail on right.
    GPS: N31°20.73′ W110°15.22′

▼ 0.2 SO Road turns to dirt.
3.0 ▲ SO Road turns to paved.

▼ 1.6 SO Cross through wash on concrete ford.
1.6 ▲ SO Cross through wash on concrete ford.

▼ 3.2 SO Cattle guard, then Montezuma Pass. Parking area on left and short hiking trail to the ramada. Crest hiking trail on right after cattle guard. Zero trip meter.
0.0 ▲   Continue down from the saddle to the northeast.
    GPS: N31°21.05′ W110°17.09′

▼ 0.0   Continue down from the saddle to the northwest.
3.5 ▲ SO Montezuma Pass. Parking area on right and short hiking trail to the ramada. Crest hiking trail on left, then cross cattle guard. Zero trip meter.

▼ 1.3 SO Track on right up Copper Canyon and track on left; then cross through Copper Canyon Wash.
2.2 ▲ SO Cross through Copper Canyon Wash; then track on left up Copper Canyon and track on right.
    GPS: N31°21.74′ W110°17.97′

▼ 1.8 SO Cattle guard, end of descent from pass.
1.7 ▲ SO Cattle guard, trail starts to climb toward Montezuma Pass.

South Trail #12: Mexican Border Road

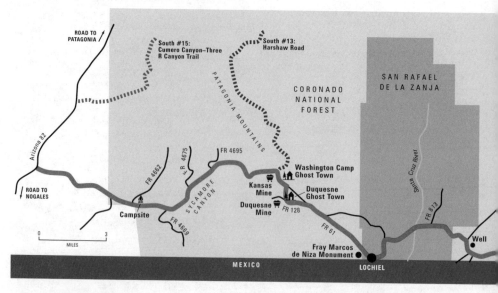

▼ 2.1   SO   Track on left.
1.4 ▲   SO   Track on right.

▼ 2.3   SO   Track on left.
1.2 ▲   SO   Track on right.

▼ 3.5   SO   Track on right is FR 771 to Huachuca
                  Mountain Trailhead. Zero trip meter.
0.0 ▲   Continue to the northeast.
                  GPS: N31°22.31′ W110°19.91′

▼ 0.0   Continue to the southwest.
4.9 ▲   SO   Track on left is FR 771 to Huachuca
                  Mountain Trailhead. Zero trip meter.

▼ 0.3   SO   Track on right.
4.6 ▲   SO   Track on left.

▼ 0.6   SO   Cattle guard; then track on left.
4.3 ▲   SO   Track on right; then cattle guard.

▼ 0.9   SO   Track on left.
4.0 ▲   SO   Track on right.

▼ 1.0   SO   Track on right, then cross over Cave
                  Canyon Creek on bridge.
3.9 ▲   SO   Cross over Cave Canyon Creek on
                  bridge, then track on left.
                  GPS: N31°22.36′ W110°20.72′

▼ 1.1   SO   Track on left.
3.8 ▲   SO   Track on right.

▼ 1.7   SO   Track on right and track on left; then
                  cattle guard.
3.2 ▲   SO   Cattle guard; then track on right and
                  track on left.

▼ 2.0   SO   Track on left.
2.9 ▲   SO   Track on right.

▼ 2.3   SO   Cross over Bear Creek on bridge.
2.6 ▲   SO   Cross over Bear Creek on bridge.
                  GPS: N31°22.80′ W110°21.76′

▼ 2.4   SO   Well-used track on right.
2.5 ▲   SO   Well-used track on left.

▼ 2.6   SO   Track on left.
2.3 ▲   SO   Track on right.

▼ 3.0   SO   Cross over creek.
1.9 ▲   SO   Cross over creek.

▼ 3.1   SO   Track on left.
1.8 ▲   SO   Track on right.

▼ 3.2   SO   Cattle guard.

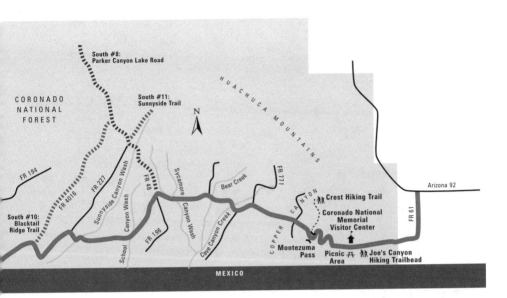

1.7 ▲   SO   Cattle guard.

▼ 3.4   SO   Cross through wash; then track on
             right.
1.5 ▲   SO   Track on left, then cross through
             wash.

▼ 3.7   SO   Track on left.
1.2 ▲   SO   Track on right.

▼ 4.0   SO   Cross over wash; then track on right.
0.9 ▲   SO   Track on left; then cross over wash.

▼ 4.1   SO   Track on left; then cross through
             Sycamore Canyon Wash.
0.8 ▲   SO   Cross through Sycamore Canyon
             Wash; then track on right.
             GPS: N31°22.63′ W110°23.45′

▼ 4.3   SO   Cross through Joaquin Canyon Wash,
             track on right; then cattle guard.
0.6 ▲   SO   Cattle guard, track on left; then cross
             through Joaquin Canyon Wash.

▼ 4.9   TL   Graded road straight on is South #8:
             Parker Canyon Lake Road, FR 48. Zero
             trip meter.
0.0 ▲   Continue southeast following the sign
             for Sierra Vista.

GPS: N31°22.79′ W110°24.13′

▼ 0.0   Continue south following the sign to
             Nogales.
5.1 ▲   TR   Graded road on left is South #8:
             Parker Canyon Lake Road, FR 48. Zero
             trip meter.

▼ 0.1   SO   FR 196 on left goes to ranch.
5.0 ▲   SO   FR 196 on right goes to ranch.

▼ 2.2   SO   Track on left; then cattle guard, cross-
             ing through School Canyon.
2.9 ▲   SO   Cattle guard; then track on right, cross-
             ing through School Canyon.

▼ 2.3   SO   Track on right; then cross through
             School Canyon Wash; then track on
             left.
2.8 ▲   SO   Track on right; then cross through
             School Canyon Wash; then track on
             left.
             GPS: N31°21.15′ W110°25.47′

▼ 2.6   SO   Track on left.
2.5 ▲   SO   Track on right.

▼ 2.8   SO   Track on right.
2.3 ▲   SO   Track on left.

▼ 3.3   SO   Track on left and track on right along fence line.

1.8 ▲   SO   Track on left and track on right along fence line.

▼ 3.8   SO   Cattle guard.

1.3 ▲   SO   Cattle guard.

▼ 4.5   SO   Cattle guard, entering Santa Cruz County.

0.6 ▲   SO   Cattle guard, entering Cochise County.
     GPS: N31°21.23′ W110°27.56′

▼ 4.6   SO   Cross through Sunnyside Canyon Wash.

0.5 ▲   SO   Cross through Sunnyside Canyon Wash.

▼ 4.7   SO   Track on left.

0.4 ▲   SO   Track on right.

▼ 5.1   BL   Graded road on right is FR 227 to Parker Canyon Lake. Zero trip meter at sign and continue following the sign to Nogales.

0.0 ▲   Continue toward the Coronado National Memorial.
     GPS: N31°21.43′ W110°28.04′

▼ 0.0   Continue toward Lochiel.

2.3 ▲   BR   Graded road on left is FR 227 to Parker Canyon Lake. Zero trip meter and continue following the sign to Sierra Vista.

▼ 0.1   SO   Cattle guard.

2.2 ▲   SO   Cattle guard.

▼ 0.2   SO   Track on left.

2.1 ▲   SO   Track on right.

▼ 0.5   SO   Track on right.

1.8 ▲   SO   Track on left.

▼ 1.8   SO   Cross through Bodie Canyon Wash.

0.5 ▲   SO   Cross through Bodie Canyon Wash.
     GPS: N31°20.46′ W110°29.42′

▼ 2.2   SO   Track on left.

0.1 ▲   SO   Track on right.

▼ 2.3   SO   Track on right is South #10: Blacktail Ridge Trail, FR 4016. Zero trip meter.

0.0 ▲   Continue to the south.
     GPS: N31°20.91′ W110°29.67′

▼ 0.0   Continue to the north.

3.9 ▲   SO   Track on left is South #10: Blacktail Ridge Trail, FR 4016. Zero trip meter.

▼ 0.6   SO   Track on right.

3.3 ▲   SO   Track on left.

▼ 1.7   SO   Track on left.

2.2 ▲   SO   Track on right.

▼ 1.9   SO   Cross through wash.

2.0 ▲   SO   Cross through wash.

▼ 2.0   SO   Cattle guard; then track on left.

1.9 ▲   SO   Track on right; then cattle guard.

▼ 3.3   SO   Track on left, cattle guard, then track on left.

0.6 ▲   SO   Track on right, cattle guard, then track on right.

▼ 3.7   SO   Well on right; then cross through wash.

0.2 ▲   SO   Cross through wash; then well on left.

▼ 3.8   SO   Track on left.

0.1 ▲   SO   Track on right.

▼ 3.9   TL   Turn onto graded road following the sign to Lochiel and Patagonia. Graded road straight on is FR 194. Zero trip meter.

0.0 ▲   Continue to the south.
     GPS: N31°20.79′ W110°33.02′

▼ 0.0   Continue to the west.

5.3 ▲   TR   Turn onto graded road following the sign to Parker Canyon Lake and Sierra Vista. Graded road on left is FR 194. Zero trip meter.

▼ 0.4   SO   Track on right.

4.9 ▲   SO   Track on left.

▼ 0.7   SO   Cattle guard. Entering private land, remain on road.

4.6 ▲   SO   Cattle guard, entering national forest.

▼ 1.8   SO   Graded road on right is FR 813, track on left is for authorized vehicles only.

3.5 ▲   SO   Graded road on left is FR 813, track on right is for authorized vehicles only.

     GPS: N31°21.28′ W110°34.72′

▼ 2.1   SO   Cattle guard.

3.2 ▲   SO   Cattle guard.

▼ 2.4   SO   Cross over the Santa Cruz River on bridge. Then cattle guard and track on right.

2.9 ▲   SO   Track on left and cattle guard. Then cross over the Santa Cruz River on bridge.

     GPS: N31°21.35′ W110°35.34′

▼ 2.8   SO   Track on left is for authorized vehicles only.

2.5 ▲   SO   Track on right is for authorized vehicles only.

▼ 3.0   SO   Cross through wash.

2.3 ▲   SO   Cross through wash.

▼ 3.2   SO   Track on left is for authorized vehicles only.

2.1 ▲   SO   Track on right is for authorized vehicles only.

▼ 4.0   TL   Graded road straight ahead is for authorized vehicles only. Turn left following signs for Lochiel and Nogales.

1.3 ▲   TR   T-intersection. Graded road on left is for authorized vehicles only.

     GPS: N31°20.86′ W110°36.71′

▼ 4.3   SO   Track on left is for authorized vehicles only, then cattle guard.

1.0 ▲   SO   Cattle guard, then track on right is for authorized vehicles only.

▼ 4.6   SO   Cattle guard.

0.7 ▲   SO   Cattle guard.

▼ 4.7   SO   Track on left.

0.6 ▲   SO   Track on right.

▼ 4.8   SO   Track on right.

0.5 ▲   SO   Track on left.

▼ 5.2   SO   Cattle guard.

0.1 ▲   SO   Cattle guard.

▼ 5.3   BR   Graded road on left is Lochiel Road, which goes 0.2 miles to Lochiel, the old customs house and border crossing. Zero trip meter.

0.0 ▲   Continue to the east on FR 61.

     GPS: N31°20.14′ W110°37.40′

▼ 0.0   Continue to the northwest on FR 61.

3.4 ▲   BL   Graded road on right is Lochiel Road, which goes 0.2 miles to Lochiel, the old customs house, and border crossing. Zero trip meter.

▼ 0.1   SO   Monument to Fray Marcos de Niza on left of road.

3.3 ▲   SO   Monument to Fray Marcos de Niza on right of road.

     GPS: N31°20.35′ W110°37.60′

▼ 0.4   SO   Track on left.

3.0 ▲   SO   Track on right.

▼ 0.6   SO   Cattle guard, entering San Antonio Ranch.

2.8 ▲   SO   Cattle guard, leaving San Antonio Ranch.

▼ 1.6   SO   Cattle guard, entering Coronado National Forest. FR 4911 on left after cattle guard.

1.8 ▲   SO   FR 4911 on right; then cattle guard, entering San Antonio Ranch.

     GPS: N31°21.20′ W110°38.61′

▼ 2.5   SO   Private road on right.

0.9 ▲   SO   Private road on left.

▼ 2.9   SO   Cattle guard.

0.5 ▲   SO   Cattle guard.

▼ 3.1   SO   Track on left.

0.3 ▲   SO   Track on right.

▼ 3.3   SO Track on left.
0.1 ▲   SO Track on right.

▼ 3.4   TL Turn onto smaller graded road, FR 128,
             signed to Duquesne. Zero trip meter.
0.0 ▲   Continue toward Lochiel.
             GPS: N31º22.06' W110º40.13'

▼ 0.0   Continue toward Duquesne.
1.8 ▲   TR Turn right and rejoin FR 61.

▼ 0.1   SO Track on left.
1.7 ▲   SO Track on right.

▼ 0.2   SO Track on left and campsite on left.
1.6 ▲   SO Track on right and campsite on right.

▼ 0.3   SO Cross through Washington Gulch.
1.5 ▲   SO Cross through Washington Gulch.
             GPS: N31º22.13' W110º40.45'

▼ 0.8   SO Cross through wash.
1.0 ▲   SO Cross through wash.

▼ 1.0   BR Graded road on left is FR 7015, which
             goes past Duquesne Mine.
0.8 ▲   BL Graded road on right is FR 7015, which
             goes past Duquesne Mine.
             GPS: N31º22.19' W110º41.07'

▼ 1.1   SO Duquesne. Old timber houses on left
             and right.
0.7 ▲   SO Duquesne. Old timber houses on left
             and right.

▼ 1.2   SO Mine on left.
0.6 ▲   SO Mine on right.

▼ 1.3   SO Track on right.
0.5 ▲   SO Track on left.

▼ 1.8   TL Turn left and rejoin FR 61. Zero trip
             meter.
0.0 ▲   Continue toward Duquesne.
             GPS: N31º22.74' W110º41.18'

▼ 0.0   Continue to the west.
0.7 ▲   TR Turn right onto graded road, FR 128,
             signed to Duquesne. Zero trip meter.

▼ 0.1   SO Trail enters Washington Camp.
0.6 ▲   SO Leave Washington Camp.

▼ 0.4   SO Track on left. Leave Washington
             Camp.
0.3 ▲   SO Track on right. Trail enters Washington
             Camp.

▼ 0.7   BL Graded road on right is South #13:
             Harshaw Road to Patagonia and
             Harshaw. Zero trip meter.
0.0 ▲   SO Continue to the southeast toward
             Duquesne.
             GPS: N31º23.19' W110º41.47'

▼ 0.0   Continue to the northwest toward
             Nogales.
7.7 ▲   SO Graded road on left is South #13:
             Harshaw Road to Patagonia and
             Harshaw. Zero trip meter.

▼ 0.3   SO Loading hopper of the Kansas Mine on
             left of trail, mine remains on right,
             below trail.
7.4 ▲   SO Loading hopper of the Kansas Mine on
             right of trail, mine remains on left,
             below trail.
             GPS: N31º23.22' W110º41.80'

▼ 0.4   SO Track on left.
7.3 ▲   SO Track on right.

▼ 0.5   SO FR 4704 on right.
7.2 ▲   SO FR 4704 on left.
             GPS: N31º23.31' W110º41.95'

▼ 1.3   SO Cross through wash.
6.4 ▲   SO Cross through wash.

▼ 1.5   SO Cattle guard on saddle.
6.2 ▲   SO Cattle guard on saddle.
             GPS: N31º23.17' W110º42.83'

▼ 3.4   SO FR 4695 on right.
4.3 ▲   SO FR 4695 on left.
             GPS: N31º23.39' W110º44.32'

▼ 3.8   SO FR 4677 on right.
3.9 ▲   SO FR 4677 on left.

GPS: N31°23.19' W110°44.69'

▼ 4.0   SO   Track on left, enter Sycamore Canyon.
3.7 ▲   SO   Track on right, leave Sycamore Canyon.

▼ 4.4   SO   Cattle guard; then track on left.
3.3 ▲   SO   Track on right; then cattle guard.

▼ 4.7   SO   FR 4675 on right.
3.0 ▲   SO   FR 4675 on left.
        GPS: N31°22.64' W110°45.42'

▼ 5.1   SO   Track on left is FR 4763.
2.6 ▲   SO   Track on right is FR 4763.

▼ 5.5   SO   Cross through Sycamore Wash.
2.2 ▲   SO   Cross through Sycamore Wash.

▼ 5.6   SO   FR 4671 on left.
2.1 ▲   SO   FR 4671 on right.

▼ 6.1   SO   Track on left to corral, cattle guard; then FR 4668 on left. Leaving Sycamore Canyon.
1.6 ▲   SO   Track on right is FR 4668, cattle guard; then track on right to corral. Entering Sycamore Canyon.

▼ 6.3   SO   Track on right is FR 4669.
1.4 ▲   SO   Track on left is FR 4669.
        GPS: N31°21.82' W110°46.52'

▼ 7.3   SO   Two tracks on left are FR 4902 followed by FR 4667.
0.4 ▲   SO   Two tracks on right are FR 4667 followed by FR 4902.
        GPS: N31°21.85' W110°47.51'

▼ 7.5   SO   Cattle guard; then large camping area on right.
0.2 ▲   SO   Large camping area on left; then cattle guard.
        GPS: N31°21.92' W110°47.80'

▼ 7.6   SO   Track on left and FR 4662 on right.
0.1 ▲   SO   Track on right and FR 4662 on left.
        GPS: N31°21.97' W110°47.90'

▼ 7.7   SO   Exiting the Sierra Vista Ranger District

        at sign. Zero trip meter.
0.0 ▲   Continue to the east.
        GPS: N31°22.00' W110°48.00'

▼ 0.0   Continue to the west.
4.0 ▲   SO   Entering the Sierra Vista Ranger District at sign. Zero trip meter.

▼ 0.4   SO   Graded road on left.
3.6 ▲   SO   Graded road on right.

▼ 1.3   SO   FR 4516 on left, leaving Coronado National Forest at sign.
2.7 ▲   SO   Entering Coronado National Forest, then FR 4516 on right.
        GPS: N31°22.47' W110°49.29'

▼ 1.5   SO   Cattle guard.
2.5 ▲   SO   Cattle guard.

▼ 2.5   SO   Cross through wash.
1.5 ▲   SO   Cross through wash.

▼ 2.6   SO   Cross through wash.
1.4 ▲   SO   Cross through wash.

▼ 3.0   SO   Track on right, road is now paved.
1.0 ▲   SO   Road turns to graded dirt. Track on left.

▼ 4.0   Trail ends at intersection with Arizona 82. Turn left for Nogales, turn right for Patagonia.
0.0 ▲   Trail commences on Arizona 82 at Bayerville, 4.1 miles northeast of Nogales. Zero trip meter and turn southeast on paved road, signed Duquesne Road. Turn is next to the school, 0.1 miles south of mile marker 6 and 0.1 miles north of the Santa Cruz River Bridge.
        GPS: N31°23.30' W110°52.29'

Harshaw Road

STARTING POINT	Arizona 82 in Patagonia
FINISHING POINT	South #12: Mexican Border Road at Washington Camp, 12.3 miles from the eastern end of the trail
TOTAL MILEAGE	15.6 miles
UNPAVED MILEAGE	9.9 miles
DRIVING TIME	1 hour
ELEVATION RANGE	4,100–5,600 feet
USUALLY OPEN	Year-round
BEST TIME TO TRAVEL	October to May
DIFFICULTY RATING	1
SCENIC RATING	7
REMOTENESS RATING	+0

Special Attractions

- Harshaw town site and cemetery.
- Views to the south over grasslands toward Mexico.
- Trail can be combined with either South #14: Flux Canyon Trail or South #12: Mexican Border Road for an interesting day's drive.

History

Harshaw sprang up in 1877 principally because of the Hermosa Mine, discovered by a rancher, David Tecumseh Harshaw. Harshaw grazed cattle on Apache land and was asked to relocate. He moved his herd to the valley around what is now Harshaw. While tending his cattle, David discovered the rich silver vein that became the Hermosa Mine. Soon after operations began, 150 men and a 20-stamp mill were employed. The town at one time had 30 buildings ranging from hotels and saloons to stores, blacksmith shops, and corrals. Flooding, a major fire, and the closing of the Hermosa Mine in 1881 quieted Harshaw for a while, but it persisted until the early 1900s.

The surrounding area was rich in silver and lead. One of the most famous mines in the region was the Patagonia, which dated back to Spanish times. Army Lt. Sylvester

Mowry, known for his flamboyance, left the military and bought the mine in 1859, changing the name to the Mowry Mine. Under Mowry's leadership in the early 1860s, it was one of the richest mines in the nation, producing $1.5 million of silver and lead and employing more than 100 workers. Mowry was arrested as a Confederate sympathizer during the Civil War and jailed in Fort Yuma. Meanwhile, his mine was pillaged, and Mowry spent the rest of his life trying to raise capital in the East and Europe to refurbish and reopen the looted mine. Apache wars closed most mining in the area in the late 1860s, but Harshaw and other mining camps and towns in the area, including Washington Camp and Duquesne thrived again in the last years of the nineteenth century before finally petering out in the early 1900s.

Description

This road is wide, graded, and easygoing; in dry weather, passenger vehicles can enjoy the varied scenery found along its length. The trail commences in the picturesque small town of Patagonia, where you can top up with fuel, enjoy a meal at one of several cafes, or purchase food for a picnic. The information center housed in the old railroad station is worth a visit.

The road initially is paved as it leaves Patagonia and enters the forest, running alongside Harshaw Creek, which is lined with sycamores and cottonwoods. This route is well traveled and you are likely to see many people enjoying a shady picnic alongside the creek. The town site of Harshaw is encountered after 7.5 miles. There are the remains of an adobe building on the corner, and opposite by a large parking area is the cemetery. There are many interesting stories pertaining to the lives of the pioneers of the region on the grave markers.

From Harshaw, the road continues south through the forest, passing many trails that invite exploration, including South #14: Flux Canyon Trail, and a turn to the old mine at Mowry, before descending slowly down to join South #12: Mexican Border Road at Washington Camp. From here the

A graded section of the trail in the Patagonia Mountains

exit to the highway is via the Mexican Border Road. The shortest way out is to turn right to Nogales.

Current Road Information

Coronado National Forest
Sierra Vista Ranger District
5990 South Hwy 92
Hereford, AZ 85615
(520) 378-0311

Map References

BLM   Fort Huachuca, Nogales
USFS Coronado National Forest: Nogales and Sierra Vista Ranger Districts
USGS 1:24,000   Patagonia, Mt. Hughes, Harshaw
          1:100,000 Fort Huachuca, Nogales
Maptech CD-ROM: Southeast Arizona/Tucson
Arizona Atlas & Gazetteer, p. 73
Arizona Road & Recreation Atlas, p. 54, 88
Recreational Map of Arizona

Route Directions

▼ 0.0   In Patagonia on Arizona 82 at the old Patagonia Railroad Station, zero trip meter and turn southeast on 3rd Avenue and then immediately left on McKeown Avenue.
3.0 ▲   Turn right onto 3rd Avenue in Patagonia, then the trail ends at the intersection with Arizona 82 in the center of town. Turn right for Sonoita, turn left for Nogales.
           GPS: N31°32.44' W110°45.15'

▼ 0.2   SO Road becomes Harshaw Avenue and swings east.
2.8 ▲   SO Road becomes McKeown Avenue.

▼ 1.2   SO Cross over creek on bridge, then Red Rock Drive on left.
1.8 ▲   SO Red Rock Drive on right; then cross over creek on bridge.

▼ 1.3	SO	Redrock Canyon Road on left.
1.7 ▲	SO	Redrock Canyon Road on right.

▼ 1.8	SO	Cattle guard; then graded road on left.
1.2 ▲	SO	Graded road on right; then cattle guard.

▼ 2.6	SO	Cattle guard.
0.4 ▲	SO	Cattle guard.

▼ 2.7	SO	Entering the Coronado National Forest. Track on right is trailhead and parking area for the Arizona Trail.
0.3 ▲	SO	Track on left is trailhead and parking area for the Arizona Trail. Leaving the Coronado National Forest.

GPS: N31°31.62′ W110°42.65′

▼ 2.8	SO	Cattle guard.
0.2 ▲	SO	Cattle guard.

▼ 3.0	BR	Graded road on left is FR 139. Bear right, remaining on paved road. Zero trip meter.
0.0 ▲		Continue to the northwest.

GPS: N31°31.52′ W110°42.43′

▼ 0.0		Continue to the southeast and cross over Harshaw Creek on bridge.
2.7 ▲	SO	Cross over Harshaw Creek on bridge, then graded road on right is FR 139. Bear left, remaining on paved road. Zero trip meter.

▼ 0.2	SO	Cattle guard.
2.5 ▲	SO	Cattle guard.

▼ 1.5	SO	Well on right; then cattle guard. Road is now FR 58.
1.2 ▲	SO	Cattle guard; then well on left.

▼ 1.7	SO	Track on right.
1.0 ▲	SO	Track on left.

Adobe ruin at Harshaw ghost town

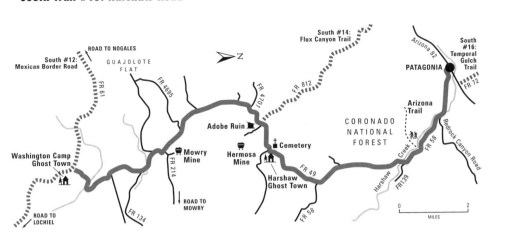

▼ 2.7   TR   Road turns to graded dirt, then turn right onto large graded dirt road FR 49, sign-posted to Harshaw and Lochiel. Zero trip meter. FR 58 continues ahead. Entering private land.

0.0 ▲   Continue to the northwest. Road becomes paved.

GPS: N31°29.32' W110° 41.52'

▼ 0.0   Continue to the southwest and cross over wash.

2.5 ▲   TL   Cross over wash; then T-intersection, turn left onto large graded dirt road FR 58, to Patagonia. Road immediately becomes paved. Re-entering the national forest. Zero trip meter.

▼ 0.5   SO   Cattle guard.
2.0 ▲   SO   Cattle guard.

▼ 0.6   SO   Cross through wash.
1.9 ▲   SO   Cross through wash.

▼ 1.1   SO   Cattle guard.
1.4 ▲   SO   Cattle guard.

▼ 1.8   SO   Track on left. The old site of Harshaw is at the intersection, marked by an adobe ruin. Harshaw Cemetery is on the right off the large parking area.

0.7 ▲   SO   Track on right. The old site of Harshaw is at the intersection, marked by an adobe ruin. Harshaw Cemetery is on the left off the large parking area.

GPS: N31°28.07' W110°42.44'

▼ 2.5   SO   Cattle guard, then track on right is South #14: Flux Canyon Road (FR 812). Zero trip meter at sign.

0.0 ▲   Continue to the northeast toward Patagonia on FR 49.

GPS: N31°27.90' W110°43.13'

▼ 0.0   Continue to the southwest toward Lochiel on FR 49.

3.8 ▲   SO   Track on left is South #14: Flux Canyon Road (FR 812), then cattle guard. Zero trip meter at sign.

▼ 0.1   SO   Adobe ruin on left; then track on left.
3.7 ▲   SO   Track on right; then adobe ruin on right.

▼ 0.3   SO   Cross through wash.
3.5 ▲   SO   Cross through wash.

▼ 0.5   SO   Cattle guard.
3.3 ▲   SO   Cattle guard.

▼ 0.6   SO   Cross through wash.
3.2 ▲   SO   Cross through wash.

▼ 0.7   SO   Track on right is FR 4701.

3.1 ▲   SO Track on left is FR 4701.

▼ 0.9   SO Cross through wash.
2.9 ▲   SO Cross through wash.

▼ 1.1   SO Track on right.
2.7 ▲   SO Track on left.

▼ 1.4   SO Cross through wash.
2.4 ▲   SO Cross through wash.

▼ 2.2   SO Cross through wash.
1.6 ▲   SO Cross through wash.

▼ 2.3   SO FR 4698 on right.
1.5 ▲   SO FR 4698 on left.
    GPS: N31°26.19′ W110°43.42′

▼ 2.5   SO Cattle guard.
1.3 ▲   SO Cattle guard.

▼ 3.1   SO Track on right is FR 4695 to Guajolote Flat. Track on left.
0.7 ▲   SO Track on right. Track on left is FR 4695 to Guajolote Flat.
    GPS: N31°25.86′ W110°42.86′

▼ 3.6   SO Track on left.
0.2 ▲   SO Track on right.

▼ 3.8   SO Graded road on left is FR 214, sign-posted to Mowry. Zero trip meter.
0.0 ▲   Continue to the west, remaining on FR 49.
    GPS: N31°25.46′ W110°42.27′

▼ 0.0   Continue to the east, passing beside ranch buildings.
3.6 ▲   SO Pass beside ranch buildings, then graded road on right is FR 214, sign-posted to Mowry. Zero trip meter.

▼ 0.4   BL FR 4695A on right through gate.
3.2 ▲   BR FR 4695A on left through gate.
    GPS: N31°25.16′ W110°42.16′

▼ 0.8   SO Cross through wash.
2.8 ▲   SO Cross through wash.

▼ 0.9   SO Track on left.

2.7 ▲   SO Track on right.

▼ 1.0   SO FR 134 on left.
2.6 ▲   SO FR 134 on right.
    GPS: N31°24.89′ W110°41.58′

▼ 1.7   SO Cattle guard; then FR 5589 on right and track on left.
1.9 ▲   SO FR 5589 on left and track on right; then cattle guard.
    GPS: N31°24.37′ W110°41.67′

▼ 2.0   SO Track on right.
1.6 ▲   SO Track on left.

▼ 2.1   SO Track on left.
1.5 ▲   SO Track on right.

▼ 2.2   SO Track on left through gate.
1.4 ▲   SO Track on right through gate.

▼ 2.3   SO Track on left.
1.3 ▲   SO Track on right.

▼ 2.9   SO Track on left; then cross through wash.
0.7 ▲   SO Cross through wash; then track on right.

▼ 3.0   SO Track on right.
0.6 ▲   SO Track on left.

▼ 3.5   SO Cattle guard.
0.1 ▲   SO Cattle guard.

▼ 3.6   Trail ends at the intersection with South #12: Mexican Border Road, FR 61, immediately west of Washington Camp. Turn right for Nogales, turn left for Lochiel.
0.0 ▲   Trail starts on South #12: Mexican Border Road, FR 61, on the west side of Washington Camp, 12.3 miles from the eastern end of the trail. Zero trip meter and turn north on graded dirt road at the sign for Patagonia. The road is marked as Harshaw Road and FR 61.
    GPS: N31°23.18′ W110°41.47′

Flux Canyon Trail

STARTING POINT	South #13: Harshaw Road, 8.2 miles from Patagonia
FINISHING POINT	Arizona 82, 2.0 miles south of Patagonia
TOTAL MILEAGE	6.9 miles
UNPAVED MILEAGE	6.9 miles
DRIVING TIME	1 hour
ELEVATION RANGE	4,000–7,000 feet
USUALLY OPEN	Year-round
BEST TIME TO TRAVEL	Year-round
DIFFICULTY RATING	4
SCENIC RATING	8
REMOTENESS RATING	+0

Special Attractions

- Views down Alum Gulch.
- Many mining remains.
- Easy trail that winds through the Patagonia Mountains.

History

The mines along this trail were mainly associated with Harshaw. One of them, the World's Fair Mine, was a big operation, but probably due to the steep terrain had no permanent settlement. Instead, the mine workers lived in nearby settlements.

Legendary Jesuit missionary, Padre Eusebio Francisco Kino was active throughout this area, first visiting local Indian villages in 1692. However, the locale was the scene of much strife between the Apache and Pima

The trail becomes more difficult as it climbs out of Alum Gulch

Indians, with the Pima eventually being forced farther west toward Tucson. Two or three miles southwest of Patagonia was the site of the Indian village of Sonoita, not to be confused with the present-day town. Sonoita is a Papago word meaning "place where corn will grow." In 1701 the Jesuits established the mission of San Gabriel de Guevavi near Sonoita. Under Chief Coro, the Sobaipuri Indians had moved there after abandoning villages a few miles away at Quiburi and Santa Cruz for fear of retaliation by the Apache, whom they had earlier defeated.

One of early Arizona's most colorful characters, Irishman James "Paddy" Graydon, operated a saloon, the U.S. Boundary Hotel, about 10 miles north of Patagonia in the 1850s, near Fort Buchanan. Graydon, a former U.S. cavalryman, immigrated to America from Ireland in 1853 and wound up in the Sonoita area after a stint with the cavalry in New Mexico Territory. At his hotel, Graydon provided enlisted men with everything from prostitutes to sardines and was a self-appointed regulator of law and order in times of strife. He was part of a vigilante party that chased down a band of Indians who were led by Cochise and accused of stealing a Mexican boy from the ranch of another Irishman, John Ward. After much bloodshed, it turned out that Cochise's band was not guilty. The boy had grown up among the Pinal Indians and was one of General Crook's foremost "Apache" scouts during the Geronimo campaign of the 1880s. There is a historical marker on Arizona 82 to mark the event. When the Civil War broke out, Fort Buchanan was abandoned and Graydon rejoined the U.S. Army as captain of an independent spy unit that operated behind Confederate lines. However, he never returned to his hotel. He died in a gunfight at Fort Stanton, New Mexico, a few months after the Civil War battle of Valverde.

Description

This trail passes through the Harshaw mining district, alongside many of the mines associated with the town of Harshaw. In addition, the trail travels in or above the deep Flux Canyon

and Alum Gulch. The trail climbs up from South #13: Harshaw Road along Alum Gulch, past rugged, red mountain scenery. The first section of the trail passes through private property, before re-entering Coronado National Forest as it climbs toward the saddle separating Alum Gulch from Flux Canyon. This first section of the trail is easygoing, roughly graded road as it winds past the tailings piles and adits of the Blue Eagle and World's Fair Mines, both large producers in their time.

Part of the trail around Alum Gulch and Flux Canyon follows an easy shelf road with ample width for one vehicle and plenty of passing places. As the trail descends toward Arizona 82, it starts to merit its 4-difficulty rating. The trail is steep and the surface is loose enough that 4WD is required for traction.

The trail finishes by running alongside Alum Gulch again, passing through a few houses before exiting onto the highway, a couple of miles south of Patagonia.

Current Road Information

Coronado National Forest
Sierra Vista Ranger District
5990 South Hwy 92
Hereford, AZ 85615
(520) 378-0311

Map References

BLM   Nogales, Fort Huachuca
USFS   Coronado National Forest: Nogales
       and Sierra Vista Ranger Districts
USGS   1:24,000   Harshaw, Cumero
       Canyon, Patagonia
       1:100,000 Nogales, Fort Huachuca
Maptech CD-ROM: Southeast Arizona/
       Tucson
Arizona Atlas & Gazetteer, p. 73
Arizona Road & Recreation Atlas, pp. 54, 88

Route Directions

▼ 0.0   From South #13: Harshaw Road, 0.7
          miles south of Harshaw town site and
          8.2 miles south of Patagonia, zero trip
          meter and turn northwest on the
          roughly graded trail, FR 812 at the sign

South Trail #14: Flux Canyon Trail

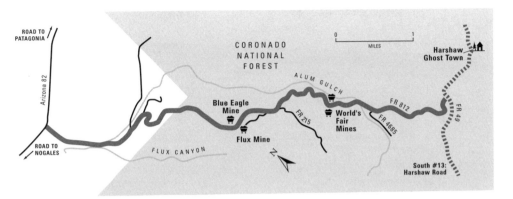

		for Flux Canyon.
3.2 ▲		Trail ends at the intersection with South #13: Harshaw Road, 0.7 miles south of Harshaw town site. Turn left for Patagonia, turn right for Washington Camp and South #12: Mexican Border Road.
		GPS: N31°27.90′ W110°43.13′

▼ 1.1	SO	Cattle guard.
2.1 ▲	SO	Cattle guard.
		GPS: N31°28.16′ W110°43.66′

▼ 1.2	BL	Cross through wash; then track on right.
2.0 ▲	BR	Track on left; then cross through wash.

▼ 1.3	SO	Track on right.
1.9 ▲	BR	Track on left.

▼ 1.5	BR	FR 4685 on left.
1.7 ▲	SO	FR 4685 on right.
		GPS: N31°28.41′ W110°43.96′

▼ 2.1	BL	Track on right to World's Fair Mine—concrete foundations and tailings.
1.1 ▲	SO	Track on left to World's Fair Mine—concrete foundations and tailings.
		GPS: N31°28.78′ W110°44.19′

▼ 3.1	SO	Adit on left.
0.1 ▲	SO	Adit on right.

▼ 3.2	BR	FR 215 on left. Zero trip meter.
0.0 ▲		Continue to the northeast.

GPS: N31°29.19′ W110°44.78′

▼ 0.0		Continue to the west.
2.4 ▲	BL	FR 215 on right. Zero trip meter.

▼ 0.1	BR	Track on left is gated. Cross saddle and start to run down the side of Flux Canyon.
2.3 ▲	SO	Cross saddle and start to run alongside Alum Gulch.

▼ 0.7	SO	Track on left goes to the Flux Mine.
1.7 ▲	BL	Track on right goes to the Flux Mine.
		GPS: N31°29.38′ W110°45.29′

▼ 0.8	SO	Track on right.
1.6 ▲	BR	Track on left.

▼ 1.1	SO	Mine shaft below track on right is part of the Blue Eagle Mine.
1.3 ▲	SO	Mine shaft below track on left is part of the Blue Eagle Mine.
		GPS: N31°29.70′ W110°45.48′

▼ 1.4	SO	Cattle guard. Exiting national forest.
1.0 ▲	SO	Sign for FR 812. Entering national forest.

▼ 1.9	SO	Cattle guard.
0.5 ▲	SO	Cattle guard.

▼ 2.3	SO	Cattle guard.
0.1 ▲	SO	Cattle guard.

▼ 2.4	SO	Join larger graded dirt road. Zero trip

	meter		▼ 1.0	SO	Cross through wash.
0.0 ▲	Continue to the east.		0.3 ▲	SO	Cross through wash.
	GPS: N31°30.24' W110°46.12'				**GPS: N31°30.65' W110°47.00'**

▼ 0.0   Continue to the west.

1.3 ▲   BR Bear right onto smaller roughly graded dirt road and zero trip meter. Intersection is unmarked.

▼ 0.1   SO Graded road on right. Trail follows along the lower end of Alum Gulch.

1.2 ▲   SO Graded road on left.

▼ 0.7   SO Cross through two washes.

0.6 ▲   SO Cross through two washes.

▼ 0.9   SO Cross through wash.

0.4 ▲   SO Cross through wash.

▼ 1.3   Cattle guard, then trail ends at intersection with Arizona 82. Turn right for Patagonia, left for Nogales.

0.0 ▲   Trail commences on Arizona 82, 2.0 miles south of Patagonia, 0.1 miles south of mile marker 17. Zero trip meter and turn south on graded dirt road marked Flux Canyon Road and cross cattle guard. Initially the trail crosses private property.

GPS: N31°30.94' W110°47.04'

A section near the beginning of the route that is bordered by private property

Cumero Canyon—Three R Canyon Trail

STARTING POINT	Arizona 82, 7.5 miles northeast of Nogales
FINISHING POINT	Arizona 82, 4.2 miles south of Patagonia
TOTAL MILEAGE	9 miles
UNPAVED MILEAGE	9 miles
DRIVING TIME	1.5 hours
ELEVATION RANGE	3,900–4,600 feet
USUALLY OPEN	Year-round
BEST TIME TO TRAVEL	September to June
DIFFICULTY RATING	3
SCENIC RATING	7
REMOTENESS RATING	+0

Special Attractions
- Tres de Mayo Mine.
- Winding trail along the western edge of the Patagonia Mountains.

Description
This pleasant trail winds along the western side of the Patagonia Mountains and offers beautiful views of the mountains as well as good backcountry camping opportunities.

Both ends of the trail cross private land; access is granted under the Sportsman Landowners respect program. Please stay on the trail and leave gates as you find them. Continued access to the trail depends on responsible trail behavior.

Once in the Coronado National Forest, the standard drops slightly and the small, well-formed trail is rougher as it undulates through open vegetation, mainly grasslands and scattered mesquite; it is not brushy to the sides of a vehicle. The trail then travels up a ridge alongside Cumero Canyon before crossing over to descend down Maggies Canyon, Cox Gulch, and finally, the well-used Three R Canyon. Navigation is easy as the major tracks have national forest route markers on them. The trail is marked on the Coronado Forest Map as FR 235 and FR 215, but the section that connects Maggies Canyon with Cox Gulch is not shown.

Approximately halfway along the trail the Tres de Mayo Mine can be reached up a short, 4-rated spur to the west. There are some stone foundations at the mine, a well, and a very deep shaft.

The historic site of Johnny Ward's Ranch is located 1.5 miles north of the northern end of the trail along Arizona 82. This early ranching pioneer had a ranch here from 1858 to 1903. A plaque sits below the family shrine of the Telles family. Started in 1941 in exchange for the safety of their sons in war, the shrine is maintained to this day.

Current Road Information
Coronado National Forest
Sierra Vista Ranger District
5990 South Hwy 92
Hereford, AZ 85615
(520) 378-0311

Map References
BLM Nogales
USFS Coronado National Forest: Nogales and Sierra Vista Ranger Districts
USGS 1:24,000 Cumero Canyon
1:100,000 Nogales
Maptech CD-ROM: Southeast Arizona/ Tucson
Arizona Atlas & Gazetteer, p. 73
Arizona Road & Recreation Atlas, pp. 54, 88

Route Directions

▼ 0.0 From Arizona 82, 7.5 miles northeast of Nogales, 0.2 miles north of mile marker 9, zero trip meter and turn northeast on unmarked, formed, red dirt road, marked FR 235, and cross cattle guard. Immediately the trail forks, bear left, passing designated access sign. Trail is crossing private property.

1.5 ▲ Trail ends on Arizona 82. Turn left for Nogales, turn right for Patagonia.
GPS: N31°25.65′ W110°50.55′

Mine foundations and well at the Tres de Mayo Mine site

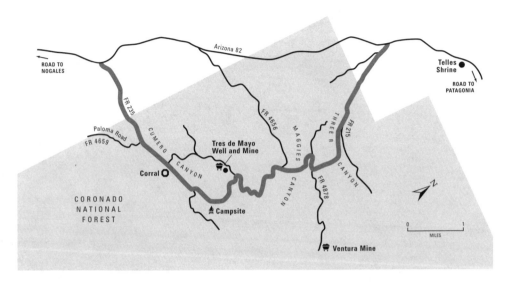

▼ 1.1   SO   Cattle guard, entering Coronado National Forest.

0.4 ▲   SO   Cattle guard, trail crosses into private property.
GPS: N31°25.72' W110°49.48'

▼ 1.5   BL   Track on right is marked Paloma Road, FR 4659. Zero trip meter.

0.0 ▲   Continue to the west.
GPS: N31°25.76' W110°49.03'

▼ 0.0   Continue to the east.

2.5 ▲   SO   Track on left is marked Paloma Road, FR 4659. Zero trip meter.

▼ 0.7   BR   Track on left is FR 4658; then corral on right.

1.8 ▲   BL   Corral on left; then track on right is FR 4658.
GPS: N31°25.96' W110°48.37'

▼ 0.8   SO   Track on right.
1.7 ▲   SO   Track on left.

▼ 1.2   BL   Cross through wash, bear left following sign for Three R Canyon, remaining on FR 235. Track on right is FR 4680.

1.3 ▲   BR   Track on left is FR 4680, bear right and cross through wash.
GPS: N31°26.14' W110°47.81'

▼ 1.7   BL   Campsite on right, bear left and cross through Cumero Canyon Wash.

0.8 ▲   BR   Cross through Cumero Canyon Wash, bear right upon exit, campsite on left.
GPS: N31°26.35' W110°47.50'

▼ 1.9   BL   Track on right.
0.6 ▲   BR   Track on left.

▼ 2.1   SO   Cross through wash.
0.4 ▲   SO   Cross through wash.

▼ 2.4   SO   Cross through wash.
0.1 ▲   SO   Cross through wash.

▼ 2.5   BR   Track on left is FR 4658 which goes 0.4 miles to Tres de Mayo well and mine. Trail continues past the mine. Zero trip meter.

0.0 ▲   Continue to the southeast.
GPS: N31°26.85' W110°47.67'

▼ 0.0   Continue to the east.
2.3 ▲   BL   Track on right is FR 4658 which goes

Shrine of the Telles family near the northern end of the trail

0.4 miles to Tres de Mayo well and mine. Trail continues past the mine. Zero trip meter.

▼ 0.5   SO Cross through wash.
1.8 ▲   SO Cross through wash.

▼ 0.9   SO Cross through wash.
1.4 ▲   SO Cross through wash.
        GPS: N31°27.27' W110°47.45'

▼ 1.0   SO Track on right to campsite.
1.3 ▲   SO Track on left to campsite.

▼ 1.4   SO Small track on left is FR 4656.
0.9 ▲   SO Small track on right is FR 4656.
        GPS: N31°27.54' W110°47.44'

▼ 1.5   SO Gate. Entering into the top end of Maggies Canyon.
0.8 ▲   SO Gate. Leaving Maggies Canyon.

▼ 1.8   SO Cross through wash.
0.5 ▲   SO Cross through wash.

▼ 1.9   SO Cross through wash.
0.4 ▲   SO Cross through wash.

▼ 2.1   BR Closed track on left.
0.2 ▲   BL Closed track on right.
        GPS: N31°28.02' W110°47.41'

▼ 2.3   TL T-intersection. Track on right is FR 4878, which goes up Cox Gulch toward Ventura Mine. Zero trip meter.
0.0 ▲   Continue to the west.
        GPS: N31°27.95' W110°47.18'

▼ 0.0   Continue to the north.
2.7 ▲   TR Turn right remaining on main trail. Track straight on is FR 4878, which goes up Cox Gulch toward Ventura Mine. Zero trip meter.

The Three R Canyon Wash crossing

▼ 0.8   SO   Cross through Three R Canyon Wash.
1.9 ▲   SO   Cross through Three R Canyon Wash.
         GPS: N31°28.51′ W110°47.46′

▼ 1.1   SO   Cross through wash. Trail is following
              alongside wash in Three R Canyon.
1.6 ▲   SO   Cross through wash.

▼ 1.2   TL   Turn left and cross through wash.
              Track on right is FR 215, which travels
              up Three R Canyon. Small track ahead.
1.5 ▲   TR   Cross through wash and turn right at
              sign onto FR 235, sign-posted to
              Palomas Mesa. FR 215 continues
              ahead to Three R Canyon. Small track
              on left.
         GPS: 31°28.69′ W110°47.72′

▼ 1.4   SO   Cross through wash. Track on right up
              wash is closed, track on left is FR
              4653.
1.3 ▲   SO   Cross through wash. Track on left up
              wash is closed, track on right is FR
              4653.
         GPS: N31°28.83′ W110°47.91′

▼ 1.5   SO   Cross through wash.
1.2 ▲   SO   Cross through wash.

▼ 1.6   SO   Track on left to concrete foundations;
              then cross through wash.
1.1 ▲   SO   Cross through wash; then track on
              right to concrete foundations.

▼ 1.8   SO   Cross through wash.
0.9 ▲   SO   Cross through wash.

▼ 1.9   SO   Cattle guard, leaving Coronado
              National Forest, then cross through
              wash. Road is now graded dirt as it
              crosses private land.
0.8 ▲   SO   Cross through wash then cattle guard,
              entering Coronado National Forest.
              Trail is marked FR 215. Road is now
              formed trail.
         GPS: N31°29.11′ W110°48.16′

▼ 2.3   SO   Cross through wash.
0.4 ▲   SO   Cross through wash.

▼ 2.6   SO   Track on left; then cross through wash.
0.1 ▲   SO   Cross through wash; then track on
              right. Trail is following alongside wash
              in Three R Canyon.

▼ 2.7   Trail ends at junction with Arizona 82.
              Turn left for Nogales, turn right for
              Patagonia.
0.0 ▲   Trail commences on Arizona 82, 4.2
              miles south of Patagonia, 0.3 miles
              south of mile marker 15. Zero trip
              meter and turn southeast across cattle
              guard on graded dirt road. Trail initially
              crosses private property and is marked
              FR 215.
         GPS: N31°29.80′ W110°48.62′

Temporal Gulch Trail

STARTING POINT	Arizona 82 in Patagonia
FINISHING POINT	Walker Basin
TOTAL MILEAGE	11.7 miles
UNPAVED MILEAGE	11.2 miles
DRIVING TIME	1.5 hours (one-way)
ELEVATION RANGE	4,100–5,800 feet
USUALLY OPEN	Year-round
BEST TIME TO TRAVEL	Year-round
DIFFICULTY RATING	5
SCENIC RATING	9
REMOTENESS RATING	+0

Special Attractions
■ Extremely scenic Temporal Gulch.
■ Prolific bird life.
■ Trail travels along a section of the Arizona
Trail.
■ Views over Temporal Gulch, the Patagonia
Mountains, and Mt. Wrightson.

Description
This spur trail travels through one of the
most scenic and varied canyons in the Santa
Rita Mountains. The fantastic views and

moderately challenging trail, coupled with excellent backcountry camping and birding opportunities, combine to make this trail a favorite among many.

The trail departs the picturesque town of Patagonia, and for the first 6.1 miles is well-graded dirt, as it travels through the open grasslands alongside Gringo Gulch and into Coronado National Forest.

The trail travels along a section of the Arizona Trail; at the parking area and information boards for the hiking trail, the vehicle trail drops in standard to become a lumpy, formed trail.

The scenery is spectacular as you climb up Temporal Gulch, which offers views of the extremely pretty canyon as well as more far-reaching views to Mt. Wrightson. There are rough spots on the trail at this stage as it winds along the canyon. Campers should note that there are excellent shady campsites under large cottonwoods in the first mile past the hiking trailhead. These are the best sites along the trail. Farther up they become fewer and farther between.

After 3.7 miles, the trail leaves Temporal Gulch and climbs up along a steep shelf road toward Walker Basin. On the return trip, this section gives excellent views back over the gulch to the Patagonia Mountains. Bird watchers may see vermilion flycatchers and Strickland's woodpeckers, among others.

After crossing a small saddle, the trail descends along the side of the wooded Walker

The trail crosses back and foorth through the wash in Temporal Gulch

Natural rock tanks above the dam at the end of the trail in Walker Basin

Canyon. It descends steeply along a well-formed trail to finish in Walker Basin. There are a series of natural tanks in the creek at the end of the trail, just above a small concrete dam. The trail continues for 0.2 miles to the wilderness boundary where all vehicle travel must stop. The final 0.2 miles are extremely steep and are beyond the scope of this book.

The major difficulties of the trail are the steep, low-traction climbs out of Temporal Gulch into Walker Basin and back out again. In spring and summer, Temporal Gulch can have water in it; 12 inches is not uncommon after summer rains. Although the latter part of the trail passes through woodland, the trail is wide and is not brushy for any vehicle. This trail is also popular with mountain bikers.

Current Road Information
Coronado National Forest
Nogales Ranger District
303 Old Tucson Road
Nogales, AZ 85621
(520) 281-2296

Map References
BLM   Fort Huachuca
USFS Coronado National Forest: Nogales and Sierra Vista Ranger Districts
USGS 1:24,000 Mt. Hughes, Patagonia, Mt. Wrightson
          1:100,000 Fort Huachuca
Maptech CD-ROM: Southeast Arizona/ Tucson
Arizona Atlas & Gazetteer, p. 73
Arizona Road & Recreation Atlas, pp. 54, 88
Recreational Map of Arizona

Route Directions

▼ 0.0   From Arizona 82 in Patagonia, zero trip meter and turn northwest on 1st Avenue, 0.2 miles north of the town center. Road is paved and leads off south of the high school. Remain on 1st Avenue, ignoring turns to the right and left.
        GPS: N31°32.64′ W110°44.85′

▼ 0.5   SO Cattle guard. Road is now graded dirt.

▼ 0.8   SO Cross through wash.
▼ 1.0   SO Cattle guard.
▼ 1.9   BR Graded road on left.
            GPS: N31°33.99′ W110°45.67′

▼ 2.2   SO Two tracks on right.
▼ 2.3   SO Entering Coronado National Forest over cattle guard. Zero trip meter. Road is now marked as FR 72.
            GPS: N31°34.35′ W110°45.67′

▼ 0.0   Continue to the north.
▼ 0.9   SO Track on right.
▼ 1.3   SO Cattle guard; then track on right.
▼ 2.2   SO Track on right.
▼ 2.7   SO Cross through wash, climb out of Gringo Gulch.
▼ 2.9   SO Cattle guard.
            GPS: N31°36.21′ W110°46.57′

▼ 3.6   SO FR 762 on left. FR 72 continues straight ahead.
            GPS: N31°36.12′ W110°47.05′

▼ 3.8   BL Cattle guard; then Arizona Trail trailhead parking on right. Information boards. Zero trip meter.
            GPS: N31°36.17′ W110°47.20′

▼ 0.0   Continue to the northwest. Trail drops in standard and becomes a formed trail.
▼ 0.1   SO Cross through wash.
▼ 0.3   SO Cross through wash.
▼ 0.5   SO Cross through wash; then track on left is FR 4094; then cross through wash again.
▼ 0.6   SO Cross through wash.
▼ 0.8   SO Cattle guard.
▼ 0.9   SO Cross through wash, track on left to campsite, then second track on left is FR 72A. Route marker at junction. Zero trip meter.
            GPS: N31°36.92′ W110°47.46′

▼ 0.0   Continue to the north and cross through wash.
▼ 0.1   SO Two tracks on right to private property; then well on left.
            GPS: N31°37.05′ W110°47.51′

South Trail #16: Temporal Gulch Trail

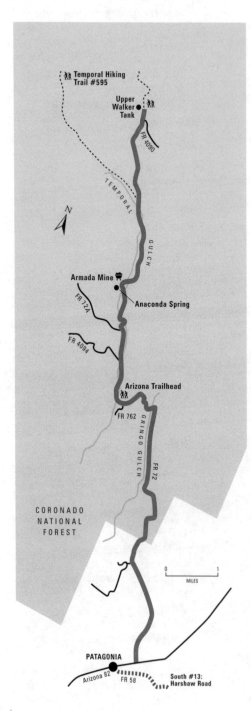

▼ 0.3   SO   Adit on right of trail.
▼ 0.4   SO   Cross through wash.
▼ 0.5   SO   Cross through wash.
     GPS: N31°37.27' W110°47.72'

▼ 0.6   SO   Cross through wash.
▼ 1.0   SO   Cross through wash. Anaconda Spring on left, then the Armada Mine on left.
     GPS: N31°37.65' W110°47.93'

▼ 1.2   SO   Cross through wash; then mine on left.
     GPS: N31°37.78' W110°47.96'

▼ 1.3   SO   Cross through wash.
▼ 1.4   SO   Faint track on right. Canyon becomes wider.
▼ 1.5   SO   Cross through wash.
▼ 1.6   SO   Cross through wash.
▼ 1.7   SO   Track on left.
     GPS: N31°38.18' W110°47.90'

▼ 2.2   SO   Cross through wash.
▼ 2.3   SO   Cross through wash.
▼ 2.4   SO   Cross through two washes.
▼ 2.6   SO   Cross through two washes; then track on left to campsite.
▼ 2.7   SO   Cross through wash. Sign on left for Temporal hiking trail #595 to Mt. Wrightson, 9.4 miles. The Arizona Trail continues along the main trail and climbs out of Temporal Gulch along shelf road.
     GPS: N31°38.92' W110°48.31'

▼ 2.9   SO   Pass through wire gate.
▼ 3.1   SO   Saddle. Track on left to small campsite with great view. Trail descends.
     GPS: N31°39.18' W110°48.52'

▼ 3.6   SO   Track on right. End of shelf road.
     GPS: N31°39.51' W110°48.67'

▼ 3.8   SO   Trail crosses saddle leaving the Temporal Gulch drainage and starts to descend to Walker Basin. Walker Canyon on right.
▼ 4.2   BR   Track on left.
     GPS: N31°39.97' W110°48.90'

| ▼ 4.3 | SO | Cross through two small washes. |
| ▼ 4.4 | TL | Track on right is FR 4090. |

GPS: N31°40.11′ W110°48.88′

| ▼ 4.7 | | Trail ends at Upper Walker Tank where there is a small concrete dam in the wash. A sign points the way to the Walker Basin Trail and Mt. Wrightson. |

GPS: N31°40.30′ W110°48.95′

SOUTH REGION TRAIL #17

Carr Canyon Trail

STARTING POINT	Arizona 92, 0.5 miles south of the national forest ranger station
FINISHING POINT	Carr Peak Hiking Trailhead
TOTAL MILEAGE	7.4 miles
UNPAVED MILEAGE	6.3 miles
DRIVING TIME	45 minutes (one-way)
ELEVATION RANGE	4,800–7,400 feet
USUALLY OPEN	April to November
BEST TIME TO TRAVEL	April to November
DIFFICULTY RATING	2
SCENIC RATING	8
REMOTENESS RATING	+0

Special Attractions

■ Panoramic views over the Sierra Vista Valley and mountains to the east.
■ Access to hiking trails and national forest campgrounds.
■ Reef town site.

History

Reef town site was a mining settlement that was active from 1893, when the first gold and silver mines were discovered, all the way through to 1926. More than 100 people lived at Reef, which had a post office, a spring for water, and a phone line to Tombstone down in the valley. Reef gained a mill for processing gold in 1899. The mill, when built, was the most advanced of its kind, but it was used for only six weeks before technical problems forced its closure. In 1903 the mill was dis-

mantled and moved down the mountain.

In World War I, Reef turned to mining tungsten, and a tungsten-processing mill was constructed on the site of the original mill. Later still, the site mined quartz; the light-colored piles of quartz left behind can be seen from the hiking trailhead opposite the Reef Town Site Campground.

Description

The higher elevations of the Huachuca Mountains near Sierra Vista provide many people the opportunity for some cooler hiking and camping in the summer months. This graded road accesses the Miller Peak Wilderness Area as well as two shady and pleasant national forest campgrounds.

The trail is graded and climbs steadily up Carr Canyon toward Carr Peak. The trail runs along a high shelf road, wide enough for two vehicles to pass with care. Rough and lumpy sections, particularly on the tight switchbacks, mean the trail is better suited to high-clearance vehicles.

As you climb, there are panoramic views east over the San Pedro Valley. The Mule Mountains are visible, as are the Dragoon Mountains and Sierra Vista down at the base of the range.

There are two national forest campgrounds near the top of the trail—Reef town site and Ramsey Vista. Both have pleasant, shady campsites, and Ramsey Vista also has good views and a public-use horse corral. A fee is required at both sites.

The hiking trailheads to Carr Peak are at the end of the trail.

Current Road Information

Coronado National Forest
Sierra Vista Ranger District
5990 South Hwy. 92
Hereford, AZ 85615
(520) 378-0311

Map References

BLM Nogales
USFS Coronado National Forest: Nogales and Sierra Vista Ranger Districts

USGS 1:24,000 Miller Peak
        1:100,000 Nogales
Maptech CD-ROM: Southeast Arizona/
    Tucson
Arizona Atlas & Gazetteer, p. 74
Arizona Road & Recreation Atlas, pp. 54, 88
Recreational Map of Arizona

Route Directions

▼ 0.0   From Arizona 92, 0.5 miles south of the national forest ranger station south of Sierra Vista, zero trip meter and turn southwest onto the paved Carr Canyon Road at the road sign for Carr Canyon.
         GPS: N31°27.22′ W110°15.43′

▼ 0.1   SO   Wild Rabbit Road on right.

▼ 1.1   SO   Pavement ends. Cross through wash, road is now graded dirt.

▼ 1.4   SO   Cattle guard, entering Coronado National Forest. Road is now marked as FR 368. Zero trip meter.
         GPS: N31°26.91′ W110°16.82′

▼ 0.0   Continue to the northwest and cross through wash.

▼ 0.2   SO   Parking area on right and left.

▼ 0.7   SO   Cross through wash on concrete ford, then Carr Information Center on left.
         GPS: N31°26.50′ W110°17.18′

▼ 1.0   SO   Closure gate, cross over creek on bridge.
         GPS: N31°26.29′ W110°17.08′

▼ 1.9   SO   Clark Spring hiking trail #124 on left

The shelf road affords some great views

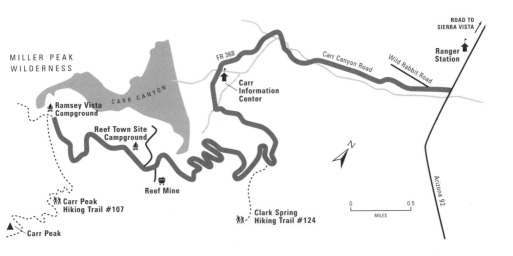

to Miller Canyon Road.
  GPS: N31°26.16′ W110°16.43′

▼ 4.1   SO   Track on left to campsite.
  GPS: N31°25.79′ W110°16.96′

▼ 4.5   SO   Information board on left. End of
      switchbacks and shelf.

▼ 4.6   SO   Track on left goes 0.1 miles to flat
      area at the quartz heaps of the Reef
      Mine.
  GPS: N31°25.66′ W110°17.30′

▼ 4.8   SO   Reef Town Site Campground on right
      and track on right to trailhead parking
      for Old Sawmill hiking trail to Carr
      Peak and Miller Peak. Zero trip meter.
  GPS: N31°25.67′ W110°17.40′

▼ 0.0   Continue to the northwest.
▼ 0.1   SO   Group campground on right.
      Reservations required.
▼ 1.1   BR   One-way section.
▼ 1.2   SO   Trail ends at the trailhead parking to
      Carr Peak hiking trail #107, which
      goes to Carr Peak, and Comfort

Springs hiking trail, #109. Ramsey
Vista Campground is straight ahead,
fee area.
  GPS: N31°25.68′ W110°18.16′

Mule Mountains Trail

STARTING POINT	Arizona 80, immediately north of the tunnel north of Bisbee
FINISHING POINT	Gate before communications tower
TOTAL MILEAGE	3.6 miles
UNPAVED MILEAGE	3.2 miles
DRIVING TIME	30 minutes (one-way)
ELEVATION RANGE	5,800–7,000 feet
USUALLY OPEN	Year-round
BEST TIME TO TRAVEL	Year-round
DIFFICULTY RATING	2
SCENIC RATING	8
REMOTENESS RATING	+0

Special Attractions

■ Short trail that climbs into the Mule Mountains.
■ Views of Bisbee.

Description

This short trail is a perfect accompaniment to a trip to Bisbee, giving a bird's-eye view over the town as well as over the lightly vegetated Mule Mountains. The trail leaves from the top of the Mule Tunnel, following along the line of the old road to Mule Pass. At the top of the pass there is a marker to the road constructed by prison labor in 1913. From the divide, the road climbs steeply up into the Mule Mountains. The standard is good. There are a few houses up the road, so although it is steep, it is well constructed and roughly graded. As the road climbs, Bisbee appears nestled in Tombstone Canyon. The Escabrosa Ridge is seen off to the west.

A view across the canyon to Escabrosa Ridge

South Trail #18: Mule Mountains Trail

Map References
BLM Douglas
USGS 1:24,000 Bisbee
1:100,000 Douglas
Maptech CD-ROM: Southeast Arizona/
Tucson
Arizona Atlas & Gazetteer, p. 74

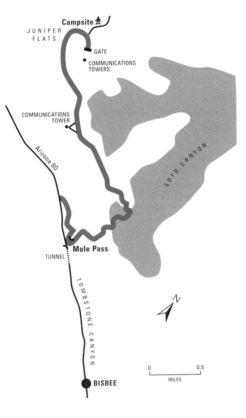

Route Directions

▼ 0.0   From Arizona 80, north of the Mule Tunnel, turn east on unmarked paved road and zero trip meter.
GPS: N31°27.78' W109°56.87'

▼ 0.4   TL   Top of old road over Mule Pass at saddle, turn sharp left onto graded dirt primitive road. Road immediately climbs steeply.
GPS: N31°27.50' W109°56.53'

▼ 1.4   BL   Track on right is private road.
▼ 1.9   SO   Track on left.
▼ 2.4   SO   Track on left to communications towers.
GPS: N31°28.35' W109°57.10'

▼ 2.5   SO   Main track on left to communications towers. Zero trip meter.
GPS: N31°28.42' W109°57.18'

▼ 0.0   Continue to the northwest.
▼ 0.1   SO   Track on left.
▼ 0.3   SO   Track on left.
▼ 0.6   SO   Two tracks on left.
GPS: N31°28.74' W109°57.65'

▼ 1.0   SO   Track on left is 4-rated and goes 0.2 miles via a couple of campsites to a viewpoint over Soto Canyon.
GPS: N31°28.96' W109°57.54'

▼ 1.1   Trail ends at gate to communications towers.

Rough spots along the road and steep grades make a high-clearance vehicle preferable as the trail switchbacks steeply up to the ridge in the Mule Mountains. The trail ends at the gate to the radio towers near the top of the mountain.

Current Road Information
Bureau of Land Management
Tucson Field Office
12661 East Broadway Blvd.
Tucson, AZ 85748
(520) 258-7200

THE SHOOT-OUT AT THE O.K. CORRAL

The shoot-out at the O.K. Corral rattled the small town of Tombstone. In the center of the shoot-out was the bitter feud between two factions: the Earps versus the Clantons and McLaurys. At the end of the day, three men lay dead in the Arizona dust and its aftermath claimed two more victims.

The feud had its roots in the cattle-rustling activities of the Clantons and McLaurys. The Earps either infringed on their rustling or threatened to stop the crimes. Ike Clanton, in testimony about the shoot-out, accused the Earps of being involved in various shady dealings, including cattle rustling. The Earps were far from angelic, but they held positions of law enforcement, so it is more likely that they were going to put a stop to the cattle rustling. Ike Clanton was also a bit fidgety about some information that the Earps had on him. For a reward, Ike had tipped off Wyatt and his brother Virgil (the town marshal of Tombstone) about three very dangerous stagecoach robbers. If word got out, Ike would either be hanging from a tree or riddled with bullets. He was worried that Wyatt in particular would tell his friend Doc Holliday. Holliday was often seen gambling with notorious men—the underbelly of society. Tom and Frank McLaury then both testified that Doc had killed two people in an attempted stagecoach robbery. To Wyatt's relief, Doc was acquitted, but now the Earps had a score to settle with the McLaurys.

Wyatt Earp

Hostilities continued to grow. Ike demanded to see Holliday. He figured that Doc knew of the bargain he had made with the law and feared that the dentist would expose him. On October 22, 1881, a hotheaded Holliday found Ike Clanton and verbally ripped him apart. The dispute would have escalated to gunplay if Virgil hadn't threatened to arrest the two. On October 26, Ike had a message that he wanted Virgil to give to Holliday: "The damned son of a bitch has got to fight." Virgil wanted nothing to do with it, wouldn't deliver the message, and told Ike that any disturbances would land him in jail. Fuming and very drunk, Ike Clanton wandered from saloon to saloon all night, wailing about the Earps and Holliday. Brandishing a shotgun, he looked for them, but couldn't find anyone upon whom to vent his anger. The next morning Virgil Earp found the irate Ike, pistol-whipped him, and tossed him into jail for carrying a weapon within city limits. Wyatt found him in the recorder's court and told him, "You damn dirty cow thief. You have been threatening our lives, and I know it. I think I would be justified in shooting you down any place I would meet you." Tom McLaury showed up at the courthouse to check on his friend and found himself at the wrong place at the wrong time. Words about a showdown were exchanged between the two. Wyatt struck him, pistol-whipped him, and left him bloody and crumpled on the floor. Resentment grew to a fervent boil. John Behan, the sheriff of Cochise County, arrived on the scene and tried to settle things, but the Earps brushed him off.

Doc Holliday

At 2:00 P.M., October 26, 1881, Wyatt, Morgan, and Virgil Earp, along with the recently deputized Doc Holliday, approached the Clantons, McLaurys, and Billy Claiborne. The two factions were fuming and armed to the teeth. The Earps and the Clantons tell differing stories about the events that followed. Virgil pro-

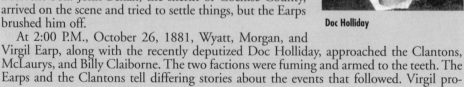

claimed that he didn't want a firefight; he just wanted the Clanton faction disarmed and out of town. The Clantons said that the Earps fired first. Whatever happened, the outcome was the same—shooting began. Morgan Earp's shot clipped Billy Clanton in the wrist. Frank McLaury went down when Wyatt shot him in the stomach. Ike Clanton ran.

Billy Claiborne ducked into a photography studio. Tom McLaury was shielded by his horse. Doc Holliday pulled a shotgun from beneath his long coat, darted around the animal, and blasted McLaury. Billy Clanton, wounded in the right wrist, drew with his left and shot Virgil in the leg. Frank McLaury, who was shot in the stomach, plugged Doc in the hip. But Frank went down for

The O.K. Corral after it burned to the ground in 1882

good when he was shot in the neck, either by Morgan or Holliday. Morgan was then shot in the shoulder by Billy Clanton. In a hail of gunfire from either Morgan or Wyatt, Billy Clanton went down. Tom McLaury, Frank McLaury, and Billy Clanton were dead. Before Billy died, he requested that his boots be taken off, "Get the doctor and put me to sleep. . . Pull off my boots. I always told my mother I'd never die with my boots on."

The battle wasn't over. Clanton supporters were vehement that the deaths of the McLaurys and Billy Clanton in the streets of Tombstone were acts of murder. They wanted revenge. On December 28, 1881, Virgil Earp was wounded by a shotgun blast as he exited a saloon. The gunman was never found. Virgil was lucky; he survived, although never fully regaining the use of his left arm. However, the Earp's luck was about to run out.

On March 18, 1882, the Earps were playing pool. Just as Morgan Earp was reaching for the chalk two shots rang out from the shadows of the saloon. Morgan went down with a fatal stomach wound; he died there surrounded by his family. The second bullet barely missed Wyatt. Virgil was still hurting from his previous wound, so the Earps decided he'd best get out of town and they took him to the train depot. While waiting for the train, the Earps spotted Frank Stilwell—a known stagecoach robber and Clanton supporter. Wyatt had a hunch that

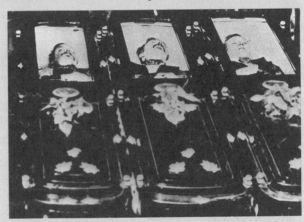

Billy Clanton and the McLaury Brothers lie dead after the shootout

Stilwell was responsible for Morgan's murder. Stilwell spotted the Earps and ran. Wyatt and four others (including Doc Holliday) gave chase. They cornered Stilwell and riddled him with bullets. His hands had powder burns, as if he'd recently fired a shotgun. With this last killing the dust finally settled in Tombstone. The O.K. Corral burnt to the ground in 1882, but the name has become indelibly linked to popular images of the wild west.

Tex Canyon Trail

STARTING POINT   Kuykendall Cutoff Road, 7.3 miles south of the intersection of Arizona 181

FINISHING POINT   Arizona 80, 0.3 miles northeast of mile marker 396

TOTAL MILEAGE   26.3 miles

UNPAVED MILEAGE   26.3 miles

DRIVING TIME   2.5 hours

ELEVATION RANGE   4,700–6,000 feet

USUALLY OPEN   Year-round

BEST TIME TO TRAVEL   Year-round

DIFFICULTY RATING   1

SCENIC RATING   9

REMOTENESS RATING   +0

Special Attractions

- Trail passes close to the site of Camp Rucker army post.
- Trail down a wide, scenic valley.
- Access to many backcountry campsites and hiking trails.

History

The northern end of this trail passes along Whitewater Draw, so-named because of the white alkaline coloring left by water. A nearby ranch and post office gained the same Whitewater name, though the post office lasted only 11 years, closing in 1918. Whitewater Draw is amply fed by the creek through Rucker Canyon, Long John Canyon, and Bruno Canyon on the western side of the Chiricahua Mountains and has been prone to flash flooding over the centuries. On one such occasion in 1878, a military party from the nearby Camp Supply was caught in a downpour and took refuge in a temporary saloon until the rains abated. Following some other travelers, Lt. Henley and Lt. John Rucker mounted their horses and proceeded across the swelling wash. Henley was swept away first with Rucker following in an attempt to save his friend. Both men drowned despite the efforts of fellow travelers and the accompanying Apache scouts who risked their own lives trying to save the officers. After this, the name of Camp Supply was changed to Camp Rucker and the canyon became known as Rucker Canyon.

Camp Rucker, originally built to protect the settlers of the region, was an important base for the military in its efforts to subdue the warring Chiricahua Apache following the wrongful killing of Cochise's tribe members at Fort Bowie in 1861. Cochise, who formerly had only fought with the Mexicans, killed his hostages and declared revenge on the settlers. The warfare lasted for many years.

One incident at Camp Rucker helped precipitate the famous Gunfight at the O.K. Corral in the notoriously rowdy town of Tombstone. In July 1880, some mules were stolen from the Camp Rucker stables by the McLaury brothers of Tombstone. The military camp enlisted the aid of U.S. Deputy Marshall Virgil Earp to find the mules. They eventually turned up with the brands altered on the McLaury ranch.

Camp Rucker developed into a small settlement by the late 1880s, gaining its own post office with the temporary name of Powers before reverting to the name Rucker Canyon in 1929, by which time most of the settlers had moved on to greener pastures.

Tex Canyon gained its name from Tex Whaley who settled there in the late 1880s. He assisted in the army's efforts to convince Geronimo to bring about peace with the Apache.

The southern end of the trail terminates in the San Bernardino Valley at the site of Chiricahua, a small community that flourished between 1907 and the early 1920s. For many years it was a cattle-loading station on the railroad to Douglas. The valley takes it name from the San Bernardino Land Grant of the 1820s, which after the Gadsden Purchase of 1853–54, straddled the international border between Mexico and the United States. The grant had been purchased by Lt. Ignacio Perez from the Mexican government for $90, springs included. He ran cattle on his ranch until the Apache raids of the 1880s became too much of a risk and he was forced to abandon his cattle for good.

In the mid-1880s the Slaughter family operated a cattle ranch on the American portion of the San Bernardino Land Grant, approximately 23,500 acres of the original 70,000. The Slaughters waged war on the cattle rustlers of this region and were so good at delivering their message that their cattle, marked with the famous "Z" brand, were left untouched by most rustlers.

To the north of Rucker Canyon, in Turkey Creek Canyon, is the grave of cattle rustler and Tombstone gunfighter Johnny Ringo. Ringo's death was shrouded in mystery. His body was found propped against an oak tree with a single bullet to the head. He was buried a few yards from the tree. Although the coroner's verdict said suicide, many believe that he was murdered, and there is an impressive and famous list of suspects to choose from. Wyatt Earp and Lou Cooley are both likely to have killed him, but most of the evidence points to a small-time gambler called Johnny-behind-the-deuce, a.k.a. John O'Rourke.

Description

This smooth road passes along two canyons within the Coronado National Forest: Rucker Canyon and Tex Canyon. Initially the graded gravel road crosses ranchland as it follows alongside the low Swisshelm Mountains. Within the national forest, the standard of the road falls slightly and it becomes narrower, but is still suitable for passenger vehicles in dry weather. It can be washboardy in sections.

A major road on the left goes to the site of Camp Rucker, 11.4 miles from the northern end of the trail. The site is now a national forest campground. This road continues on past other developed campgrounds to Rucker Lake. From the intersection, the main trail follows alongside shady Cottonwood Creek through open forest and grassland. The trail then travels along wide Tex Canyon. The vegetation is scattered: alligator juniper, oaks, yuccas, agave, and small pines. There are many excellent backcountry campsites along this section as well as many short side trails to explore. Most only go a couple of miles to the

Lichen-covered rocks beside a typical section of trail

wilderness boundary, but give access to some very pretty hiking trails.

The trail exits the forest to travel across open ranchland in the San Bernadino Valley. It finishes on Arizona 80 at the site of the old settlement of Chiricahua. Nothing remains of the settlement now except the name on the map.

Current Road Information
Coronado National Forest
Douglas Ranger District
1192 West Saddleview Rd.
Douglas, AZ 85607
(520) 364-3468

Map References
BLM Chiricahua Peak
USFS Coronado National Forest: Chiricahua-Peloncillo Mtns. Ranger District
USGS 1:24,000 Square Top Hills East, Swisshelm Mtn., Bruno Peak, Stanford Canyon, Chiricahua Peak, Swede Peak, Pedregosa Mtns. East, Paramore Crater
1:100,000 Chiricahua Peak
Maptech CD-ROM: Southeast Arizona/ Tucson
Arizona Atlas & Gazetteer, p. 75
Arizona Road & Recreation Atlas, pp. 55, 89
Recreational Map of Arizona

Velvet mesquite tree and Sunset Peak in the background

South Trail #19: Tex Canyon Trail

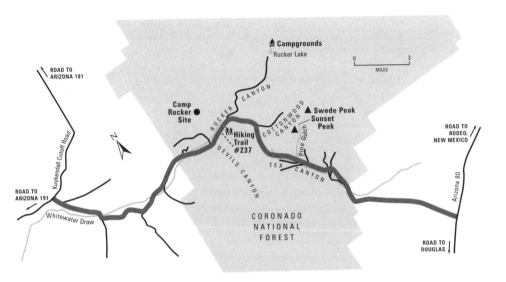

Route Directions

▼ 0.0   On the Kuykendall Cutoff Road, 7.3 miles south of Arizona 181, zero trip meter and turn east on the wide graded gravel Rucker Road signed to Rucker. Intersection is also 9 miles from Arizona 191 to the west.

5.0 ▲   Trail ends at the intersection of Rucker Road and the Kuykendall Cutoff Road. Turn left to exit to Arizona 191, turn right to exit to Arizona 181.
         GPS: N31°47.07′ W109°32.34′

▼ 0.3   SO Cattle guard; then track on left.
4.7 ▲   SO Track on right; then cattle guard.

▼ 1.7   SO Cattle guard.
3.3 ▲   SO Cattle guard.

▼ 2.6   BL Cross Whitewater Draw on concrete ford; then bear left on the far side. Track on right after crossing.
2.4 ▲   BR Track on left; then cross Whitewater Draw on concrete ford.
         GPS: N31°45.18′ W109°30.79′

▼ 2.8   SO Two cattle guards.
2.2 ▲   SO Two cattle guards.

▼ 2.9   SO Cattle guard.
2.1 ▲   SO Cattle guard.

▼ 4.0   SO Cattle guard.
1.0 ▲   SO Cattle guard.

▼ 5.0   TL T-intersection. Turn left following sign to Rucker. Zero trip meter.
0.0 ▲   Continue to the northwest.
         GPS: N31°44.22′ W109°28.59′

▼ 0.0   Continue to the northeast.
3.4 ▲   TR Turn right onto wide gravel road. Zero trip meter. Intersection is unmarked in this direction.

▼ 0.7   SO Cross through Whitewater Draw.
2.7 ▲   SO Cross through Whitewater Draw.

▼ 0.9   SO Cross over Whitewater Draw on bridge.
2.5 ▲   SO Cross over Whitewater Draw on bridge.

▼ 1.7   SO Track on right.
1.7 ▲   SO Track on left.

▼ 2.0   SO Cattle guard.
1.4 ▲   SO Cattle guard.

▼ 2.5   SO Cattle guard.
0.9 ▲   SO Cattle guard.

▼ 2.7   SO Cross through wash.
0.7 ▲   SO Cross through wash.

▼ 3.4   BR Graded road on left is private. Zero trip
            meter and bear right following sign to
            Rucker Recreation Area.
0.0 ▲   Continue to the west.
            GPS: N31°45.30′ W109°25.27′

▼ 0.0   Continue to the east.
3.0 ▲   SO Graded road on right is private. Zero
            trip meter.

▼ 0.2   SO Cattle guard; then cross through wash
            on concrete ford.
2.8 ▲   SO Cross through wash on concrete ford;
            then cattle guard.

▼ 1.6   SO Track on left is designated access
            route.
1.4 ▲   SO Track on right is designated access
            route.
            GPS: N31°44.98′ W109°23.56′

▼ 2.4   SO Hiking trail #237 on right to Devils
            Canyon, marked as a forest trail.
0.6 ▲   SO Hiking trail #237 on left to Devils
            Canyon, marked as a forest trail.
            GPS: N31°45.20′ W109°22.85′

▼ 3.0   SO Cattle guard, then graded road on left
            goes to Rucker, Rucker Lake, and
            USFS campgrounds. Zero trip meter
            and carry on following sign to Douglas
            and Arizona 80. (Douglas is sign-post-
            ed in both directions at this point.)
0.0 ▲   Continue to the southwest.
            GPS: N31°45.39′ W109°22.18′

▼ 0.0   Continue to the northeast.

▼ 5.9   SO Graded road on right goes to Rucker,
            Rucker Lake, and USFS campgrounds.
            Zero trip meter and continue following
            sign to Douglas. (Douglas is sign-post-
            ed in both directions at this point.)

▼ 0.5   SO Cattle guard.
5.4 ▲   SO Cattle guard.

▼ 0.6   SO Track on left to corral.
5.3 ▲   SO Track on right to corral.

▼ 0.7   SO Track on left through gate—hiking
            access only.
5.2 ▲   SO Track on right through gate—hiking
            access only.

▼ 1.1   SO Cross through wash; then tracks on
            left and right.
4.8 ▲   SO Tracks on left and right; then cross
            through wash.

▼ 1.2   SO Track on left.
4.7 ▲   SO Track on right.

▼ 1.4   SO Track on left continues alongside
            Cottonwood Canyon.
4.5 ▲   SO Track on right continues alongside
            Cottonwood Canyon.
            GPS: N31°44.72′ W109°21.08′

▼ 1.9   SO Track on right.
4.0 ▲   SO Track on left.

▼ 2.5   SO Cattle guard at saddle; then track on
            right.
3.4 ▲   SO Track on left; then cattle guard at sad-
            dle.
            GPS: N31°43.86′ W109°21.18′

▼ 3.4   SO Track on right.
2.5 ▲   SO Track on left.

▼ 3.8   SO Track on left.
2.1 ▲   SO Track on right.
            GPS: N31°42.89′ W109°21.05′

▼ 4.0   SO Cross over creek on bridge.
1.9 ▲   SO Cross over creek on bridge.

▼ 4.2   SO   Track on right. Sunset Peak is on the left.
1.7 ▲   SO   Track on left. Sunset Peak is on the right.

▼ 4.3   SO   Track on right.
1.6 ▲   SO   Track on left.

▼ 4.6   SO   Track on left.
1.3 ▲   SO   Track on right.

▼ 4.7   SO   Cattle guard.
1.2 ▲   SO   Cattle guard.

▼ 5.3   SO   Track on right is private.
0.6 ▲   SO   Track on left is private.

▼ 5.7   SO   Track on right.
0.2 ▲   SO   Track on left.

▼ 5.9   SO   Track on left goes to Pine Gulch, Sunset Peak, and Swede Peak. Zero trip meter at sign.
0.0 ▲   Continue to the northwest.
      GPS: N31°41.61′ W109°19.72′

▼ 0.0   Continue to the southeast.
2.6 ▲   SO   Track on right goes to Pine Gulch, Sunset Peak, and Swede Peak. Zero trip meter at sign.

▼ 0.7   SO   Track on right.
1.9 ▲   SO   Track on left.

▼ 0.8   SO   Track on left.
1.8 ▲   SO   Track on right.
      GPS: N31°41.03′ W109°19.18′

▼ 1.0   SO   Track on right; then cattle guard.
1.6 ▲   SO   Cattle guard; then track on left.

▼ 1.1   SO   Track on left.
1.5 ▲   SO   Track on right.

▼ 1.2   SO   Cross over creek.
1.4 ▲   SO   Cross over creek.

▼ 1.3   SO   Track on right and track on left.
1.3 ▲   SO   Track on right and track on left.

▼ 2.1   SO   Cattle guard; then track on left.
0.5 ▲   SO   Track on right; then cattle guard.

▼ 2.2   SO   Cross through wash.
0.4 ▲   SO   Cross through wash.

▼ 2.6   SO   Track on right; then cattle guard. Leaving Coronado National Forest into private land. Zero trip meter at cattle guard.
0.0 ▲   Continue to the north.
      GPS: N31°39.68′ W109°18.64′

▼ 0.0   Continue to the south.
6.4 ▲   SO   Cattle guard, entering Coronado National Forest; then track on left. Zero trip meter at cattle guard.

▼ 0.2   SO   Cross through wash.
6.2 ▲   SO   Cross through wash.

▼ 0.7   SO   Cattle guard.
5.7 ▲   SO   Cattle guard.

▼ 1.4   SO   Cattle guard.
5.0 ▲   SO   Cattle guard.

▼ 6.4   SO   Cattle guard. Then trail ends on Arizona 80 in the San Bernadino Valley. Turn right for Douglas, turn left for Rodeo, NM.
0.0 ▲   Trail commences on Arizona 80, approximately 28 miles northeast of Douglas, 0.3 miles northeast of mile marker 396. Zero trip meter and turn northwest over a cattle guard onto the graded dirt road at the sign for Rucker Canyon. Road is called Krentz Ranch Road.
      GPS: N31°35.63′ W109°14.34′

Pinery Canyon Trail

STARTING POINT	Southwestern Research Station, 5.1 miles from Portal
FINISHING POINT	Arizona 181, 2.8 miles east from Arizona 186, immediately before the entrance to Chiricahua National Monument
TOTAL MILEAGE	18 miles
UNPAVED MILEAGE	17.9 miles
DRIVING TIME	1.5 hours
ELEVATION RANGE	5,200–7,600 feet
USUALLY OPEN	April to December
BEST TIME TO TRAVEL	April to December
DIFFICULTY RATING	1
SCENIC RATING	8
REMOTENESS RATING	+0

Special Attractions

- One of the prime bird-watching areas in southeastern Arizona.
- Easy, graded trail through spectacular, sky island scenery.
- Many backcountry campsites and developed campgrounds.
- Chiricahua National Monument at the western end of the trail.

History

Portal, the settlement near the start of this trail, is descriptively named after the town's location at the mouth of Cave Creek Canyon and is thought to have been founded by the Duffener brothers, who came from Paradise, just about the turn of the 20th century. Their mining activities drew them toward what became known as Portal. The tiny post office was opened in 1905 and still operates today.

Pinery Canyon developed its name because it was a good source for fine pine timbers used in 1862 for the construction of Fort Bowie near Apache Pass. The fort was an important stronghold in the continued conflict and warfare with the Chiricahua Apaches.

The trail runs up alongside Cave Creek on the eastern side of the range. Cave Creek got its name not only from the many caves along its striking bluffs but also from an impressive underground cavern named Crystal Cavern, which is upstream from where the trail enters the creek line. Around 1878, one of the earliest pioneers in the region, a man named Reed, sold out to the Hands brothers. The brothers are credited with the development of the original trail that traverses this part of the Chiricahua Mountains from Pinery Canyon up, over, and down to the Portal region.

Onion Saddle is also a descriptive name as the original trail passed by a creek that was noted for its wild onions.

As you enter the mouth of Pinery Canyon, you pass close to Riggs Spring, named after one of the earliest pioneer families in the area. Ed and Lilian Riggs were active in the creation of the Chiricahua National Monument in 1924, and Ed is credited with being one of the first Americans to discover many of the eerie, towering, rhyolite rock shapes now within the monument. Ed's father-in-law, Neil Erickson, had accidentally entered this magnificent wonderland in the late 1880s while tracking an Apache who had stolen one of the army's horses. Though it was many months before the horse was found, the real find was the region's unique, rocky terrain. The Chiricahua Apache whom Erickson had trailed was known as Massai and was one of the last of the Chiricahua Indians to be relocated to Florida. Ed Riggs later suggested the name of Massai Point for the high point within the national monument.

Description

The Chiricahua Mountains are one of the sky islands of Arizona's southeast mountain ranges where the elevation of the range creates mini-climate zones of flora and fauna typically found much farther to the north. These islands stand out as cool oases in the summer heat, refuges where outdoor enthusiasts can hike, 4WD, and camp in relative coolness.

In winter, these sky islands can often re-

BASIN TRAIL NO. 247   1
← WELCH SEEP
← GREENHOUSE CANYON 3 1/2
← HERB MARTYR DAM   4 1/2

Basin Hiking Trail begins on the western side of the range

A view of the trail as it climbs toward Onion Saddle

ceive several inches of snow; consequently many of these high altitude trails can be closed to vehicles in winter months. Some are open to snowmobiles; others are limited to skis and snowshoes.

The Pinery Canyon Trail is one of only two graded roads that cross the range from east to west. The drive is suitable for passenger vehicles in dry weather, and there are some smaller, more difficult trails that lead off from the main trail. The trail passes many primitive campsites as well as five developed national forest campgrounds along or near the trail; three of them along the paved road to Portal at the eastern end of the trail. These can be extremely popular in summer.

The Chiricahuas are a prime destination for bird watchers from around the world. More than 330 species of birds can be seen in the mountains, including 14 different types of hummingbirds and 10 species of owls. The rare and elegant trogon nests in the Chiricahuas, one of its few nesting sites in the United States. A popular time for birders to visit is during the spring migration in late April to early May, when many thousands of colorful songbirds make their annual move northward. Hummingbirds and other tropical species are best seen between April and September. The Southwestern Research Station at the western end of this trail is a research station of the American Museum of Natural History, which opened in 1955.

Other wildlife that can be seen are mule deer, javelina, bobcats, coyotes, and black bears. Like all the sky islands, the Chiricahuas support a flourishing population of black bears, which can be active around the campgrounds in summer. Take due precautions with food, and of course, never ever feed a bear!

From Portal, the graded road winds alongside Cave Creek. A major graded road leads back to Paradise, a small settlement within the Chiricahuas, which at one time had thirteen saloons. The original jail there was in the open air; prisoners were shackled to a chain running between two trees. The

mines closed in 1907 but the town still has a few residents.

The main trail climbs up to Onion Saddle at 7,600 feet before descending along Pinery Canyon through cool stands of pine, oak, and alligator juniper to finish on Arizona 181 at the entrance to Chiricahua National Monument.

To reach the start of the trail, proceed south from Portal on the main paved road, passing the ranger station on the right. Continue for 3.1 miles, then swing right remaining on the paved road. Continue for another 2.0 miles, then at the junction of FR 42A to the left, zero trip meter. The start of the trail is immediately past the cluster of buildings on the left that is the Southwestern Research Station.

The graves of Frank and Grace Hands, who are connected with Hilltop, are near the beginning of the trail over Hands Pass. For more information about the Hands family, see South #21: Hands Pass Trail.

This road is not maintained for winter travel and may be impassable in winter months. Call ahead for information. However, it may be open for longer than the dates given above.

Current Road Information

Coronado National Forest
Douglas Ranger District
1192 West Saddleview Rd.
Douglas, AZ 85607
(520) 364-3468

Map References

BLM Willcox, Chiricahua Peak
USFS Coronado National Forest: Chiricahua-Peloncillo Mts. Ranger Districts
USGS 1:24,000 Portal, Rustler Park, Fife Peak, Bowie Mountain South
1:100,000 Willcox, Chiricahua Peak
Maptech CD-ROM: Southeast Arizona/ Tucson
Arizona Atlas & Gazetteer, p. 75
Arizona Road & Recreation Atlas, pp. 55, 89
Recreational Map of Arizona

Route Directions

▼ 0.0   At the intersection of FR 42 and FR 42A, at the Southwestern Research Station, zero trip meter and continue northwest on the paved FR 42, following the signs for Rustler Park and Arizona 181.

3.7 ▲   Trail ends at the intersection of FR 42 and FR 42A at the Southwestern Research Station. Continue along the road and follow the signs for 5.1 miles to Portal.

       GPS: N31°53.07′ W109°12.34′

▼ 0.1   SO   Road turns to graded dirt. Dispersed camping now permitted. Entering Coronado National Forest.

3.6 ▲   SO   Camping in designated campgrounds only. Road is crossing private land.

▼ 1.1   SO   Track on right.
2.6 ▲   SO   Track on left.

▼ 1.7   SO   Cross over creek.
2.0 ▲   SO   Cross over creek.

▼ 2.0   SO   Track on left.
1.7 ▲   SO   Track on right.

▼ 2.2   SO   Track on right.
1.5 ▲   SO   Track on left.

▼ 2.6   SO   Basin Trail #247 on left goes to Herb Martyr Dam—hiking and pack trail.
1.1 ▲   SO   Basin Trail #247 on right goes to Herb Martyr Dam—hiking and pack trail.

       GPS: N31°53.98′ W109°14.28′

▼ 2.8   SO   Track on left.
0.9 ▲   SO   Track on right.

▼ 3.1   SO   Cattle guard; then loop of old road on right.
0.6 ▲   SO   Loop of old road on left; then cattle guard.

▼ 3.7   SO   Graded road on right is FR 42B to Paradise. Zero trip meter.
0.0 ▲   Continue to the east toward Portal.

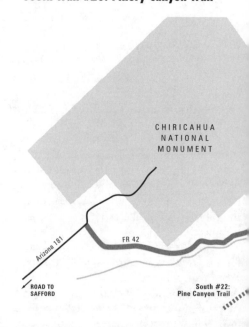

       GPS: N31°54.52′ W109°15.03′

▼ 0.0   Continue to the west and cross over East Turkey Creek; then track on left.

3.1 ▲   SO   Track on right; then cross over East Turkey Creek. Then graded road on left is FR 42B to Paradise. Zero trip meter.

▼ 3.1   SO   Onion Saddle. Track on right is also start of Shaw Peak hiking trail #251, graded road on left is FR 42D to Rustler Park and South #23: Barfoot Park Trail. Continue straight on, following the sign for Arizona 181. Zero trip meter at saddle.

0.0 ▲   Continue to the southeast.

       GPS: N31°55.99′ W109°15.78′

▼ 0.0   Continue on to the northwest and cross cattle guard.

4.5 ▲   SO   Cattle guard; then Onion Saddle. Track on left is also start of Shaw Peak hiking trail #251, graded road on right is FR 42D to Rustler Park and South #23: Barfoot Park Trail. Continue straight on, following the sign for Portal. Zero trip

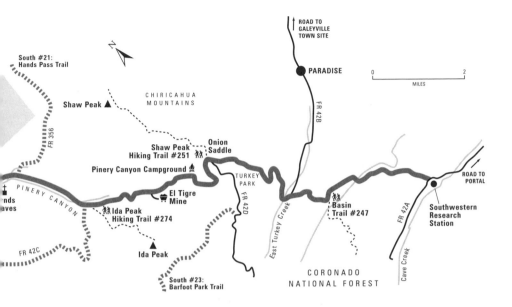

meter at saddle.

▼ 1.7   SO   Pinery Canyon Campground on right.

2.8 ▲   SO   Pinery Canyon Campground on left.

             GPS: N31°55.97' W109°16.30'

▼ 2.8   SO   Track on left goes 0.2 miles to El Tigre
                Mine and continues past it. There is a
                large timber-framed adit and two
                smaller ones.

1.7 ▲   BL   Track on right goes 0.2 miles to El
                Tigre Mine and continues past it. There
                is a large timber-framed adit and two
                smaller ones.

             GPS: N31°56.31' W109°17.22'

▼ 3.2   SO   Track on right.

1.3 ▲   SO   Track on left.

▼ 3.3   SO   Cross over creek on bridge.

1.2 ▲   SO   Cross over creek on bridge.

             GPS: N31°56.41' W109°17.55'

▼ 4.0   SO   Cross over creek on bridge.

0.5 ▲   SO   Cross over creek on bridge.

             GPS: N31°56.63' W109°18.01'

▼ 4.4   SO   Ida Peak hiking trail #274 on left.

0.1 ▲   SO   Ida Peak hiking trail #274 on right.

             GPS: N31°56.82' W109°18.36'

▼ 4.5   SO   Track on right to concrete footings and
                large camping area followed by South
                #22: Pine Canyon Trail (FR 42C) on
                left at sign to Methodist Camp. Also
                track on right to camping area. Zero
                trip meter.

0.0 ▲   Continue to the southeast, track on left
                to concrete footings and large camping
                area.

             GPS: N31°56.89' W109°18.43'

▼ 0.0   Continue to the northwest and cross
                through wash.

1.6 ▲   SO   Cross through wash; then graded road
                on right is South #22: Pine Canyon
                Trail (FR 42C) at sign to Methodist
                Camp. Also track on left to camping
                area. Zero trip meter.

▼ 0.9   SO   Cross over wash.

0.7 ▲   SO   Cross over wash.

| ▼ 1.4 | SO | Cattle guard. |
| 0.2 ▲ | SO | Cattle guard. |

| ▼ 1.6 | SO | Track on right is South #21: Hands Pass Trail (FR 356) signed to North Fork. Also track on left to camping area. Continue following sign to Arizona 181. Zero trip meter. |
| 0.0 ▲ | | Continue to the southeast following sign for Portal. |

GPS: N31°58.16' W109°19.20'

| ▼ 0.0 | | Continue to the northwest and cross through Pinery Creek wash. |
| 1.4 ▲ | SO | Cross through Pinery Creek wash; then track on left is South #21: Hands Pass Trail (FR 356) signed to North Fork. Track on right goes to camping area. Zero trip meter. |

| ▼ 0.3 | SO | Graves of Frank and Grace Hands are on the left surrounded by a wire fence. |
| 1.1 ▲ | SO | Graves of Frank and Grace Hands are on the right surrounded by a wire fence. |

GPS: N31°58.25' W109°19.54'

| ▼ 1.0 | SO | Cattle guard. |
| 0.4 ▲ | SO | Cattle guard. |

| ▼ 1.4 | SO | Leaving Coronado National Forest at sign. Zero trip meter. |
| 0.0 ▲ | | Continue to the east. |

GPS: N31°58.29' W109°20.69'

| ▼ 0.0 | | Continue to the west. |
| 3.7 ▲ | SO | Entering Coronado National Forest at sign. Zero trip meter. |

| ▼ 0.1 | SO | Cattle guard. |
| 3.6 ▲ | SO | Cattle guard. |

| ▼ 0.2 | SO | Cross over creek. |
| 3.5 ▲ | SO | Cross over creek. Trail is running along-side Pinery Creek. |

| ▼ 0.4 | SO | Cross over creek. |
| 3.3 ▲ | SO | Cross over creek. |

| ▼ 1.6 | SO | Two cattle guards. |
| 2.1 ▲ | SO | Two cattle guards. |

GPS: N31°58.89' W109°22.21'

| ▼ 3.6 | SO | Cattle guard, road is now paved. |
| 0.1 ▲ | SO | Cattle guard, road turns to graded gravel. |

| ▼ 3.7 | | Trail ends at the intersection of Arizona 181 and Pinery Canyon road, immediately before the entrance into the Chiricahua National Monument. Turn right to visit the national monument, turn left to exit to Safford. |
| 0.0 ▲ | | At the junction of Arizona 181 and Pinery Canyon road, immediately before the entrance into the Chiricahua National Monument, zero trip meter and turn east on the paved Pinery Canyon road at the sign. |

GPS: N32°00.41' W109°23.34'

SOUTH REGION TRAIL #21

Hands Pass Trail

STARTING POINT	South #20: Pinery Canyon Trail, 5.1 miles from the western end
FINISHING POINT	San Simon–Paradise Road, 5 miles north of Paradise
TOTAL MILEAGE	12 miles
UNPAVED MILEAGE	12 miles
DRIVING TIME	3.5 hours
ELEVATION RANGE	4,600–6,700 feet
USUALLY OPEN	Year-round
BEST TIME TO TRAVEL	April to October
DIFFICULTY RATING	6
SCENIC RATING	8
REMOTENESS RATING	+0

Special Attractions

■ Access to the Kasper Tunnel—important in the history of Hilltop ghost town.
■ Picturesque trail through the Chiricahua Mountains.
■ Backcountry camping.
■ Hands Pass and views of Cochise Head.

A narrow section of trail along East Whitehall Creek

The western entrance to Kasper Tunnel

History

Originally from England, Frank, John, and Alfred Hands were partly responsible for opening up this region to mining in the 1890s. They were also behind the early construction of trails that linked the mining settlements in this region; Hands Pass, named after them, is one such trail. They acquired the Hilltop Mine, formerly known as Ayers Camp, from its founder, Jack Dunn, who struck upon it some ten years earlier. The mine developed farther into Hilltop Town when the brothers sold their interests to a St. Louis investor in 1913. Frank Hands and his wife, Grace, are buried very close to the southern end of Hands Pass. The site is noted on South #20: Pinery Canyon Trail.

Hilltop had developed on both sides of Shaw Peak by the late 1910s, with the small Kasper Tunnel serving as the link. The later-developing east side of the town grew even more than the original west side. No buildings remain on the western slopes except for several concrete footings and the outlet of the Kasper Tunnel. In its prime, Hilltop hosted a dance hall, restaurant, pool hall, an impressive manager's house, bunkhouses, and more. By the 1930s mining activities were greatly reduced and the town was losing its residents. Various small groups attempted to continue mining through to the late 1940s but the closure of the post office in 1945 marked the final years of Hilltop. A few remnants of the town on the eastern side of the Kasper Tunnel survive on private land; permission is required to visit these.

Harris Mountain, at the eastern end of the trail, is named after a family who unwisely tried to take a short cut through the Chiricahua Mountains in 1873 and died at the hands of Chiricahua Apaches. Traveling by themselves from the San Simon Wash up Hunt Canyon toward Hands Pass, the parents and their two youngest children were killed and their 15- year-old daughter was abducted. Their disappearance remained a mystery until the daughter retold the tragic events when she was found in Mexico by the army many years later. She was able to lead a party to the Hunt Canyon site and to the bones of her family.

Jhus Canyon is a reminder of one of the leading Chiricahua Apache. Jhus was instrumental in encouraging the Apache to leave the San Carlos Reservation and to attempt to reclaim lands they considered stolen.

Five miles south of the end of the trail is the small settlement of Paradise. Supposedly it was named by a young couple, George and Reed Walker, who were so happy with their chosen home site that they felt they lived in paradise. In 1901 a mine developed near Paradise, which altered the solitude of this remote settlement completely. The mine attracted some of the more colorful and wild characters from Tombstone and forever altered the peaceful existence of the settlers. The saloons were busy and the jail tree (later the jailhouse) was well-used. The mines were considered economically unsound by the 1910s and the miners departed, yet the settlement of Paradise lingered. By the early 1940s, Paradise was all but deserted and the post office closed its doors. Perhaps there is something contagious in the name or the peaceful mountainside location as a few lights have managed to linger on in this tiny settlement as it enters into the twenty-first century.

Description

This challenging trail skirts below Chiricahua National Monument, traveling over Hands Pass and heading steeply down to join East Whitetail Creek. Although it is an exciting drive, most carefully driven, high-clearance SUVs with good tires can safely navigate the trail. Those driving vehicles with side steps, long overhangs, or low-hanging brush or towbars should think twice. There are several places along the trail where these are a distinct disadvantage and there is a risk of damage.

The trail commences on South #20: Pinery Canyon Trail, very close to the graves of Frank and Grace Hands. The intersection is sign-posted to North Fork, FR 356, and leads off alongside the creek, passing some good campsites along the way.

After 1.9 miles, a spur trail leads off to the southwest end of the Kasper Tunnel, a long tunnel dug through the hillside, which allowed for the relocation of Hilltop to its current location. The spur trail is rated a 5, mainly because of its eroded nature and sections of narrow shelf road. It ends at the Kasper Tunnel, which appears now as a small hole dug in the solid rock. The turnout for vehicles is on a huge pile of excavated rock that came out of the tunnel. An idea of the length of the tunnel can be gained by studying the enormous amount of material that came out of such a small hole. The hiking trail to Shaw Peak also starts here.

From the main trail, you start to climb in earnest up to Hands Pass. The shelf road is a comfortable width for a single vehicle and there are adequate passing places. The surface on the north side of the pass is loose and there are a couple of small rock ledges, but this side of the pass is the easier of the two. In wet weather, or after a sprinkle of snow, the red soil can become very greasy. There are views of the Kasper Tunnel and its workings to the east, Shaw Peak to the southeast, and as you crest the top of Hands Pass, Cochise Head can be seen directly ahead. The oddly shaped mountain resembles a face looking upwards with the top of the head pointing east. The rock formations make the nose, eyebrows, and lips. It is so named because the famous Chiricahua Apache chief eluded capture for many years in this region.

Once over the crest of Hands Pass the difficult descent down the south side begins. The trail here is rocky and very stony, and traction is low. The most challenging section is 0.7 miles south of the pass. There the trail is badly eroded on one side, leaving a trail too narrow for most SUVs to traverse. ATVs and possibly the smallest subcompacts may fit, but check carefully before you attempt this route, as it is very off-camber with a deep gully at the end. Most vehicles will need to bridge the eroded section, putting the passenger-side wheels up tight to the bank where there is a narrow edge for tires to grab. This section needs a driver with good nerves and tires with good tread; otherwise there is a risk that the vehicle will slip down into the gully, risking possible body damage. A spotter is a big advantage. The trail is informally and actively maintained; however, previous drivers have placed rocks to build up an edge for tires to grab and in other strategic places to try to control further trail erosion.

The trail continues 6-rated for 0.3 miles as it travels along a narrow channel strewn with large boulders. You will need to watch your wheel placements carefully. A farther 0.3 miles along the trail, there is a very deep, ditchy wash crossing. Be extremely careful with front and rear overhangs. If you are driving this trail in the reverse direction and you don't like the look of this wash, then turn back at this point.

After the wash, the major difficulties are past. The trail now follows alongside or in the bed of East Whitetail Creek. There are still some slow-going sections as the trail crawls over large river-rock boulders. This end of the trail passes through private property. The boundaries are clearly marked, and the property owners request that you fill in your vehicle details in order to pass through. Please comply with their reasonable request and treat the access through the property as a privilege not a right. It can be rescinded at any time. Considerate use of the trail will help ensure access for future users.

The site of Hilltop is just off the main trail. It too stands on private property, and vehicle access is by permission only. The final section of the trail travels past private property, open forest, and ranchland to end at the intersection with the San Simon–Paradise Road, 5 miles north of Paradise.

Current Road Information

Coronado National Forest
Douglas Ranger District
1192 West Saddleview Rd.
Douglas, AZ 85607
(520) 364-3468

South Trail #21: Hands Pass Trail

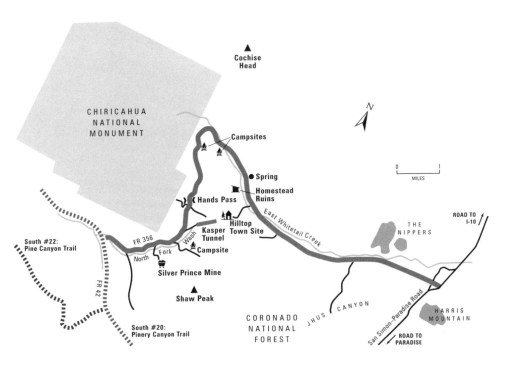

Map References

BLM Chiricahua Peak, Willcox
USFS Coronado National Forest: Chiric-
ahua-Peloncillo Mtns. Ranger Dis-
tricts
USGS 1:24,000 Rustler Park, Cochise
Head, Portal, Blue Mtn.
1:100,000 Chiricahua Peak, Willcox
Maptech CD-ROM: Southeast Arizona/
Tucson
Arizona Atlas & Gazetteer, p. 75
Arizona Road & Recreation Atlas, pp. 55, 89
Recreational Map of Arizona (incomplete)

Route Directions

▼ 0.0   From South #20: Pinery Canyon Trail,
1.4 miles east of Coronado National
Forest boundary, zero trip meter and
turn east onto small formed trail at the
marker for FR 356, signed to North
Fork. Small track on right at intersection goes to camping area.

1.9 ▲   Trail ends at the junction with South
#20: Pinery Canyon Trail. Turn right for
Arizona 181, turn left to follow the
Pinery Canyon Trail to Portal. Small
track straight on goes to camping area.
GPS: N31°58.16' W109°19.20'

▼ 0.1   SO Cattle guard.
1.8 ▲   SO Cattle guard.

▼ 0.2   SO Cross through North Fork Wash.
1.7 ▲   SO Cross through North Fork Wash.

▼ 0.4   SO Track on right; then cross through
North Fork Wash.
1.5 ▲   SO Cross through North Fork Wash; then
track on left.
GPS: N31°58.08' W109°18.78'

▼ 0.6   BL Corral, cabin, and well on left followed
by track on right. Bear left and cross
through wash.
1.3 ▲   SO Cross through wash; then track on left.

Corral, cabin, and well on right.
GPS: N31°56.06′ W109°18.57′

▼ 0.7   SO   Track on left underneath power lines. Trail is following alongside North Fork Wash.

1.2 ▲   SO   Track on right underneath power lines.

▼ 0.9   SO   Enter North Fork Wash.

1.0 ▲   BR   Exit wash to the right.

▼ 1.0   BL   Bear left on trail out of wash, tracks continue in wash.

0.9 ▲   SO   Enter North Fork Wash, vehicle tracks go up the wash to the left.

▼ 1.1   SO   Cross through wash.

0.8 ▲   SO   Cross through wash.

▼ 1.3   SO   Well-used track on right goes 0.4 miles to Silver Prince Mine and private cabin. Nothing remains of mine. Continue to the northeast along wash course. Trail immediately forks and rejoins again.

0.6 ▲   SO   Trails rejoin, then well-used track on left goes 0.4 miles to Silver Prince Mine and private cabin. Nothing remains of mine.
GPS: N31°58.40′ W109°18.08′

▼ 1.4   SO   Trails rejoin.

0.5 ▲   SO   Trail immediately forks and rejoins again.

▼ 1.5   SO   Pass through fence line; then track on right at well.

0.4 ▲   SO   Track on left at well; then pass through fence line.
GPS: N31°58.52′ W109°17.89′

▼ 1.6   SO   Cross through two washes.

0.3 ▲   SO   Cross through two washes.

▼ 1.7   SO   Track on right at concrete pad.

0.2 ▲   SO   Track on left at concrete pad.

▼ 1.8   BL   Cross through wash; then bear left and climb away from the creek. Track on right goes to campsite.

0.1 ▲   SO   Track now follows alongside North Fork Wash. Track on left at bottom of

hill goes to campsite.
GPS: N31°58.63′ W109°17.66′

▼ 1.9   SO   Track on right goes 0.7 miles to the southwest end of the Kasper Tunnel. Zero trip meter. Coordinates at Kasper Tunnel—GPS: N31°59.14′ W109°17.39′

0.0 ▲   Continue to the southwest.
GPS: N31°58.72′ W109°17.61′

▼ 0.0   Continue to the north.

5.5 ▲   SO   Track on left goes 0.7 miles to the southwest end of the Kasper Tunnel. Zero trip meter. Coordinates at Kasper Tunnel—GPS: N31°59.14′ W109°17.39′
GPS: N31°59.14′ W109°17.39′

▼ 0.1   SO   Second entrance to spur trail to Kasper Tunnel on right.

5.4 ▲   SO   Track on left joins spur trail to Kasper Tunnel.
GPS: N31°58.79′ W109°17.61′

▼ 0.5   SO   View to the right of workings of Kasper Tunnel.

5.0 ▲   SO   View to the left of workings of the Kasper Tunnel.

▼ 1.0   SO   Hands Pass. Pass through gate; then track on right and left. Views ahead to Cochise Head. Trail descends the north side of Hands Pass.

4.5 ▲   SO   Track on right and left at top of Hands Pass. Pass through gate. Trail descends the south side of Hands Pass.
GPS: N31°59.45′ W109°17.71′

▼ 1.7   SO   Difficult rutted section.

3.8 ▲   SO   Difficult rutted section.
GPS: N32°00.05′ W109°17.73′

▼ 1.8   SO   Cross through wash.

3.7 ▲   SO   Cross through wash.

▼ 2.0   SO   End of difficult section.

3.5 ▲   SO   Start of difficult section.
GPS: N32°00.26′ W109°17.94′

▼ 2.3   SO   Cross through deep, ditchy wash.

Watch overhangs and fuel tanks.

3.2 ▲ SO Cross through deep, ditchy wash. If you don't like the look of this wash, then go no farther.
GPS: N32°00.43' W109°18.10'

▼ 2.5 SO Campsite at small saddle.
3.0 ▲ SO Campsite at small saddle.

▼ 3.0 SO Cross through wash.
2.5 ▲ SO Cross through wash.
GPS: N32°00.94' W109°18.15'

▼ 3.1 SO Cross through two washes.
2.4 ▲ SO Cross through two washes.

▼ 3.2 SO Cross through wash.
2.3 ▲ SO Cross through wash.

▼ 3.3 TR Track on left crosses wash. Turn right and follow alongside East Whitetail Creek, trail enters or runs alongside it.
2.2 ▲ TL Exit creek. Turn left before wash crossing and start to climb toward saddle, leaving East Whitetail Creek. Track on right crosses wash.
GPS: N32°01.07' W109°18.00'

▼ 3.5 SO Exit creek wash and follow alongside above creek.
2.0 ▲ SO Enter creek wash.
GPS: N32°00.93' W109°17.86'

▼ 3.7 SO Campsite on far side of creek.
1.8 ▲ SO Campsite on far side of creek.

▼ 3.8 SO Gate, entering private land. Please remain on trail, then cross through wash. Please keep gate closed. Please respect the landowners' conditions of entry that are posted at the gate.
1.7 ▲ SO Entering Coronado National Forest.
GPS: N32°00.83' W109°17.54'

▼ 3.9 SO Cross through two washes.
1.6 ▲ SO Cross through two washes.

▼ 4.0 SO Cross through wash.
1.5 ▲ SO Cross through wash.

▼ 4.2 SO Track on left through gate is private. Trail standard improves.
1.3 ▲ BL Bear left following sign for trailhead parking. Re-enter wash course. Trail standard becomes more difficult. Track on right through gate is private.
GPS: N32°00.69' W109°17.20'

▼ 4.7 SO Exit wash, spring on left.
0.8 ▲ SO Spring on right, enter wash.
GPS: N32°00.42' W109°16.78'

▼ 4.8 SO Gate, exiting private property into national forest. Please keep gate closed. Track on left.
0.7 ▲ SO Track on right. Entering private property through gate. Please keep gate closed and respect landowners' conditions of entry that are posted at the gate.
GPS: N32°00.39' W109°16.77'

▼ 4.9 SO Track on right crosses creek to small ruin of adobe homestead in paddock; then faint track on left.
0.6 ▲ SO Faint track on right; then track on left crosses creek to small ruin of adobe homestead in paddock.
GPS: N32°00.28' W109°16.66'

▼ 5.3 SO Entering private property.
0.2 ▲ SO Exiting private property.

▼ 5.4 SO Gate, leaving private property. Remain on trail.
0.1 ▲ SO Gate, trail passes through private property, remain on trail.
GPS: N32°00.01' W109°16.32'

▼ 5.5 TL Cross through East Whitetail Creek, then turn left in front of house. Zero trip meter. Track on right goes to Hilltop. Vehicle access to Hilltop by permission only.
0.0 ▲ Continue to the northwest.
GPS: N31°59.97' W109°16.25'

▼ 0.0 Continue to the east.
4.6 ▲ TR Track straight on goes to Hilltop. Turn right in front of house and cross

through East Whitetail Creek. Zero trip meter. Vehicle access to Hilltop by permission only.

▼ 0.1 SO Cattle guard, crossing private property.
4.5 ▲ SO Cattle guard.

▼ 0.3 SO Property boundary. Track on right.
4.3 ▲ SO Crossing private property. Track on left.

▼ 0.6 SO Track on left; then track on right.
4.0 ▲ SO Track on left; then track on right.

▼ 0.8 SO Track on right.
3.8 ▲ SO Track on left.

▼ 1.7 SO Cattle guard; then track on left.
2.9 ▲ SO Track on right; then cattle guard.

▼ 2.4 SO Cattle guard.
2.2 ▲ SO Cattle guard.

▼ 2.6 SO Track on right.
2.0 ▲ SO Track on left.

▼ 3.0 SO Track on right; then cattle guard.
1.6 ▲ SO Cattle guard; then track on left.
    GPS: N32°00.14' W109°13.19'

▼ 3.4 SO Cattle guard.
1.2 ▲ SO Cattle guard.

▼ 3.7 SO Cattle guard.
0.9 ▲ SO Cattle guard.

▼ 4.3 SO Cross through wash.
0.3 ▲ SO Cross through wash.

▼ 4.4 SO Cattle guard; then track on left.
0.2 ▲ SO Track on right; then cattle guard.

▼ 4.5 SO Track on right joins Paradise Road.
0.1 ▲ SO Track on left joins Paradise Road.

▼ 4.6 Trail ends at junction with San Simon–Paradise Road. Harris Mountain is ahead; to the left are The Nippers. Turn right for Paradise, turn left for I-10.
0.0 ▲ Trail commences on the San

Simon–Paradise Road, 5 miles north of Paradise, 18 miles south of San Simon. Zero trip meter at the sign and turn southwest on the well-graded, dirt road following the sign for East Whitetail Canyon. Harris Mountain is on the west side of the San Simon–Paradise Road and The Nippers are on the right.
GPS: N32°00.21' W109°11.44'

Pine Canyon Trail

STARTING POINT	South #20: Pinery Canyon Trail, 6.7 miles west of Arizona 181
FINISHING POINT	Oak Ranch on Arizona 181, 0.1 miles north of mile marker 56
TOTAL MILEAGE	12.1 miles
UNPAVED MILEAGE	12.1 miles
DRIVING TIME	2 hours
ELEVATION RANGE	4,900–6,400 feet
USUALLY OPEN	Year-round
BEST TIME TO TRAVEL	Year-round
DIFFICULTY RATING	3
SCENIC RATING	8
REMOTENESS RATING	+0

Special Attractions

■ Views of the jagged rock formations that form Pine Canyon.
■ Shady trail that crosses Pine Creek numerous times.
■ Access to hiking trails into the Chiricahua Wilderness.
■ Many pleasant backcountry camping sites.

History

This trail approaches the Chiricahua Mountains from the eastern flats and offers a good view of Fife Peak before heading up Fife Canyon. Both features were named in remembrance of a Mrs. Fife, one of two wives of a Mormon polygamist who ranched locally. She was approached by one of her Mexican employees for food, and though she offered the food, the employee shot and killed her. He was captured soon after near Fort Bowie, was identified, and hung.

Description

Pine Canyon Trail is a rough, rocky single track that travels through two canyons—Pine Canyon and the wider Fife Canyon. Initially the trail follows a roughly graded, single-lane dirt road as it travels across Downing Pass, past some spectacular, jagged red rock formations. At one point there is a view ahead looking down into narrow Pine Canyon.

The trail then turns onto a small, formed track that winds alongside Pine Creek, crossing it often. All the crossings have firm, stony bottoms. Normally the creek has a few inches of water, but in spring and after summer storms, depths of 18 inches or more are not uncommon, and the difficulty of the trail increases accordingly. The canyon is tight and passes below the red rock formations glimpsed earlier from Downings Pass. The vegetation is predominantly oak, pine, and alligator juniper, and the entire trail is moderately brushy for most vehicles, the lower section of Pine Canyon being the worst. The lower section of Pine Canyon is also the slowest going as the trail crawls over small but lumpy river rocks.

The trail opens out as it exits Pine Canyon. It is wider and travels through manzanita, alligator juniper, and low shrubs. It crosses into the wider, lower Fife Canyon and becomes smoother as it follows alongside Fife and Fivemile Creeks.

The lower end of the trail spills out into open grasslands and runs along the national forest boundary before crossing private property for the final two miles. Access through the private property is granted under the Sportsman-Landowners Respect Program. The designated route passes through the ranch yards and right past the ranch house. Access is not permitted after dark. Please respect this restriction to avoid disturbing the owners, and drive slowly to avoid making unnecessary dust.

There are several good campsites along

One of the many crossings of Pine Creek

this trail; the best ones are at the north end of Pine Creek where there are several good sites along the creek, underneath mature trees, and farther down alongside Fivemile Creek where there are several more open ones.

Current Road Information
Coronado National Forest
Douglas Ranger District
1192 West Saddleview Rd.
Douglas, AZ 85607
(520) 364-3468

Map References
BLM Chiricahua Peak
USFS Coronado National Forest: Chiric-
ahua-Peloncillo Mtns. Ranger Dis-
tricts
USGS 1:24,000 Rustler Park, Fife Peak
1:100,000 Chiricahua Peak
Maptech CD-ROM: Southeast Arizona/
Tucson
Arizona Atlas & Gazetteer, p. 75
Arizona Road & Recreation Atlas, pp. 55, 89

Route Directions

▼ 0.0   From South #20: Pinery Canyon Trail, 6.7 miles from western end, turn southwest on graded dirt road FR 42C at sign for the Methodist Camp and zero trip meter.
1.4 ▲   Trail finishes at the intersection with South #20: Pinery Canyon Trail. Turn left to exit to Arizona 181, turn right to follow along Pinery Canyon to Portal.
      GPS: N31°56.89' W109°18.43'

▼ 0.1 SO Cross through wash.
1.3 ▲ SO Cross through wash.

▼ 0.8 SO Track on left.
0.6 ▲ SO Track on right.

▼ 0.9 SO Saddle at Downings Pass.
0.5 ▲ SO Saddle at Downings Pass.
      GPS: N31°56.44' W109°18.88'

▼ 1.4 TR At sign for Pine Canyon, turn right onto small formed trail. Zero trip meter.
0.0 ▲   Continue to the northeast.
      GPS: N31°56.11' W109°19.15'

▼ 0.0   Continue to the northwest.
2.5 ▲ TL T-intersection, turn left onto larger graded trail, following sign for Pinery Road. Zero trip meter.

▼ 0.2 SO Track on right to campsite; then cross through Pine Creek.
2.3 ▲ SO Cross through Pine Creek; then track on left to campsite.

▼ 0.6 SO Cross through creek.
1.9 ▲ SO Cross through creek.

▼ 0.7 SO Cross through creek.
1.8 ▲ SO Cross through creek.

▼ 0.9 SO Gate.
1.6 ▲ SO Gate.
      GPS: N31°56.61' W109°19.69'

▼ 1.2 SO Cross through creek.
1.3 ▲ SO Cross through creek.

▼ 1.3 SO Cross through creek.
1.2 ▲ SO Cross through creek.

▼ 1.8 SO Cross through creek.
0.7 ▲ SO Cross through creek.

▼ 2.2 SO Cross through creek.
0.3 ▲ SO Cross through creek.

▼ 2.3 SO Track on left goes to Hoovey Canyon hiking trailhead.
0.2 ▲ SO Track on right goes to Hoovey Canyon hiking trailhead.
      GPS: N31°57.13' W109°20.89'

▼ 2.5 BR Track on left goes to Green Canyon. Bear right following sign to Fife Canyon and zero trip meter.
0.0 ▲   Continue to the southeast.
      GPS: N31°57.24' W109°21.12'

▼ 0.0   Continue to the north; and cross

A view of the rock crags that form the walls of Pine Canyon

South Trail #22: Pine Canyon Trail

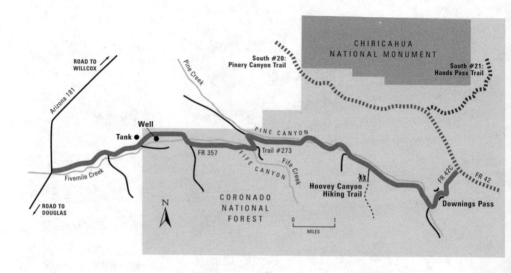

through creek.

2.6 ▲ BL Cross through creek, then track on right goes to Green Canyon. Bear left; there is a sign at the junction for Green and Fife Canyons. Zero trip meter.

▼ 0.3 SO Track on left to campsite.
2.3 ▲ SO Track on right to campsite.

▼ 0.6 SO Cross through creek.
2.0 ▲ SO Cross through creek.

▼ 0.8 SO Cross through creek.
1.8 ▲ SO Cross through creek.
       GPS: N31°57.54′ W109°21.85′

▼ 1.0 SO Enter creek.
1.6 ▲ SO Exit creek.

▼ 1.1 SO Exit creek.
1.5 ▲ SO Enter creek.

▼ 1.3 SO Cross through creek.
1.3 ▲ SO Cross through creek.

▼ 1.6 SO Clearing on left.
1.0 ▲ SO Clearing on right.

▼ 1.8 SO Cross through Pine Creek.

0.8 ▲ SO Cross through Pine Creek.

▼ 2.6 TL Turn left, following the USFS sign for Fife Canyon, FR 357. Faint track on right and track ahead to campsite. Intersection is in small clearing. Zero trip meter.
0.0 ▲   Continue to the northeast.
         GPS: N31°57.70′ W109°23.64′

▼ 0.0   Continue to the southeast, leaving Pine Canyon.
3.4 ▲ TR Turn right in clearing. Track on left goes to campsite, faint track straight on. There is a USFS sign pointing to Fife Canyon (the direction you have come). Zero trip meter. There is an old fallen down sign for Green Canyon and Rustler Park FR 357. Trail now enters Pine Canyon.

▼ 0.2 SO Gate. Entering Fife Canyon.
3.2 ▲ SO Leaving Fife Canyon. Gate.
         GPS: N31°57.54′ W109°23.48′

▼ 0.3 TR Track on left is Trail #273 into Fife Canyon. It is used by vehicles at the lower end and then enters wilderness. Turn right, following the sign to Oak Ranch.

3.1 ▲ TL Turn left following the sign for Pine Canyon. Ahead is Trail #273 into Fife Canyon. It is used by vehicles at the lower end and then enters wilderness.
GPS: N31°57.46' W109°23.47'

▼ 0.5 SO Cross through Fife Creek.
2.9 ▲ SO Cross through Fife Creek.
GPS: N31°57.48' W109°23.66'

▼ 0.8 SO Cross through wash.
2.6 ▲ SO Cross through wash.

▼ 1.8 SO Faint track on right.
1.6 ▲ SO Faint track on left.

▼ 2.0 SO Track on left is Trail #258.
1.4 ▲ SO Track on right is Trail #258.
GPS: N31°57.63' W109°25.19'

▼ 2.1 SO Cross through Fivemile Creek; then track on left.
1.3 ▲ SO Track on right; then cross through Fivemile Creek.

▼ 2.2 BL Track on right, bear left along fence line—the national forest boundary.
1.2 ▲ BR Track on left, bear right toward Fivemile Creek.
GPS: N31°57.76' W109°25.22'

▼ 2.7 SO Track on left to campsite.
0.7 ▲ SO Track on right to campsite.

▼ 2.9 SO Well on left.
0.5 ▲ SO Well on right.
GPS: N31°57.77' W109°25.89'

▼ 3.4 SO Tank on right; then track on left across Fivemile Creek. Continue straight on through gate into private property. Access is granted under the Sportsman-Landowners Respect Program. Please close gate. There is no access to the private property after dark. Zero trip meter.
0.0 ▲ Continue to the north. Track on right along Fivemile Creek; then tank on left. Continue straight on.
GPS: N31°57.58' W109°26.38'

▼ 0.0 Continue to the south and pass through second gate and track on right.
2.2 ▲ SO Track on left; then pass through gate. Then pass through second gate, leaving private property into the national forest. Zero trip meter at second gate. Please close gates.

▼ 0.2 SO Well on left.
2.0 ▲ SO Well on right.

▼ 0.8 SO Track on left.
1.4 ▲ SO Track on right.

▼ 1.0 SO Cattle guard; then gate.
1.2 ▲ SO Gate; then cattle guard.

▼ 1.9 SO Track on left through gate.
0.3 ▲ SO Track on right through gate.

▼ 2.0 BL Track on right, bear left and cross cattle guard and pass through ranch yard, keeping residences on right. Please go very slowly to avoid dust or disturbing the owners.
0.2 ▲ BR Pass through ranch yard, keeping residences on the left; then cross cattle guard and bear right, track on left.
GPS: N31°57.08' W109°28.39'

▼ 2.1 SO Track on right; then cattle guard.
0.1 ▲ SO Cattle guard; then track on left.

▼ 2.2 Trail ends at junction of paved Arizona 181. Turn right for Willcox, turn left for Douglas.
0.0 ▲ Trail commences on Arizona 181, 0.1 miles north of mile marker 56. Turn east through the gate of Oak Ranch and zero trip meter. Access is granted under the Sportsman-Landowners Respect Program. The trail initially passes through the ranch yard past the houses, so please drive very slowly to avoid dust or disturbing the owners. Access through the private property is not permitted after dark.
GPS: N31°57.11' W109°28.61'

Barfoot Park Trail

STARTING POINT	Intersection of FR 357 and FR 42D, 2 miles south of Onion Saddle
FINISHING POINT	Pine Creek
TOTAL MILEAGE	3.1 miles
UNPAVED MILEAGE	3.1 miles
DRIVING TIME	45 minutes (one-way)
ELEVATION RANGE	7,000–8,400 feet
USUALLY OPEN	April to December
BEST TIME TO TRAVEL	April to December
DIFFICULTY RATING	4
SCENIC RATING	7
REMOTENESS RATING	+0

Special Attractions

■ Cool woodland trail that offers excellent birding.
■ Remote backcountry camping at Barfoot Park.
■ Barfoot Lookout.

Description

This short trail is part of a through route that connects Barfoot Park to South #22: Pine Canyon Trail near the Methodist Camp lower down in Pine Canyon. However, Pine Creek heavily washed out a few years ago and a short section is considered impassable to most vehicles, most unmodified 4WDs included.

The trail starts from the Rustlers Park Road, FR 42D, 2 miles south of Onion Saddle. In the 1870s and 1880s, rustling cattle from Mexico for resale in Arizona was a common activity. Rustler Park was a favorite stopover point for rustlers, who had time to re-brand, rest up, and feed the cattle on the park's higher-elevation green pastures.

A hiking trail near the start of the trail goes a short but steep distance to the old lookout and a great view. Barfoot Park is a small, pretty meadow, which in late spring is studded with wild iris. A spring trickles across the meadow and at one end there are the remains of an old national forest campground. The concrete picnic tables and benches remain, and there is plenty of shade and many spots in which to camp under the pines. An unmarked hiking trail climbs back up to the Barfoot Lookout on Buena Vista Peak. Barfoot Peak can be seen to the north. Birders will enjoy searching for some of the high elevation species, such as Mexican chickadees, red crossbills, and red-faced warblers.

The trail standard gets tougher as it becomes a small, well-formed narrow trail and starts to descend toward Pine Canyon on a shelf road. Views are limited as it travels within the woodland canopy. Three miles from the start, as the trail enters Pine Creek, there is a white Road Closed sign, which marks the start of the extremely challenging section. The forest service placed the sign there to warn most road users that the road is impassable ahead. However, it is not currently an official road closure (which would be denoted by a national forest closed trail sign), and experienced drivers in modified rigs may wish to continue along the forest road, which exits through the Methodist Camp near the start of South #22: Pine Canyon Trail. This section of the trail is beyond the scope of this book and is not mapped.

For drivers without the modified equipment necessary to treat the trail as a through road, it is possible to drive in from the south end through the Methodist Camp to access some pleasant shady campsites along Pine Creek and the hiking trail to Rattlesnake Peak.

Current Road Information

Coronado National Forest
Douglas Ranger District
1192 West Saddleview Rd.
Douglas, AZ 85607
(520) 364-3468

Map References

BLM Chiricahua Peak
USFS Coronado National Forest: Chiricahua-Peloncillo Mtns. Ranger Districts

The narrow trail as it descends through the woods beside Pine Creek

South Trail #23: Barfoot Park Trail

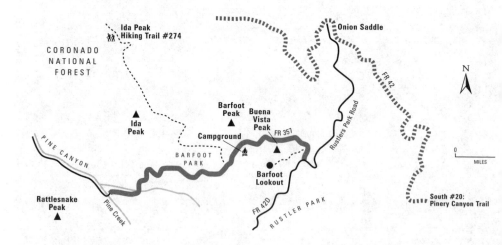

USGS 1:24,000 Rustler Park
 1:100,000 Chiricahua Peak
Maptech CD-ROM: Southeast Arizona/
 Tucson
Arizona Atlas & Gazetteer, p. 75
Arizona Road & Recreation Atlas, pp. 55, 89

Route Directions

▼ 0.0   From FR 42D, 2 miles south of Onion
        Saddle, zero trip meter and turn north
        on FR 357, following the sign for
        Barfoot Park. The road is roughly grad-
        ed at this point. Second small track on
        right at junction.
        GPS: N31°54.88′ W109°16.08′

▼ 0.1   SO Hiking trail at sign on left to Barfoot
        Lookout.
        GPS: N31°55.01′ W109°16.05′

▼ 0.5   SO Cattle guard on saddle.

▼ 0.9   BR Barfoot Park. Barfoot Peak is directly to
        the north. Concrete footings on right,
        then track on left to campsite. Hiking
        trail to Barfoot Lookout on left is
        unsigned, but is edged with rocks at the
        start.

GPS: N31°55.03′ W109°16.75′

▼ 1.0   BL Track on right.

▼ 1.1   SO Track on left; then track on right goes
        0.2 miles to Barfoot Helispot and Ida
        Peak hiking trail #274 to South #20:
        Pinery Canyon Trail. Old corral and pic-
        nic tables at junction.

▼ 1.9   BL Track on right goes 0.1 miles to camp-
        site.
        GPS: N31°54.92′ W109°17.55′

▼ 2.1   SO Track on left.
        GPS: N31°54.82′ W109°17.62′

▼ 2.5   SO Cross through the head of Pine Creek.
        GPS: N31°54.74′ W109°17.80′

▼ 3.1   Trail ends at Road Closed sign where
        trail meets Pine Creek. Past this point
        the trail is suitable for modified 4WDs
        only.
        GPS: N31°54.70′ W109°18.10′

Swift Trail

STARTING POINT	US 191 at Swift Trail Junction
FINISHING POINT	Clark Peak Hiking Trailhead #301
TOTAL MILEAGE	32.4 miles
UNPAVED MILEAGE	11.8 miles
DRIVING TIME	2.5 hours (one-way)
ELEVATION RANGE	3,200–9,500 feet
USUALLY OPEN	April 15 to November 15
BEST TIME TO TRAVEL	April 15 to November 15
DIFFICULTY RATING	1
SCENIC RATING	8
REMOTENESS RATING	+0

Special Attractions

■ Easy trail traveling through many life zones, ultimately climbing to 9,531 feet.
■ Cool summer camping opportunities.
■ Summer wildflower viewing.
■ Trout fishing in Riggs Flat Lake.

History

The towns of Safford and Thatcher were first settled in 1872 and quickly became substantial agricultural communities, utilizing water from the Gila River to irrigate the surrounding countryside. Residents sought a refuge from the blistering summer heat of the valley and looked to Mt. Graham to provide the escape. The Swift Trail was constructed initially as a timber road for the pioneers, but later the settlers used it as their route up the mountain for their annual summer migration.

The road was later upgraded by the forest service and the Civilian Conservation Corps (CCC), which had many camps in the region.

There are many historical points of interest along the Swift Trail: the first comes at the boundary of the Coronado National Forest. A historical plaque commemorates P. J. and George Jacobson who constructed a sawmill farther up the canyon. The mill commenced operations in 1895 and provided the lumber for many of the buildings in the region. A second plaque commemorates Theodore T. Swift, who was supervisor of the Crook National Forest, now called the Coronado National Forest, from 1908 to 1923. Swift was the major force behind the upgrade of the original logging trail, and today the trail bears his name.

The first picnic ground to be reached, Noon Creek, is named as it was the mid-day rest stop for the early pioneers on their way up the mountains for the summer. The major CCC camp of the region was located near the picnic ground. Two hundred workers were housed in eight barracks in the complex. The summer camp was at Columbine; the winter camp was at Noon Creek. Some of the work completed by the CCC included fire lookouts and improvements to the Swift Trail. The Noon Creek Camp housed World War II German prisoners of war after its closure.

Twenty miles from the start of the trail is Heliograph Peak, so called because the army used it as a signaling point in the Apache War. Signals were flashed across southern Arizona by using mirrors to reflect the bright sunlight.

Shortly after Heliograph Peak, a side trail leads to Treasure Park, which has one of the most exciting stories of the trail. Supposedly, Mexican bandits buried nineteen bags of gold and silver here before the Gadsden Purchase. The gold has never been recovered. This is also the site of the first CCC camp in Arizona.

Hospital Flat, a short distance farther, gets its name from its use as a hospital in the summer by the soldiers from Fort Grant at the base of the north side of the mountain. Fort Grant was constructed as a military post in 1872 and housed soldiers who were active in the Indian Wars. It is now a state prison.

The University of Arizona's Steward Observatory houses three world-class telescopes and is a world-ranking astrophysical research organization. As well as housing its own equipment, the observatory also houses the Vatican Advanced Technology Telescope and Germany's Max Planck Submillimeter Telescope. A fourth telescope is under construction.

The next two sites along the trail commemorate early settlers. Peters Flat is named after Scottish-born Peter McBride, an early Gila Valley settler. While working as a logger on the mountain, McBride, as any good Scot would, planted potatoes. He stored them in long, earthen trenches before carrying them down the mountain to Safford for sale.

The second plaque is at Chesley Flat, which is named after the Chesley family, which had a cabin here in the 1890s. The family grazed cattle. Sarah Jane Chesley made and sold cheese from the milk.

The 11-acre Riggs Flat Lake was put in by the Arizona Game and Fish Department in 1957. The lake is named after Lew Riggs, who used the area as summer pasture for his cattle in the late 1870s and early 1880s.

Description

This easy trail is paved for two-thirds of its length and the remainder is a well-graded gravel road, making it a pleasant trail for those in passenger vehicles or anyone wanting to experience some cooler mountain temperatures and spectacular scenery. The trail commences on US 191, seven miles south of Safford at a well-marked intersection. Almost immediately the paved road starts to climb, switchbacking its way up into the Pinaleño Mountains. The creosote bush, mesquite, and cactus desert plains are quickly left behind, as the road passes through the pinyon pine, alligator juniper, and desert oak of the slightly higher elevations.

As the trail continues to climb into the national forest, there are many cool and shady picnic areas. Noon Creek is at the lowest elevation. Although shown on the forest maps as a campground, Noon Creek is now for picnicking only. A short distance farther along is the start of the Round-the-Mountain pack trail. There are horse corrals and a couple of pleasant picnic sites at the start. A historical plaque commemorates the work done by the boys who lived at the CCC camps located in the Pinaleño Mountains.

Most of the side trails leading off the main Swift Trail are either very short, only a

Riggs Flat Lake

View across Suphur Springs Valley toward the Galiuro Mountains

mile or two in length, or are inaccessible to the public by vehicle. The higher elevations have been designated as a refuge for the endangered Mt. Graham red squirrel since 1988. The forest service is currently considering whether to permit foot access into the area. Check with the national forest office in Safford for details.

Another road leads to the site of the University of Arizona Astrophysical Site. No public access is permitted to the observatory site.

There are many camping opportunities along this trail at any of several developed U.S. Forest Service campgrounds or at undeveloped sites that can be found along many of the short spur trails. In addition, there are undeveloped sites along the main trail, particularly around the turnoff to Riggs Flat Lake.

Riggs Flat Lake is an 11-acre lake devel-oped by the Arizona Game and Fish Department in 1957. The lake is stocked with trout. The popular campground surrounding it is one of the most pleasant along the trail. Campers should be aware that black bears abound in the Pinaleño Mountains and can be troublesome around the campgrounds. Normal and sensible precautions should be taken, and of course no food should be left outside at night unless it is in a bear-proof container. All trash containers at the picnic and camping ground are bear-proof.

The vehicle trail ends shortly after the turn to Riggs Flat Lake at the hiking trailhead for Taylor Pass.

The closure gate at the end of the paved road is locked each year from November 15 to April 15 due to snow. Snowmobiles can use the road during these months.

South Trail #24: Swift Trail

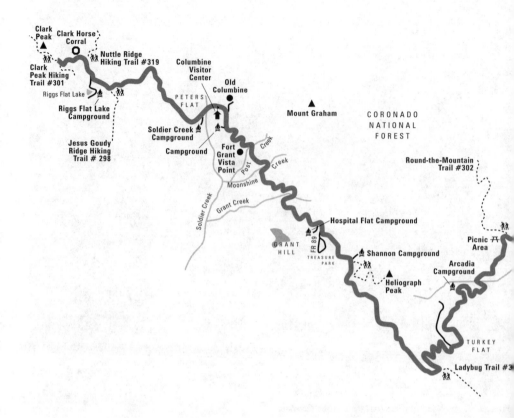

Current Road Information

Coronado National Forest
Safford Ranger District
711 14th Avenue, Suite D
Safford, AZ 85546
(928) 428-4150

Map References

BLM Safford
USFS Coronado National Forest: Safford
and Santa Catalina Ranger Districts
USGS 1:24,000 Artesia, Mt. Graham,
Stockton Pass, Webb Peak
1:100,000 Safford
Maptech CD-ROM: East Central Arizona/
White Mountains
Arizona Atlas & Gazetteer, pp. 68-69
Arizona Road & Recreation Atlas, pp. 48, 49,
82, 83
Recreational Map of Arizona

Route Directions

▼ 0.0   From US 191, 7 miles south of Safford
and 0.3 miles south of mile marker
114, zero trip meter and turn southwest on paved road sign-posted for the
Swift Trail (AZ 366).
GPS: N32°43.82' W109°42.85'

▼ 1.3   SO Cattle guard.
▼ 1.7   SO Graded road on left; then cattle guard.
▼ 3.1   SO Track on right.
GPS: N32°41.58' W109°45.03'

▼ 3.7   SO Cattle guard, road starts to climb and
switchback.
▼ 4.5   SO Entering Coronado National Forest.
Two historical plaques on right before
the sign commemorate P. J. and
George Jacobson and Theodore T.
Swift.

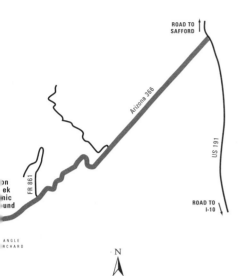

ROAD TO
SAFFORD ↑

Arizona 366

FR 861

US 191

ROAD TO
I-10

on
ek
nic
und

ANGLE
RCHARD

▲N

0 ━━━━━ 2
MILES

GPS: N32°41.14' W109°45.95'

▼5.5　SO　FR 861 on right goes to Jacobson
Overlook and a view of the Gila Valley.
GPS: N32°40.55' W109°46.65'

▼6.2　SO　FR 667 on left.
GPS: N32°40.20' W109°47.19'

▼6.7　SO　Noon Creek Picnic Ground on right. Zero
trip meter.
GPS: N32°40.08' W109°47.65'

▼0.0　　　Continue along paved road up the
mountain.

▼0.3　SO　T 329 Road on left goes to Angle
Orchard and Ladybug Trail.
GPS: N32°39.92' W109°47.75'

▼0.4　SO　Picnic area on right. Round-the-
Mountain Trail #302 to Marijalda

Creek (3.5 miles) and Frye Canyon Trail
#36 lead off through picnic ground.

▼2.3　BL　Picnic area on right. Bear left and
cross over creek. Closure gate.
GPS: N32°39.07' W109°48.75'

▼4.0　SO　Arcadia Campground on right. Fee area
on right. Zero trip meter.
GPS: N32°38.95' W109°49.07'

▼0.0　　　Continue to climb up mountain followed by road on left.

▼0.1　SO　Track on right to Upper Arcadia Group
Area.

▼0.6　SO　Track on left before closure gate.
GPS: N32°38.66' W109°49.01'

▼2.3　SO　Track on left and track on right. Turkey
Flat hiking trail #330 and Ladybug Trail
#329 on left. Start of Turkey Flat sum-
mer home area, many tracks on left
and right to private cabins.
GPS: N32°37.94' W109°48.93'

▼2.7　SO　Track on right before closure gate.

▼5.1　SO　Hiking trailhead #329, Ladybug Trail
on left, then closure gate. Ladybug
Saddle.
GPS: N32°37.34' W109°49.38'

▼6.3　SO　Road starts to level off. Views to south
over Sulphur Springs Valley.

▼8.9　SO　Snow Flat Road on left marked by a
sign. Zero trip meter.
GPS: N32°38.94' W109°51.71'

▼0.0　　　Continue along paved road.

▼0.6　SO　Graded road on right goes to
Heliograph Peak. The road is closed to
vehicles but you can hike up. Second
track on right leads to Shannon
Campground.
GPS: N32°39.38' W109°51.58'

▼1.0　SO　Track on right is closed road to High
Peak, road turns to graded dirt. Closure
gate, road is closed past this point
from Nov. 15 to April 15. Zero trip
meter.
GPS: N32°39.58' W109°51.87'

▼ 0.0   Continue on graded dirt road.
▼ 0.7   SO Track on left is FR 89, a short loop to Treasure Park.
         GPS: N32°39.88' W109°52.36'

▼ 0.9   SO Track on right to group campsite; then track on left to Hospital Flat Campground and nature trail.
▼ 1.6   SO Track on right and track on left. Track on left is closed to vehicles after a short distance, parking for Grant Hill loop trail #322 for mountain bikes and hiking.
         GPS: N32°40.11' W109°52.78'

▼ 2.7   SO Cross over Grant Creek.
▼ 3.1   SO Two tracks on left.
▼ 3.2   SO Cunningham Loop hiking trail #316 which goes to Grant Hill on right, for mountain bikes and hiking.
         GPS: N32°40.80' W109°53.56'

▼ 3.3   SO Track on left to Cunningham Campground and corrals. Crane Creek hiking trailhead #305 leads off through campground.
▼ 3.9   SO Cross over Moonshine Creek and track on left.
▼ 4.7   SO Cross over Post Creek.
▼ 5.0   SO Fort Grant Vista Point, elevation 9,356 feet. Views to Fort Grant at the foot of the mountain.
         GPS: N32°41.54' W109°54.24'

▼ 5.6   SO Graded road on right leads to observatory site.
▼ 5.9   SO Track on left to campsites.
         GPS: N32°41.88' W109°54.56'

▼ 6.3   SO Track on right goes to Old Columbine. Zero trip meter and continue following the sign to Riggs Flat Lake. Columbine Work Center on the left at the intersection.
         GPS: N32°42.23' W109°54.71'

▼ 0.0   Continue to the northwest.
▼ 0.1   SO Columbine Visitor Center on left, track on right to Ash Creek trailhead and public corral.

▼ 0.4   SO Track on left; then track on right.
▼ 0.5   SO Soldier Creek Campground on left.
         GPS: N32°42.13' W109°55.15'

▼ 0.9   SO Track on right.
▼ 1.4   SO Historical marker on left for Peters Flat.
▼ 2.4   SO Chesley Flat. Historical marker on right.
         GPS: N32°42.96' W109°56.35'

▼ 3.0   SO Track on right.
▼ 3.6   SO Track on right and campsite on right.
▼ 3.7   SO Jesus Goudy Ridge hiking trail #298 on left.
▼ 3.8   SO Riggs Flat Lake is glimpsed through the trees on the left.
▼ 4.4   SO Track on left is FR 287, which goes 0.4 miles to Riggs Flat Lake and campground.
         GPS: N32°42.83' W109°57.82'

▼ 4.5   SO Track on left.
▼ 4.7   SO Nuttle Ridge hiking trail #319 on right, several campsites. Then tracks on left and right.
▼ 4.9   SO Clark Horse Corral and two campsites with picnic tables and fire rings on right.
         GPS: N32°43.17' W109°58.15'

▼ 5.5   Trail ends at a small turnaround, with a view to the northwest. A small vehicle trail does a short loop back to the road. Carter Nuttle #315 and Clark Peak #301 hiking trailheads commence here and travel 7 miles to West Peak Lookout and 4 miles to Taylor Pass.
         GPS: N32°43.04' W109°58.60'

Tripp Canyon Road

STARTING POINT	US 70, immediately west of Pima
FINISHING POINT	Blue Jay Peak
TOTAL MILEAGE	26.4 miles
UNPAVED MILEAGE	25.7 miles
DRIVING TIME	2 hours (one-way)
ELEVATION RANGE	2,900–8,600
USUALLY OPEN	April to November
BEST TIME TO TRAVEL	April to November
DIFFICULTY RATING	3
SCENIC RATING	8
REMOTENESS RATING	+0

Special Attractions

- Fire lookout tower.
- Popular backcountry camping at the sawmill.
- Access to many hiking trails.

Description

This is one of two roads that access the top of the Pinaleño Mountains; other roads access the side canyons but do not climb to the top. The Tripp Canyon Road is the quieter and shorter of the two, climbing high along the side of Tripp Canyon, winding its way to the fire lookout at the top.

The trail leaves just west of Pima on US 70 at the sign for Tripp Canyon Road. The first few miles are graded dirt road as it sweeps around the bajada on the west side of the Pinaleño Mountains. The road can be extremely washboardy depending on when it last saw a grader. There are some pleasant views to the north and over eroded washes to Bear Springs Flat.

After 14.5 miles it enters the Coronado National Forest and starts to follow alongside wide Tripp Canyon. Here the trail starts to climb along a wide shelf road above Tripp Canyon. The vegetation changes quickly as you start to climb, leaving behind the cre-osote bush, prickly pear, and chollas of the lower slopes to enter manzanita and oak, and then on to enter the alligator juniper and pine of the higher elevations.

Campers will enjoy the plentiful sites to be found near Sawmill Canyon. There is a large, flat, shady area with many pleasant, informal sites both alongside the graded road and down a side trail.

The final section of the trail, as it ascends to the fire lookout, is the steepest and roughest. Passenger vehicles should stop at the hiking trail to Blue Jay Ridge #314. High-clearance 2WD vehicles can continue although 4WD is preferred on the loose surface.

At the top, there is a trail on the left to the lookout. It is gated shut, but you can hike the 0.2 miles to the lookout tower on West Peak. The vehicle trail continues past the tower for another 1.7 miles as a smaller formed trail before becoming a hiking trail.

Current Road Information

Coronado National Forest
Safford Ranger District
711 14th Avenue, Suite D
Safford, AZ 85546
(928) 428-4150

Bureau of Land Management
Safford Field Office
711 14th Ave.
Safford, AZ 85546
(928) 348-4400

Map References

BLM Safford
USFS Coronado National Forest: Safford and Santa Catalina Ranger Districts
USGS 1:24,000 Pima, Thatcher, Shingle Mill Mtn., Tripp Canyon
1:100,000 Safford
Maptech CD-ROM: East Central Arizona/ White Mountains
Arizona Atlas & Gazetteer, p. 68
Arizona Road & Recreation Atlas, pp. 49, 48, 83, 82
Recreational Map of Arizona

South Trail #25: Tripp Canyon Road

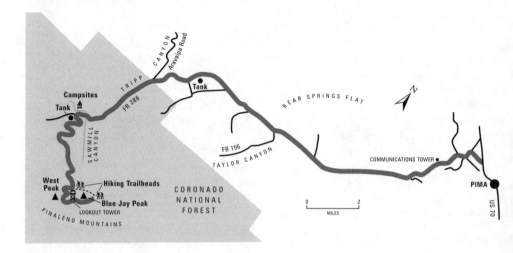

Route Directions

▼ 0.0   From US 70, immediately west of Pima, zero trip meter and turn west on the paved Tripp Canyon Road. Immediately cross railroad.
GPS: N32°54.00' W109°50.40'

▼ 0.7   TL   T-intersection. Turn left onto graded dirt road.
GPS: N32°54.01' W109°51.08'

▼ 0.9   TR   Crossroads, turn right, ahead is a dead end.
GPS: N32°53.80' W109°51.10'

▼ 1.2   BL   Cattle guard; then bear left, remaining on main graded road. Two tracks on right.

▼ 1.8   SO   Track on left.

▼ 2.1   SO   Communications tower on right.
GPS: N32°53.05' W109°51.80'

▼ 2.8   SO   Track on left; then cattle guard.

▼ 3.4   SO   Track on left.

▼ 4.3   SO   Communications tower on left; then cattle guard.

▼ 6.0   SO   Graded road on left and track on right.
GPS: N32°50.76' W109°54.64'

▼ 7.1   SO   Well-used track on right.
GPS: N32°50.51' W109°55.74'

▼ 8.1   SO   Track on right.

▼ 8.9   BR   Cattle guard, then bear right, following sign to Tripp Canyon, FR 286. Track on left is FR 156 to Taylor Canyon. Zero trip meter.
GPS: N32°50.36' W109°57.57'

▼ 0.0   Continue to the west.

▼ 0.4   SO   Track on right.

▼ 1.1   SO   Track on left.
GPS: N32°50.35' W109°58.78'

▼ 1.8   SO   Track on left is private.

▼ 2.0   SO   Track on left.

▼ 2.1   SO   Cattle guard.

▼ 2.4   SO   Track on left.

▼ 3.5   SO   Tank on left.
GPS: N32°50.19' W110°01.25'

▼ 4.1   SO   Track on left.

▼ 5.4   SO   Cattle guard.

▼ 5.6   SO   Track on right is Aravaipa Road, then cattle guard. Entering Coronado National Forest. Zero trip meter.
GPS: N32°48.95' W110°02.58'

▼ 0.0   Continue to the southwest.

The upper end of the trail winds through pine forest

▼ 0.9	SO	Corral on right.
▼ 3.2	SO	Cross over wash; then cattle guard. Entering Sawmill Canyon.
		GPS: N32°46.64' W110°03.80'

▼ 3.3	SO	Corral and two tracks on right (both to campsites).
		GPS: N32°46.65' W110°03.87'

▼ 3.4	SO	Concrete and stone footings on right. Large camping area.
		GPS: N32°46.58' W110°03.96'

▼ 3.5	SO	Two tracks on right at mile marker 7. Zero trip meter.
		GPS: N32°46.56' W110°04.00'

▼ 0.0		Continue to the south.
▼ 0.1	SO	Concrete tank on right.
▼ 0.3	SO	Small track on left.
▼ 1.2	SO	Faint track on right.
▼ 3.9	SO	Track on left at mile marker 3 goes to shady campsites and dry lake. Zero trip meter.
		GPS: N32°45.26' W110°03.20'

▼ 0.0		Continue to the south.
▼ 1.5	SO	Hiking trail on left is Blue Jay Ridge hiking trail #314.
		GPS: N32°44.65' W110°02.35'

▼ 2.8	SO	Track on left is gated and goes to the lookout tower. It is 0.2 miles to the tower, which is staffed during the wildfire season.
		GPS: N32°44.15' W110°02.40'

▼ 3.9	SO	Hiking trail straight on is Blue Jay Ridge hiking trail #314; small hiking trail out to right at this point.
		GPS: N32°44.45' W110°01.46'

▼ 4.5		Trail ends for vehicles at turn around at base of Blue Jay Peak. It continues as a single-track, hiking trail.
		GPS: N32°44.83' W110°01.56'

Willow Springs Road

STARTING POINT	Arizona 177 at Kelvin
FINISHING POINT	Arizona 77, 5.8 miles southwest of Oracle
TOTAL MILEAGE	49.8 miles
UNPAVED MILEAGE	48.2 miles
DRIVING TIME	1.5 hours
ELEVATION RANGE	1,800–3,200 feet
USUALLY OPEN	Year-round
BEST TIME TO TRAVEL	October to June
DIFFICULTY RATING	2
SCENIC RATING	7
REMOTENESS RATING	+0

Special Attractions

■ Long, easy trail through scenic ranchland.
■ Site of the old settlement of Barkerville.
■ Sweeping vistas and grasslands.

Description

A glance at the maps of the region gives an indication of what some of the earliest travelers and settlers thought of this area. Suffering Wash, Bloodsucker Wash, Rattlesnake Tank, and Hot Boy Mine tell their own tales. This trail runs through an arid region of southern Arizona, passing through some old, established ranches and grasslands, giving views of the Tortilla Mountains and the Santa Catalinas.

The trail leaves Kelvin, initially following the well-graded Florence–Kelvin Highway. The views are sweeping as the trail climbs up to the plateau. Jumbled rocks and cacti combine to provide an interesting and scenic landscape.

The trail turns down alongside Box O Wash and heads toward small Cottonwood Hill, which is the site of Barkerville. Between 1924 and 1933 Barkerville had a small store and post office run by the Barker family. At the time there was still a motor stage between Florence and Tucson. There was also a small school serving the children of the surrounding ranches. Nowadays the children attend school in Winkelman and Superior.

The trail is easygoing and roughly graded its entire length. Much of it passes through private ranchland, only some of which is posted. If you take any side trails or make camp, make certain that you are on public lands. Part of the trail runs through state land and a valid permit is required.

The final part of the trail passes through Willow Springs Ranch and eventually joins with Arizona 77 near Oracle. There are excellent views of the Santa Catalinas from this section of the trail.

Current Road Information

Bureau of Land Management
Tucson Field Office
12661 East Broadway Blvd.
Tucson, AZ 85748
(520) 258-7200

Map References

BLM   Globe, Mesa, Casa Grande, Mammoth

USGS   1:24,000   Kearny, Grayback, Ninetysix Hills NE, Ninetysix Hills SE, Black Mtn., Fortified Peak, North of Oracle, Oracle
1:100,000 Globe, Mesa, Casa Grande, Mammoth

A view across the trail to a corral and Black Mountain beyond

Maptech CD-ROM: East Central Arizona/
    White Mountains; Phoenix/Superstition Mountains
Arizona Atlas & Gazetteer, pp. 59, 67
Arizona Road & Recreation Atlas, pp. 48, 82
Recreational Map of Arizona

Route Directions

▼ 0.0   From Arizona 177, at the turn for
           Kelvin, turn southwest immediately
           north of the railroad crossing and zero
           trip meter. Road is paved and is known
           as the Florence–Kelvin Highway. Cross
           cattle guard, and follow along the north
           side of the railroad, remaining on
           paved road.
12.4 ▲   Trail ends at the intersection with
           Arizona 177 at Kelvin. Turn left for
           Superior, turn right for Winkelman.
           GPS: N33°07.28′ W110°58.49′

▼ 1.2   SO Cross railroad; then cross over Gila
              River on bridge.
11.2 ▲   SO Cross over Gila River on bridge; then
              cross railroad.

▼ 1.3   SO Road on left is Riverside Road.
              Continue straight ahead on paved
              Florence–Kelvin Highway.
11.1 ▲   SO Road on right is Riverside Road.
              Continue straight ahead to Kelvin.
           GPS: N33°06.14′ W110°58.43′

▼ 1.6   SO Road turns to graded dirt.
10.8 ▲   SO Road is now paved.

▼ 1.8   SO Cattle guard.
10.6 ▲   SO Cattle guard.

▼ 3.7   SO Cross through Ripsey Wash, track on
              left up wash.
8.7 ▲   SO Cross through Ripsey Wash, track on
              right up wash.
           GPS: N33°05.81′ W111°00.39′

▼ 4.0   BL Ranch road on right.
8.4 ▲   BR Ranch road on left.
           GPS: N33°05.85′ W111°00.62′

▼ 5.6   SO Cross through Zelleweger Wash,
              tracks on right and left down wash.
6.8 ▲   SO Cross through Zelleweger Wash,
              tracks on right and left down wash.

▼ 7.1   SO Cross through wash.
5.3 ▲   SO Cross through wash.

▼ 7.3   SO Track on left.
5.1 ▲   SO Track on right.

▼ 7.8   SO Track on left.
4.6 ▲   SO Track on right.

▼ 8.2   BL Graded road on right goes to radio
              tower.
4.2 ▲   BR Graded road on left goes to radio
              tower.
           GPS: N33°02.73′ W111°02.78′

▼ 9.8   SO Track on left.
2.6 ▲   SO Track on right.

▼ 10.1   SO Track on left.
2.3 ▲   SO Track on right.

▼ 10.8   SO Track on right.
1.6 ▲   SO Track on left.

▼ 11.1   SO Track on right; then cattle guard.
1.3 ▲   SO Cattle guard; then track on left.

▼ 11.2   SO Cross through wash.
1.2 ▲   SO Cross through wash.

▼ 11.3   SO Cross through wash.
1.1 ▲   SO Cross through wash.

▼ 11.5   SO Cross through wash.
0.9 ▲   SO Cross through wash.

▼ 11.7   SO Track on right to Teacup Ranch.
0.7 ▲   SO Track on left to Teacup Ranch.

▼ 12.4   SO Track on left through gate onto well-
              used, formed track. Zero trip meter.
0.0 ▲   Continue to the northeast.
           GPS: N33°00.04′ W111°03.84′

▼ 0.0   Continue to the southwest.
4.1 ▲   SO Track on right through gate onto well-used formed track. Zero trip meter.

▼ 0.1   SO Cattle guard; then private access road on left.
4.0 ▲   SO Private access road on right; then cattle guard.

▼ 2.0   SO Track on right.
2.1 ▲   SO Track on left.

▼ 2.2   SO Cross through wide Donnelly Wash.
1.9 ▲   SO Cross through wide Donnelly Wash.

▼ 2.8   SO Track on right to rock formations.
1.3 ▲   SO Track on left to rock formations.

▼ 3.1   BL Graded road on right is Cochran Road, leads out to an area of tumbled boulders.
1.0 ▲   BR Graded road on left is Cochran Road, leads out to area of tumbled boulders.
      GPS: N32°59.23′ W111°06.84′

▼ 3.5   SO Track on right.
0.6 ▲   SO Track on left.

▼ 4.1   TL At crossing of Box O Wash, turn left onto graded road alongside wash, signed Barkerville Road. Zero trip meter.
0.0 ▲   Continue to the northeast.
      GPS: N32°58.49′ W111°07.47′

▼ 0.0   Continue to the south.
13.9 ▲   TR Turn right onto wide, graded dirt road, signed Florence–Kelvin Highway. Zero trip meter.

▼ 0.1   SO Cattle guard, road swings away from wash.
13.8 ▲   SO Cattle guard, road runs alongside Box Wash.

▼ 0.4   SO Track on right.
13.5 ▲   SO Track on left.

▼ 1.3   SO Track on right; then track on left.
12.6 ▲   SO Track on right; then track on left.

▼ 1.6   SO Track on left.
12.3 ▲   SO Track on right.

▼ 1.7   SO Track on left.
12.2 ▲   SO Track on right.

▼ 2.4   BL Track on right.
11.5 ▲   BR Second entrance to track on left.
      GPS: N32°56.79′ W111°06.05′

▼ 2.5   SO Second entrance to track on right, then track left.
11.4 ▲   SO Track on right; then track on left.

▼ 5.3   SO Cattle guard.
8.6 ▲   SO Cattle guard.

▼ 5.6   SO Cross through wash.
8.3 ▲   SO Cross through wash.

▼ 6.0   SO Track on left; then cross through wash.
7.9 ▲   SO Cross through wash; then track on right.

▼ 6.3   SO Cross through wash; then track on right.
7.6 ▲   SO Track on left; then cross through wash.
      GPS: N32°54.20′ W111°03.39′

▼ 7.3   SO Track on left.
6.6 ▲   SO Track on right.

▼ 8.8   SO Track on right.
5.1 ▲   SO Track on left.
      GPS: N32°52.82′ W111°01.44′

▼ 9.9   SO Track on left.
4.0 ▲   SO Track on right.
      GPS: N32°52.49′ W111°00.34′

▼ 11.1   SO Cattle guard, well on left, then track on left past well. Second track left and track on right.
2.8 ▲   SO Track on left, track on right, then second track on right at well, then cattle guard.
      GPS: N32°51.82′ W110°59.27′

South Trail #26: Willow Springs Road

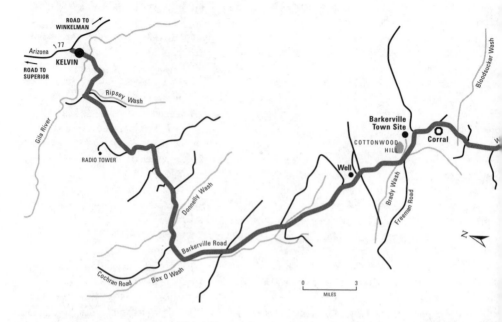

▼11.3 SO Cross gas pipeline, tracks on right and left along pipeline.

2.6 ▲ SO Cross gas pipeline, tracks on right and left along pipeline.

▼11.7 SO Cattle guard, track on left along fence line.

2.2 ▲ SO Cattle guard, track on right along fence line.

▼12.2 SO Track on right.

1.7 ▲ SO Track on left.

▼12.6 SO Track on left.

1.3 ▲ SO Track on right.

▼12.9 SO Cross through wash.

1.0 ▲ SO Cross through wash.

▼13.6 SO Track on left.

0.3 ▲ SO Track on right.

▼13.8 SO Cross through Brady Wash, track on right up wash. Traveling through Haystack Valley, Cottonwood Hill is on left.

0.1 ▲ SO Cross through Brady Wash, track on

left up wash. Traveling through Haystack Valley, Cottonwood Hill is on the right.

GPS: N32°50.13' W110°57.66'

▼13.9 BL Graded road on right is Freeman Road. Zero trip meter.

0.0 ▲ Continue to the northwest on Barkerville Road.

GPS: N32°50.03' W110°57.53'

▼0.0 Join Freeman Road and continue to the east.

1.5 ▲ BR Graded road on left is Freeman Road. Zero trip meter.

▼0.1 SO Track on right, then cross through Haystack Valley Wash.

1.4 ▲ SO Cross through Haystack Valley Wash, then track on left.

▼0.3 SO Two tracks on right to corral.

1.2 ▲ SO Two tracks on left to corral.

▼0.4 SO Cross through wash.

1.1 ▲ SO Cross through wash.

and track on right.

8.2 ▲ SO Several tracks on right, corral on left and track on left.

GPS: N32°49.07′ W110°54.94′

▼ 1.6 SO Cattle guard.
8.1 ▲ SO Cattle guard.

▼ 1.9 SO Track on left.
7.8 ▲ SO Track on right.

▼ 2.1 SO Cross through wash; then track on right.
7.6 ▲ SO Track on left; then cross through wash.

▼ 2.6 SO Cattle guard.
7.1 ▲ SO Cattle guard.

▼ 3.1 SO Track on right; then track on left.
6.6 ▲ SO Track on right; then track on left.

▼ 3.7 SO Track on right.
6.0 ▲ SO Track on left.

GPS: N32°47.43′ W110°55.52′

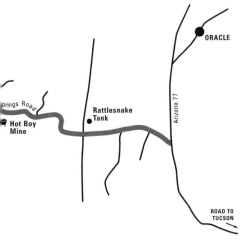

▼ 0.6 SO Cattle guard.
0.9 ▲ SO Cattle guard.

▼ 0.7 SO Track on left. Barkerville town site.
0.8 ▲ SO Track on right. Barkerville town site.

▼ 1.1 SO Cattle guard.
0.4 ▲ SO Cattle guard.

▼ 1.2 SO Track on right.
0.3 ▲ SO Track on left.

▼ 1.5 TR Turn onto graded dirt Willow Springs Road. Zero trip meter.
0.0 ▲ Continue southwest on Freeman Road.

GPS: N32°50.08′ W110°55.93′

▼ 0.0 Continue south on Willow Springs Road.
9.7 ▲ TL Turn left onto graded dirt Freeman Road. Zero trip meter.

▼ 0.5 SO Track on right.
9.2 ▲ SO Track on left.

▼ 1.5 SO Several tracks on left, corral on right

▼ 3.8 SO Track on left; then cattle guard.
5.9 ▲ SO Cattle guard; then track on right.

▼ 4.3 SO Track on right.
5.4 ▲ SO Track on left.

▼ 4.8 SO Cattle guard.
4.9 ▲ SO Cattle guard.

▼ 5.4 SO Track on right.
4.3 ▲ SO Track on left.

GPS: N32°45.98′ W110°55.12′

▼ 5.8 SO Cattle guard.
3.9 ▲ SO Cattle guard.

▼ 6.5 SO Track on left.
3.2 ▲ SO Track on right.

GPS: N32°45.29′ W110°54.17′

▼ 6.8 SO Track on right.
2.9 ▲ SO Track on left.

▼ 7.2 SO Track on left.

2.5 ▲   SO Track on right.

▼ 7.5   SO Remains of Hot Boy Mine on right.
2.2 ▲   SO Remains of Hot Boy Mine on left.
          GPS: N32º44.50' W110º53.77'

▼ 8.1   SO Cross through wash, tracks on right and left up and down wash.
1.6 ▲   SO Cross through wash, tracks on left and right up and down wash.

▼ 8.3   SO Track on right.
1.4 ▲   SO Track on left.

▼ 8.7   SO Track on left; then cattle guard.
1.0 ▲   SO Cattle guard; then track on right.

▼ 9.0   SO Cross through wash.
0.7 ▲   SO Cross through wash.

▼ 9.7   SO Major graded road on left goes into Willow Springs Ranch. Zero trip meter.
0.0 ▲   Continue to the north.
          GPS: N32º42.80' W110º53.61'

▼ 0.0   Continue to the south.
8.8 ▲   SO Major graded road on right goes into Willow Springs Ranch. Zero trip meter.

▼ 0.1   SO Track on right.
8.7 ▲   SO Track on left.

▼ 0.5   SO Track on right follows gas pipeline.
8.3 ▲   SO Track on left follows gas pipeline.

▼ 1.6   SO Cross through wash.
7.2 ▲   SO Cross through wash.

▼ 2.7   SO Track on right.
6.1 ▲   SO Track on left.

▼ 2.8   SO Exit Willow Springs Ranch.
6.0 ▲   SO Enter Willow Springs Ranch under archway.
          GPS: N32º41.20' W110º53.83'

▼ 3.8   SO Track on left and track on right along pipeline.
5.0 ▲   SO Track on left and track on right along pipeline.

▼ 4.5   SO Track on left.
4.3 ▲   SO Track on right.

▼ 4.6   SO Track on left.
4.2 ▲   SO Track on right.

▼ 4.9   SO Track on left.
3.9 ▲   SO Track on right.

▼ 5.1   SO Track on left; then cross through wash.
3.7 ▲   SO Cross through wash; then track on right.

▼ 6.0   SO Track on right, cattle guard; then track on right.
2.8 ▲   SO Track on left, cattle guard; then track on left.

▼ 7.5   SO Track on right.
1.3 ▲   SO Track on left.

▼ 7.6   SO Track on right underneath power lines; then cattle guard.
1.2 ▲   SO Cattle guard; then track on left underneath power lines.

▼ 8.0   SO Track on right; then cross through wash.
0.8 ▲   SO Cross through wash; then track on left.

▼ 8.5   SO Track on right.
0.3 ▲   SO Track on left.

▼ 8.8   Trail ends at the intersection with Arizona 77, turn left for Oracle, turn right for Tucson.
0.0 ▲   Trail commences on Arizona 77, just south of mile marker 96, at sign for Willow Springs Road. Zero trip meter and turn north over cattle guard on graded dirt road.
          GPS: N32º36.03' W110º52.26'

Oracle Control Road

STARTING POINT	Catalina Highway at Summerhaven
FINISHING POINT	American Avenue in Oracle
TOTAL MILEAGE	26.9 miles
UNPAVED MILEAGE	23.7 miles
DRIVING TIME	2.5 hours
ELEVATION RANGE	4,500–7,900 feet
USUALLY OPEN	Year-round
BEST TIME TO TRAVEL	Year-round
DIFFICULTY RATING	2
SCENIC RATING	8
REMOTENESS RATING	+0

Special Attractions

■ Less-traveled dirt road that accesses Summerhaven at the top of Mt. Lemmon.
■ Historic site of the American Flag Mine.

History

The Santa Catalina Mountains have been a magnet for many people over the years because of their cool, lofty heights that offer a respite from summer heat. Some of the earliest people to visit the mountains were the Hohokam Indians and later the Apache, who reaped food and made clothing and medicine from the various plants in this magnificent range. The Tohono O'odham tribe to the south thought the mountain range was shaped like an enormous frog and named it Babad Do'ag (Frog Mountain in their language).

One of the early mining pioneers in this region, Albert Weldon, had traveled west around Cape Horn aboard the *The Oracle*. When he finally settled in a likely spot in the early 1880s, he gave the name Oracle to the region around his small adobe homestead where he prospected on a small scale. Later the Apache Mine started producing bigger returns. Another early mine was the American Flag just south of Oracle. It was founded and developed by Isaac Lorraine in the late 1870s. He worked it until he was bought out by the Richardson Mining Company in the East. Lorraine developed a ranch with the proceeds. The mine had played out by the mid-1880s and the small community of American Flag dwindled.

Nevertheless, Oracle continued to slowly evolve and by 1895 a successful rancher, Bill Neal, and his wife had built the comfortable Mountain View Hotel, which soon attracted many travelers en route to Tucson. Bill had spent time riding with Buffalo Bill Cody in his earlier years, so one of their regular guests was Buffalo Bill himself, who took an interest in the local mines until his death in 1917.

The most famous peak in the Santa Catalina Mountains is undoubtedly Mt. Lemmon. It was named after botanist John Lemmon who, along with his new bride, came from California in 1881 to study the plant life in the Santa Catalinas. Having unsuccessfully attempted to reach the peak from the southern side, they completed their ascent from the north with the assistance of a local pioneer miner and rancher named Oliver Stratton. Lemmon documented six new plants on their journey and identified the less-common Arizona variety of ponderosa pine as having needles clumped in groups of five; the more regular variety had three. Their guide, Stratton, has given his name to several features on the north side of the mountain, including Stratton Wash, Stratton Camp Spring, and Stratton Mine.

In the late 1880s and early 1890s a number of people tried to develop ranches in the Santa Catalina Mountains. Others came to log trees to supply the mines and feed the growing housing construction in the valley below. The name Summerhaven is attributed to a reporter from the *Arizona Star*, Fred Kimball, who like others saw the high elevations as a summer retreat from the heat and named the area Summerhaven. Early summer vacationers made the long haul up this southern approach from Oracle by mule and horse to be rewarded with the cooler climate. The first inn was constructed on the mountain in the 1920s and was located in what is now Summerhaven.

The original route was a lot narrower and more twisty than it is today. The switchbacks near the top were so tight that vehicles had to back up several times to make the turns. The road was only wide enough for a single vehicle; as the area gained popularity traffic jams were not uncommon. A novel solution to the problem was adopted. A timber arch at the bottom and top marked the start of a controlled section of the road where travelers were required to drive in a set direction for a specified time interval. For a certain number of hours a day only uphill travel was permitted. Then the direction was reversed for the next few hours. Fines were imposed on anyone who broke the honor system. This unique system of traffic flow led to the name in use today: the Oracle Control Road.

By the early 1930s, Summerhaven residents and merchants craved a speedier road to their summer retreat, and an alternative route from Tucson was sought. Under the suggestion of Frank Hitchcock, the general postmaster at the time, discussions took place regarding the use of prison labor to construct a new route from the south at a reduced cost. President Herbert Hoover authorized the use of thousands of non-violent prison inmates to build the Hitchcock Highway, also known as the Catalina Highway. Construction of the new southerly approach began in 1933 and was completed in 1950.

The original Oracle Control Road remained as an emergency escape route from wildfire on the mountain, as well as a scenic drive for recreationalists. Many have complained of its condition over the decades, yet it remains a peaceful northerly approach to the Santa Catalina Mountains.

Description
The Oracle Control Road provides alterna-

An old corral at the start of the Arizona Trail

tive access to the paved Catalina Highway, which climbs up Mt. Lemmon from Tucson. The graded dirt road travels the north side of the mountain and gives access to other 4WD trails, campsites, and hiking trails. At the highest elevations of the trail, on Mt. Lemmon, travelers pass through oak and pine forests. The trail gradually descends, giving great views of Marble Peak and farther down the San Pedro River Valley with the San Manuel Copper Mine visible in front of the Galiuro Mountains. The trail surface is rough enough that a high-clearance vehicle is preferred as the trail follows a shelf road down toward Oracle. The shelf road is wide enough for a single vehicle with plenty of passing places.

As the trail gradually descends, it leaves behind the pine trees of the higher elevations and passes through scrubby oak, mesquite, and grassland. The vegetation is more open and the views more wide-ranging. The trail winds around the east side of Oracle Ridge, passing Rice Peak (7,575 feet). Tracks lead off in both directions from this section and there are many campsites with excellent views, although little shade.

The US Forest Service campground at Peppersauce Wash is passed opposite the start of the Rice Peak Trail, a challenging trail that climbs to the top of Rice Peak. The campground can get full very quickly on weekends. A fee is required. Peppersauce Wash was named by a group of hot sauce-loving cowboys who used to stash their bottle of pepper sauce in a hollow tree near where they traditionally camped.

After the campground, the trail standard improves to a wide, graded road. Passenger vehicles will have no difficulty traveling from Oracle to Peppersauce USFS Campground.

The lower end of the trail passes by the remains of American Flag. A historical marker is affixed to the major surviving building, the old post office, which is still in use today as a private cabin.

The trail can be open year-round, but snowfall may close the trail briefly some winters. Call ahead if in doubt.

Current Road Information

Coronado National Forest
Santa Catalina Ranger District
5700 North Sabino Canyon Rd.
Tucson, AZ 85750
(520) 749-8700

Map References

BLM   Tucson, Mammoth
USFS   Coronado National Forest: Safford
       and Santa Catalina Ranger Districts
USGS   1:24,000 Mt. Lemmon, Mt.
       Bigelow, Campo Bonito, Oracle
       1:100,000 Tucson, Mammoth
Maptech CD-ROM: Southeast Arizona/
       Tucson; Phoenix/Superstition Mountains
Arizona Atlas & Gazetteer, p. 67
Arizona Road & Recreation Atlas, pp. 48, 82
Recreational Map of Arizona

Route Directions

▼ 0.0		From Summerhaven, at the end of the Catalina Highway from Tucson, zero trip meter and turn north on the paved Oracle Control Road sign-posted to Peppersauce USFS Campground and Oracle. The intersection is north of mile marker 21.
	6.3 ▲	Trail ends at Summerhaven, on the Catalina Highway from Tucson. Turn right for Summerhaven, turn left for Tucson.
		GPS: N32°26.88′ W110°45.24′
▼ 0.1		SO Pass through fire stations and closure gate. Road turns to graded dirt.
	6.2 ▲	SO Road is now paved. Pass through closure gate and fire stations.
▼ 0.2		SO Oracle Ridge hiking trail #1 on left and parking area, then cattle guard.
	6.1 ▲	SO Cattle guard, then Oracle Ridge hiking trail #1 on right and parking area.
		GPS: N32°27.09′ W110°45.21′
▼ 1.5		SO Track on left to campsites.
	4.8 ▲	SO Track on right to campsites.
▼ 2.3		SO Track on right to campsite.

South Trail #27: Oracle Control Road

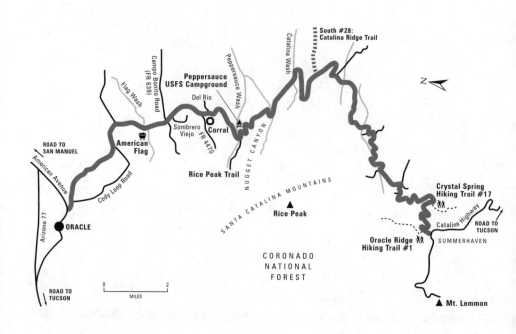

4.0 ▲	SO	Track on left to campsite.

▼ 2.7	SO	Closure gate; then track on left.
3.6 ▲	SO	Track on right; then closure gate.

▼ 2.8	SO	Track on left; then Crystal Spring hiking trail #17 on right.
3.5 ▲	SO	Crystal Spring hiking trail #17 on left; then track on right.
		GPS: N32°26.95' W110°44.20'

▼ 5.0	SO	Track on left.
1.3 ▲	SO	Track on right.
		GPS: N32°27.82' W110°44.13'

▼ 5.4	SO	Track on right; then cattle guard, then second well-used track on right.
0.9 ▲	SO	Well-used track on left; then cattle guard, then second track on left.
		GPS: N32°27.82' W110°43.89'

▼ 6.3	TR	Well-used track on left is private road to Oracle Ridge Mine. Zero trip meter.
0.0 ▲		Continue to climb toward

		Summerhaven.
		GPS: N32°28.42' W110°43.55'

▼ 0.0		Continue to descend toward Oracle, then small track on right.
2.4 ▲	TL	Small track on left; then well-used track straight ahead is private road to Oracle Ridge Mine. Zero trip meter.

▼ 0.4	SO	Pipeline on left and right.
2.0 ▲	SO	Pipeline on left and right.

▼ 1.0	SO	Cross over wash.
1.4 ▲	SO	Cross over wash.

▼ 1.4	SO	Campsite on right with good views.
1.0 ▲	SO	Campsite on left with good views.

▼ 1.6	SO	Track on right.
0.8 ▲	SO	Track on left.

▼ 2.4	SO	Graded road on right through gate. Zero trip meter
0.0 ▲		Continue to the southwest on FR 38.

▼ 0.0   Continue to the northeast.
4.5 ▲ SO Graded road on left through gate, continue straight on remaining on FR 38. Zero trip meter.

▼ 0.2 SO Cross through wash.
4.3 ▲ SO Cross through wash.

▼ 0.5 SO Track on left.
4.0 ▲ SO Track on right.

▼ 0.7 SO Cross over Gibb Wash on bridge.
3.8 ▲ SO Cross over Gibb Wash on bridge.

▼ 1.0 SO Track on right.
3.5 ▲ SO Track on left.

▼ 1.8 SO Cattle guard.
2.7 ▲ SO Cattle guard.
GPS: N32º29.35' W110º41.71'

▼ 2.1 SO Cross over wash.
2.4 ▲ SO Cross over wash.

▼ 2.9 SO Cross over wash on bridge.
1.6 ▲ SO Cross over wash on bridge.
GPS: N32º29.66' W110º41.05'

▼ 3.0 SO Private drive on left; then cattle guard.
1.5 ▲ SO Cattle guard; then private drive on right.

▼ 3.1 SO Cross through wash.
1.4 ▲ SO Cross through wash.

▼ 3.3 SO Track on right is private.
1.2 ▲ SO Track on left is private.

▼ 3.5 SO Cross through wash.
1.0 ▲ SO Cross through wash.
GPS: N32º30.04' W110º40.89'

▼ 4.2 SO Track on right.
0.3 ▲ SO Track on left.

▼ 4.4 SO Track on right.
0.1 ▲ SO Track on left.

▼ 4.5 SO Track on right is South #28: Catalina Ridge Trail. Zero trip meter.
0.0 ▲   Continue to the southeast.
GPS: N32º30.33' W110º40.88'

▼ 0.0   Continue to the northwest.
5.7 ▲ SO Track on left is South #28: Catalina Ridge Trail. Zero trip meter. Intersection is unmarked.

▼ 0.5 SO Cattle guard.
5.2 ▲ SO Cattle guard.

▼ 1.5 SO Cattle guard.
4.2 ▲ SO Cattle guard.
GPS: N32º30.82' W110º41.01'

▼ 1.8 SO Track on right.
3.9 ▲ SO Track on left.

▼ 2.2 SO Cross through Catalina Wash.
3.5 ▲ SO Cross through Catalina Wash.
GPS: N32º30.98' W110º41.15'

▼ 3.3 SO Track on right.
2.4 ▲ BR Track on left.
GPS: N32º31.42' W110º41.92'

▼ 3.4 SO Track on right and track on left.
2.3 ▲ SO Track on right and track on left.
GPS: N32º31.39' W110º42.03'

▼ 3.7 SO Track on right; then cross over Nugget Canyon on bridge.
2.0 ▲ SO Cross over Nugget Canyon on bridge; then track on left.

▼ 4.3 SO Cross through wash.
1.4 ▲ SO Cross through wash.

▼ 4.4 SO Track on left and track on right.
1.3 ▲ SO Track on left and track on right.

▼ 4.7 SO Track on right.
1.0 ▲ SO Track on left.

▼ 5.5 SO Cross over wash on bridge.
0.2 ▲ SO Cross over wash on bridge.

▼ 5.7 SO Peppersauce USFS Campground on

A large alligator juniper beside the trail

right, track on left is Rice Peak Trail.
Zero trip meter.

0.0 ▲ Continue to the southeast.

GPS: N32°32.26' W110°43.05'

▼ 0.0 Continue to the northwest and cross through Peppersauce Wash.

3.3 ▲ SO Cross through Peppersauce Wash; then Peppersauce USFS Campground on left. Track on right is Rice Peak Trail. Zero trip meter.

▼ 0.5 SO Track on right.
2.8 ▲ SO Track on left.

▼ 1.0 SO Cattle guard.
2.3 ▲ SO Cattle guard.

▼ 1.5 SO Track on left.
1.8 ▲ SO Track on right.

▼ 1.7 SO Road on right is Del Rio, corral on left.
1.6 ▲ SO Road on left is Del Rio, corral on right.

GPS: N32°33.13' W110°42.46'

▼ 2.0 SO Track on left is FR 4470.
1.3 ▲ SO Track on right is FR 4470.

GPS: N32°33.35' W110°42.51'

▼ 2.4 SO Private road on left, cross through wash.
0.9 ▲ SO Cross through wash, private road on right.

▼ 2.7 SO Private road on left, two tracks on right.
0.6 ▲ SO Private road on right, two tracks on left.

▼ 3.0 SO Road on left is Sombrero Viejo.
0.3 ▲ SO Road on right is Sombrero Viejo.

▼ 3.3 SO Large graded road on left and right is Campo Bonito Road, FR 639. Road is now Mt. Lemmon Road. Zero trip meter.
0.0 ▲ Continue to the southeast toward Peppersauce USFS Campground.

GPS: N32°34.23' W110°42.88'

▼ 0.0 Continue to the northwest toward Oracle.

4.7 ▲ BL Large graded road on left and right is Campo Bonito Road, FR 639. Zero trip meter.

▼ 0.2 SO Track on left.
4.5 ▲ SO Track on right.

▼ 0.7 SO Track on left; then cross through Flag Wash. Arizona Trail trailhead #9 on left beside corral and on right. This section is for hikers only. This is the site of American Flag.

4.0 ▲ SO Arizona Trail trailhead #9 on right beside corral and on left. This section is for hikers only. Cross through Flag Wash; then track on right. This is the site of American Flag Mine.

GPS: N32°34.85' W110°43.18'

▼ 0.8 SO Track on left.
3.9 ▲ SO Track on right.

▼ 1.1 SO Cattle guard.
3.6 ▲ SO Cattle guard.

▼ 1.6 SO Paved road joins on right. Road is now paved.
3.1 ▲ BR Bear right onto graded dirt road, following the sign for the YMCA Ranch Camp.

GPS: N32°35.59' W110°43.16'

▼ 2.2 SO Track on right and track on left; then Cody Loop Road on left.
2.5 ▲ SO Cody Loop Road on right; then track on right and track on left.

▼ 3.0 SO Leaving Coronado National Forest.
1.7 ▲ SO Entering Coronado National Forest.

GPS: N32°35.97' W110°44.41'

▼ 3.6 SO Cross through wash, Oracle State Park, Center for Environmental Education on right. Many roads on right and left, remain on main road.
1.1 ▲ SO Oracle State Park, Center for Environmental Education on left, then cross through wash.

▼ 4.7   Trail ends at the T-intersection with American Avenue in Oracle. Turn right for San Manuel, turn left for Tucson.

0.0 ▲   Trail commences on American Avenue on the east side of Oracle. Zero trip meter and turn east on the paved Mt. Lemmon Road sign-posted for Mt. Lemmon. Many roads on right and left for first 1.1 miles, remain on main road. American Avenue is the main street running through Oracle. Oracle is bypassed by Arizona 77. The turn is immediately south of the post office.
GPS: N32°36.60' W110°45.89'

SOUTH REGION TRAIL #28

Catalina Ridge Trail

STARTING POINT   South #27: Oracle Control Road, 5.7 miles southeast of Peppersauce USFS Campground
FINISHING POINT   Arizona 76, 2.7 miles south of San Manuel
TOTAL MILEAGE   10.1 miles
UNPAVED MILEAGE   10.1 miles
DRIVING TIME   2 hours
ELEVATION RANGE   3,000–4,600 feet
USUALLY OPEN   Year-round
BEST TIME TO TRAVEL   October to June
DIFFICULTY RATING   2
SCENIC RATING   7
REMOTENESS RATING   +0

Special Attractions

- Gently sloping trail offers views of the San Pedro River Valley and Galiuro Mountains.
- Alternative access to the trails on the east side of the Santa Catalina Mountains.

Description

This 2-rated trail travels down a long, gently sloping ridge between Stratton Wash and Catalina Wash. Although a very small, formed trail, it is easygoing and suitable for high-clearance 2WD vehicles. It is entirely contained within state land, and a valid state land use permit is required.

The trail leaves South #27: Oracle Control Road (also called the Mt. Lemmon Back Trail) south of Peppersauce USFS Campground. Although small, the trail is well defined as it heads toward a large water tank, which is easily visible farther along the trail. The trail heads directly east, giving striking views of the San Pedro River Valley and the Galiuro Mountains on the far side. Travelers in the opposite direction will have equally panoramic views of the Santa Catalina Mountains.

The state lands are grazed by cattle and horses, and the many tanks and dams are for their use. Much of the lower portion of the trail does not appear on BLM or topographic maps. The trail joins the graded dirt road that leads past closed mine workings before ending at the intersection with Arizona 76, south of the BHP mining town of San Manuel. The copper mine closed in July 1999, but most facilities are available in San Manuel.

Current Road Information

Coronado National Forest
Santa Catalina Ranger District
5700 North Sabino Canyon Rd.
Tucson, AZ 85750
(520) 749-8700

Map References

BLM   Mammoth
USFS   Coronado National Forest: Safford and Santa Catalina Ranger Districts
USGS   1:24,000   Campo Bonito, Peppersauce Wash
1:100,000 Mammoth
Maptech CD-ROM: Phoenix/Superstition

Prickly pear and mesquite border the trail

South Trail #28: Catalina Ridge Trail

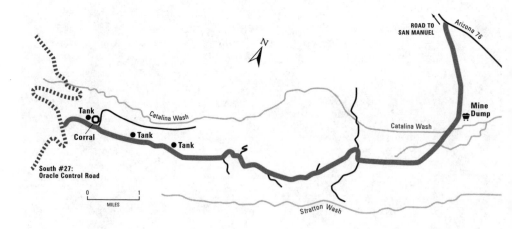

Mountains

Arizona Atlas & Gazetteer, p. 67
Arizona Road & Recreation Atlas, pp. 48, 82

Route Directions

▼ 0.0   From South #27: Oracle Control Road,
5.7 miles southeast of Peppersauce
USFS Campground, zero trip meter and
turn northeast on unmarked, formed
trail. There is a large iron tank visible
farther down the trail that acts as a
marker.

4.1 ▲   Trail ends at the intersection with the
South #27: Oracle Control Road. Turn
left for Mt. Lemmon, turn right for
Oracle.
GPS: N32°30.34' W110°40.89'

▼ 0.2   BR   Trail follows fence line heading for iron
tank.

3.9 ▲   BL   Trail swings away from fence line.
GPS: N32°30.53' W110°40.72'

▼ 0.6   SO   Large iron tank on left.

3.5 ▲   SO   Large iron tank on right.
GPS: N32°30.54' W110°40.42'

▼ 0.7   SO   Small dam on left; then corral on left.
Pass through gate continuing in a
northeasterly direction.

3.4 ▲   SO   Pass through gate, continuing in a
southwesterly direction. Corral on
right; then small dam on right.
GPS: N32°30.54' W110°40.25'

▼ 0.8   SO   Track on left.
3.3 ▲   SO   Track on right.

▼ 1.4   SO   Concrete tank on left.
2.7 ▲   SO   Concrete tank on right.

▼ 2.2   SO   Concrete tank and dam on left.
1.9 ▲   SO   Concrete tank and dam on right.
GPS: N32°30.70' W110°38.66'

▼ 3.0   SO   Small dam on right; then track on right.
1.1 ▲   SO   Track on left; then small dam on left.
GPS: N32°30.92' W110°37.85'

▼ 3.3   BR   Concrete tank on left.
0.8 ▲   BL   Concrete tank on right.

▼ 3.5   SO   Track on left.
0.6 ▲   SO   Track on right.
GPS: N32°31.06' W110°37.44'

▼ 3.9   SO   Small dam on right.
0.2 ▲   SO   Small dam on left.

▼ 4.1 BL Fork in trail, well-used track on right
               goes 0.3 miles to a tank. Zero trip
               meter.

0.0 ▲   Proceed to the southwest.
               GPS: N32°31.02' W110°36.84'

▼ 0.0   Proceed to the northeast.
1.9 ▲ SO Well-used track on left goes 0.3 miles
               to a tank. Zero trip meter.

▼ 1.0 SO Track on left.
0.9 ▲ SO Track on right.
               GPS: N32°31.35' W110°35.94'

▼ 1.3 BL Fork in trail, track on right.
0.6 ▲ SO Track on left.
               GPS: N32°31.59' W110°35.70'

▼ 1.4 SO Cross gas pipeline, tracks on left and
               right follow pipeline.
0.5 ▲ SO Cross gas pipeline, tracks on left and

               right follow pipeline.
               GPS: N32°31.67' W110°35.69'

▼ 1.7 BL Track on right through gate into well.
0.2 ▲ SO Track on left through gate into well.
               GPS: N32°31.92' W110°35.52'

▼ 1.9 TR T-intersection. Zero trip meter
0.0 ▲   Continue to the west.
               GPS: N32°31.94' W110°35.37'

▼ 0.0   Continue to the southeast.
1.3 ▲ TL Turn left toward well, which is visible
               over the creosote bushes. Zero trip
               meter.

▼ 0.1 SO Cross through wash.
1.2 ▲ SO Cross through wash.

▼ 0.2 TL Two tracks on right.
1.7 ▲ TR Turn right, track on left and track

Cattle at a tank beside the trail

straight on.
GPS: N32°31.82' W110°35.28'

▼ 1.3   TL   Turn onto wide graded road. There is a small track opposite. Zero trip meter.
0.0 ▲   Continue to the southwest.
GPS: N32°32.19' W110°34.17'

▼ 0.0   Continue to the north.
2.8 ▲   TR   Turn right onto unmarked, well-used, formed trail at the top of slight rise; there is a small track opposite. Zero trip meter.

▼ 0.4   SO   Cattle guard; then cross through wash.
2.4 ▲   SO   Cross through wash; then cattle guard.
GPS: N32°32.56' W110°34.02'

▼ 0.6   SO   Track on right.
2.2 ▲   SO   Track on left.

▼ 0.7   SO   Cross through Catalina Wash.
2.1 ▲   SO   Cross through Catalina Wash.
GPS: N32°32.84' W110°33.93'

▼ 1.0   BL   Small track on left, cattle guard, then bear left with mine dump on right.
1.8 ▲   BR   Bear right past mine dump, then cattle guard, small track on right.
GPS: N32°33.11' W110°33.84'

▼ 2.5   SO   Track on left.
0.3 ▲   SO   Track on right.

▼ 2.8   Small track on left, cattle guard, then trail ends at junction with Arizona 76. Turn left for San Manuel.
0.0 ▲   Trail commences on Arizona 76 at mile marker 47, 2.7 miles south of San Manuel. On a left-hand bend, turn right into paved entrance and then immediately right again in front of the old closed road. There is a small sign for Oracle Ridge Mine. Cross cattle guard and proceed southwest along wide, graded gravel road.
GPS: N32°34.42' W110°34.86'

Copper Creek Mining District Trail

STARTING POINT	Main Street in Mammoth
FINISHING POINT	San Pedro River Road
TOTAL MILEAGE	21.2 miles
UNPAVED MILEAGE	20.7 miles
DRIVING TIME	2 hours
ELEVATION RANGE	2,400–4,500 feet
USUALLY OPEN	Year-round
BEST TIME TO TRAVEL	October to May
DIFFICULTY RATING	2
SCENIC RATING	8
REMOTENESS RATING	+0

Special Attractions
- Rugged cliffs of Sombrero Butte.
- Historic Copper Creek Mining District.
- Remains of the Bunker Hill and other mines.

History
Copper Creek Mining District was very active and was composed of many mines. Founded in 1880, by 1910 it was at its zenith, with three mining companies active in the area. As you would expect from the name, copper was the dominant mineral, but silver and lead were also present. The town of Copper Creek had about 500 people, 50 buildings, a physician, post office, stage line, and mansion. Because it was located within a deep canyon, the town was built in tiers.

The mines operated until 1917 and reopened again in 1933 when the Arizona Molybdenum Corporation took an interest in Copper Creek. However, they closed again in 1942, at which time the post office also closed after more than 35 years of service.

Copper Creek is closely associated with Roy Sibley and the Sibley Mansion. Refer to South #30: Sibley Mansion and Bluebird Mine Trail.

At the start of the trail sits the town of

Mammoth, named in the 1870s for the Old Mammoth Mine above town, where gold ore deposits were so rich they were said to be mammoth in proportion. The town had a mill, where ore was shuttled in tramway buckets from the mine above the town. The ore buckets were then filled with drinking water for the return journey to the thirsty miners.

The Galiuro Mountains form the backdrop to Copper Creek, and this remote range too has its share of history and intrigue. In 1918 it was the location of a shootout between a posse and brothers Tom and John Power. The Power brothers were charged with evading the draft and four lawmen were dispatched to bring them in. For reasons that remain a mystery, after the posse surrounded the Powers' cabin, Jeff Power, Tom and John's father, lay dead. In the gunfight that followed, three of the four lawmen were killed.

What followed was one of Arizona's greatest manhunts. The two Power brothers and a family friend, Tom Sisson, were cap-tured by the U.S. Cavalry just below the Mexican border. Local newspapers had already convicted the Power boys, public opinion was against them, and the trial was a formality. Given life sentences, they were sent to state prison in Florence. They always maintained their innocence, saying the posse had shot and killed their father without identifying itself and that they reacted in self-defense.

Despite fervent pleadings from the men's relatives at hearings, parole boards refused to release the three men. Sisson died in 1956. Five years after Sisson's death, the Power brothers were released after serving 42 years, having endured the longest sentences in Arizona history at the time. The brothers spent most of their remaining years in the Galiuro Mountains area.

The nearby San Pedro River runs through Mammoth before joining the Gila at Winkelman. Back in the 1820s, in the heyday of beaver hats when pelts were known as "hairy bank notes" and the fur trade was one of the nation's greatest eco-

Timbers in the entrance of Bunker Hill Mine

nomic engines, beavers were in such abundance in the San Pedro River that it was renamed, at least temporarily, Beaver River.

Description

This roughly graded road leads the traveler past many mining remains of the historic Copper Creek Mining District situated on the west side of the rocky Galiuro Mountains. The trail, which starts in Mammoth, climbs gradually up the gently sloping bajada to the edge of the range. As you climb, there are panoramic views back to the west over the San Pedro River Valley to the Santa Catalina Mountains. The large open pit mine at San Manuel (closed in July 1999) can also be seen.

The trail is lumpy in spots as it climbs up a ridge between the drainages of Well Canyon to the north and Copper Creek to the south. Ahead, the Galiuro Mountains rear up with the red-topped Sombrero Butte prominent to the southeast.

There is a short section of wide shelf road as you descend toward Copper Creek, with ample room for two vehicles to pass. Copper Creek normally has water in it for approximately six months of the year, and is bordered with large cottonwoods. There are a couple of pleasant picnic spots near the creek.

The trail continues as a shelf road over Copper Creek. This section is wide enough for a single vehicle, and there are limited passing places. In the mining district there are many remnants of the mining activity that made this district famous. The area is still worked actively and some areas may not be accessible to the public; please respect any restrictions placed on the private property and mining claims.

At the old Copper Creek sign, which is embedded in a rock wall, the trail leading off to the north along Copper Creek is the difficult South #30: Sibley Mansion and Bluebird Mine Trail. There is a pleasant picnic or camping spot underneath the cottonwoods at the start of the trail that can be seen from the sign.

The second half of the trail passes through the Bunker Hill Mining District and past the remains of the Bunker Hill Mine. There are excellent views of Sombrero Butte and the

Bridge and loading chute at the Childs and Atwilkle Mine

jagged escarpment of the Galiuro Mountains. The trail is smooth as it descends the bajada, following the path of Mulberry Wash to rejoin the San Pedro River Road, 3 miles south of the starting point.

The trail crosses a combination of state, private, and BLM land. A valid state land use permit is required.

Current Road Information

Bureau of Land Management
Tucson Field Office
12661 East Broadway Blvd.
Tucson, AZ 85748
(520) 258-7200

Coronado National Forest
Santa Catalina Ranger District
5700 North Sabino Canyon Rd.
Tucson, AZ 85750
(520) 749-8700

Map References

BLM   Mammoth
USGS   1:24,000   Mammoth, Clark Ranch, Holy Joe Peak, Rhodes Peak, Oak Grove Canyon
1:100,000 Mammoth
Maptech CD-ROM: Phoenix/Superstition Mountains
Arizona Atlas & Gazetteer, p. 67
Arizona Road & Recreation Atlas, pp. 48, 82

Route Directions

▼ 0.0   In Mammoth, from Arizona 77, turn east on Main Street into the business district of Mammoth. Proceed for 0.7 miles, then turn east on Bluebird Street. Zero trip meter at intersection and proceed east on Bluebird Street, graded dirt road.

0.7 ▲   Trail ends at the intersection of Bluebird Street and Main Street in the center of Mammoth. Turn left to exit to Arizona 77.
GPS: N32°43.25' W110°38.31'

▼ 0.2   SO   Cross through San Pedro River wash. Road becomes paved.
0.5 ▲   SO   Cross through San Pedro River wash. Road is now graded dirt.

▼ 0.3   SO   Track on right.
0.4 ▲   SO   Track on left.

▼ 0.7   SO   Paved San Pedro River Road on left and right, continue straight onto small, roughly graded dirt road and zero trip meter.
0.0 ▲   Continue toward Mammoth on paved road.
GPS: N32°43.39' W110°37.59'

▼ 0.0   Continue to the northeast on dirt road that follows the wash.
6.8 ▲   SO   Paved San Pedro River Road on right and left, continue straight onto unmarked paved road and zero trip meter.

▼ 0.1   SO   Pass underneath power lines.
6.7 ▲   SO   Pass underneath power lines.

▼ 0.7   SO   Exit wash.
6.1 ▲   SO   Enter wash.

▼ 1.5   SO   Track on left.
5.3 ▲   SO   Track on right.

▼ 2.0   SO   Track on right.
4.8 ▲   SO   Track on left.

▼ 2.3   SO   Track on left.
4.5 ▲   SO   Track on right.
GPS: N32°44.14' W110°35.43'

▼ 2.4   SO   Track on left and track on right.
4.4 ▲   SO   Track on left and track on right.
GPS: N32°44.15' W110°35.27'

▼ 2.5   SO   Cross through wash.
4.3 ▲   SO   Cross through wash.

▼ 2.6   SO   Corral and tanks on left.
4.2 ▲   SO   Corral and tanks on right.
GPS: N32°44.22' W110°35.07'

▼ 4.1   SO   Cattle guard.

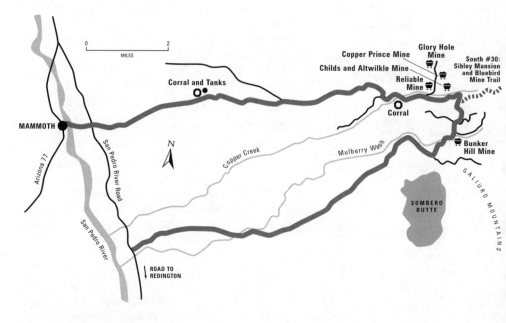

2.7 ▲　SO Cattle guard.
　　　　GPS: N32°44.39′ W110°33.63′

▼ 4.8　SO Track on left to tank.
2.0 ▲　SO Track on right to tank.
　　　　GPS: N32°44.50′ W110°33.03′

▼ 5.0　SO Track on right.
1.8 ▲　SO Track on left.

▼ 5.8　SO Tank on left.
1.0 ▲　SO Tank on right.

▼ 6.1　SO Track on left.
0.7 ▲　SO Track on right.

▼ 6.3　SO Cattle guard, entering private property, please remain on road.
0.5 ▲　SO Cattle guard, entering public land.
　　　　GPS: N32°44.82′ W110°31.50′

▼ 6.8　SO Well-used track on left leads off saddle. Zero trip meter.
0.0 ▲　　Continue to the southwest.
　　　　GPS: N32°45.03′ W110°31.04′

▼ 0.0　　Continue on around the loop to the

northeast.
1.7 ▲　SO Well-used track on right leads off saddle. Zero trip meter.

▼ 0.7　SO Track on right.
1.0 ▲　SO Track on left.
　　　　GPS: N32°44.90′ W110°30.46′

▼ 0.8　SO Track on right, then trail follows shelf road over Copper Creek.
0.9 ▲　SO Track on left, end of shelf road.

▼ 1.1　SO Tailings pile above trail on left.
0.6 ▲　SO Tailings pile above trail on right.

▼ 1.3　SO Old corral on right then track on right. Remain on main trail. End of shelf road.
0.4 ▲　SO Track on left then old corral on left. Remain on main trail. Start of shelf road.
　　　　GPS: N32°44.91′ W110°30.05′

▼ 1.4　SO Cross through Copper Creek.
0.3 ▲　SO Cross through Copper Creek.
　　　　GPS: N32°44.89′ W110°29.98′

▼ 1.7　BR Fork in trail before fenced settling ponds. The left fork drops down and

A section of shelf road above the Copper Creek Mining District crosses through Copper Creek. The sites of Reliable Mine, Copper Prince Mine, and Glory Hole Mine are up this trail. Zero trip meter.

0.0 ▲ Continue down alongside Copper Creek.
GPS: N32°45.01′ W110°29.66′

▼ 0.0 Continue past settling ponds.
1.3 ▲ SO Track on right immediately past settling ponds drops down and crosses through Copper Creek. The sites of Reliable Mine, Copper Prince Mine, and Glory Hole Mine are up this trail. Zero trip meter.

▼ 0.5 SO Tailings pile on right.
0.8 ▲ SO Tailings pile on left.

▼ 0.7 SO Loading hopper on left.
0.6 ▲ SO Loading hopper on right.
GPS: N32°45.10′ W110°28.94′

▼ 0.8 SO Iron walkway across creek; then small waterfall in creek on left.
0.5 ▲ SO Small waterfall in creek on right; then iron walkway across creek.

▼ 1.0 SO Concrete footings and timbers on right above trail.
0.3 ▲ SO Concrete footings and timbers on left above trail.

▼ 1.3 BR At tank on hill and rock wall with old Copper Creek sign embedded in it, bear right to continue the loop along the Bunker Hill Road. Track on left is South #30: Sibley Mansion and Bluebird Mine Trail. Also track on right. Zero trip meter.
0.0 ▲ Continue to the north along shelf road.
GPS: N32°45.07′ W110°28.62′

▼ 0.0 From rock wall sign, continue to the south along the shelf road.
2.2 ▲ SO Tank on hill on right, then track on right is South #30: Sibley Mansion and Bluebird Mine Trail. There is a rock wall at the junction with the old Copper Creek sign embedded in it. Also track on left. Zero trip meter.

▼ 0.3 BL Track on right, continue to climb.
1.9 ▲ SO Track on left.
GPS: N32°44.88′ W110°28.61′

▼ 0.5 SO Track on left.
1.7 ▲ BL Track on right.

▼ 0.9 SO Saddle, track on left. Sombrero Butte is directly ahead.
1.3 ▲ SO Saddle, track on right.
GPS: N32°44.57′ W110°28.58′

▼ 1.0 SO Track on right.
1.2 ▲ SO Track on left.

▼ 1.2 SO Cross through wash, well-used track on left at wash.
1.0 ▲ SO Cross through wash, well-used track on right at wash.
GPS: N32°44.38′ W110°28.64′

▼ 1.5 SO Timber-framed adit on left, track on left, then concrete footings of the Bunker Hill Mine on left.
0.7 ▲ SO Concrete footings of the Bunker Hill Mine on right, then track on right and timber-framed adit on right.
GPS: N32°44.22′ W110°28.72′

▼ 2.2 TR T-intersection with well-used dirt track. Zero trip meter.
0.0 ▲ Continue to the northwest.
GPS: N32°43.80′ W110°29.05′

▼ 0.0 Continue to the southwest.
8.5 ▲ TL Turn left on well-used dirt track, well-used track continues ahead. Zero trip meter.

▼ 0.4 SO Cross through Mulberry Wash.
8.1 ▲ BR Cross through Mulberry Wash.

▼ 1.4 SO Cattle guard. Trail is running alongside Mulberry Wash.
7.1 ▲ SO Cattle guard. Trail is running alongside Mulberry Wash.
GPS: N32°43.80′ W110°30.07′

▼ 1.8 SO Turnout on left, viewpoint for Sombrero Butte.

6.7 ▲   SO   Turnout on right, viewpoint for
             Sombrero Butte.

▼ 2.4   SO   Cattle guard; then track on right.
6.1 ▲   SO   Track on left; then cattle guard.
             GPS: N32°43.23′ W110°30.72′

▼ 2.8   SO   Track on right.
5.7 ▲   SO   Track on left.

▼ 2.9   SO   Road forks around tank and rejoins
             immediately.
5.6 ▲   SO   Road forks around tank and rejoins
             immediately.

▼ 4.9   BR   Track on left.
3.6 ▲   SO   Track on right.
             GPS: N32°41.74′ W110°32.69′

▼ 5.8   SO   Cross through Mulberry Wash, track
             on right to corral after wash.
2.7 ▲   SO   Track on left to corral, then cross
             through Mulberry Wash.
             GPS: N32°41.62′ W110°33.56′

▼ 6.0   SO   Track on right.
2.5 ▲   SO   Track on left.

▼ 6.2   SO   Track on right.
2.3 ▲   SO   Track on left.

▼ 8.0   SO   Track on right underneath power lines.
0.5 ▲   SO   Track on left underneath power lines.

▼ 8.5   Trail ends at the junction with the
             paved San Pedro River Road. Turn right
             for Mammoth via the San Pedro River
             crossing at the start of the trail, turn
             left for Redington via the San Pedro
             River Road.
0.0 ▲   Trail commences on the San Pedro
             River Road, 3 miles south of the inter-
             section with the road that crosses the
             Gila River to Mammoth. Zero trip meter
             and turn east up wide graded dirt road.
             The intersection is unmarked, but is
             immediately north of a wash crossing,
             where the road turns to dirt.
             GPS: N32°40.97′ W110°36.20′

Sibley Mansion and Bluebird Mine Trail

STARTING POINT	South #29: Copper Creek Mining District Trail at Copper Creek sign
FINISHING POINT	Sibley Mansion/Bluebird Mine
TOTAL MILEAGE	8 miles (round-trip, both spurs)
UNPAVED MILEAGE	8 miles
DRIVING TIME	3 hours
ELEVATION RANGE	3,900–4,700 feet
USUALLY OPEN	Year-round
BEST TIME TO TRAVEL	October to May
DIFFICULTY RATING	7 (Sibley Mansion); 4 (Bluebird Mine)
SCENIC RATING	8
REMOTENESS RATING:	+1

Special Attractions

■ Extremely challenging, rough, rocky trail.
■ Ruins of the 20-room Sibley Mansion.
■ Remains of the Bluebird Mine.

History

The history of the Sibley Mansion, as it came to be known, is closely intertwined with that of the Copper Creek Mining District. Roy Sibley was the manager of the Minnesota Mining Company, one of the three companies active in Copper Creek around the turn of the last century. The Minnesota Mining Company eventually bought out the majority of the Copper Creek claims, and Sibley took on the role of promoting the district to potential investors. In 1908 construction (supposedly using Indian labor) began on a fabulous 20-room mansion. The extravagant estate was located a short distance up Copper Creek from the main town site. Altogether, the mansion had 20 rooms, including 2 towers, one at each end that were 3-stories high. There were polished wooden floors, fruit trees growing on the front patio, and a wooden verandah that ran around the second story and gave inhabitants views of the sycamore grove and the hills behind. Large windows to catch the breezes and opulent furnishings completed the picture. The Sibleys wanted to present a picture of refined opulence, and potential investors were invited to stay at the mansion.

The Sibleys moved out of their home in 1910 and the majority of the flooring and other furnishings of the mansion were stripped and moved elsewhere shortly afterward.

Original access to the mansion was from Klondyke, on the east side of the Galiuro Mountains. Klondyke was established in the early 1900s and was named after the famous gold rush in Alaska (which incidentally is spelled Klondike). The town once had a population of about 500 but now supports only a dozen residents. Silver and lead mines nearby were the reason for the town's existence.

Nowadays the Sibley Mansion is crum-

bling slowly back to earth. The outside walls remain, as do the 3-story towers. The surrounding vegetation is encroaching on the mansion, but you can still clearly see the size and grandeur of the original building.

Description

These two short spur trails lead off from South #29: Copper Creek Mining District Trail. The moderately rated spur to the Bluebird Mine is a scenic shelf road that leads to two old cabins and the remains of the mine. The Sibley Mansion spur travels an extremely difficult and rocky trail along Copper Creek to the remains of the 20-room Sibley Mansion.

The start of the Sibley Mansion spur starts off innocuously enough, but quickly becomes difficult. It follows the path of Copper Creek, crossing it often. The difficulty rating of the trail comes from the very

Sibley Mansion remains

A rocky section of the trail

large, loose boulders that have to be negotiated. High-clearance is essential and side steps and low-hanging brush bars risk being damaged. This trail is not suited to a novice driver. Possibly the hardest section is alongside a small pool, where there is an off-camber rock pile to be climbed.

The mansion is set slightly back from the creek. In front of it is an idyllic picnic or camping area under large sycamore trees. The mansion has two, square three-story towers still standing, as well as the remains of the outer and inner walls. Opposite, on the far side of the creek, are the remains of a stone building that housed offices and a store house.

Sibley Mansion stands on private property, but at the time of writing it is not posted and is freely visited by 4-wheelers, hikers, and horse riders. Please treat the property with respect, so that it may continue to remain open.

The second spur to the Bluebird Mine is not as challenging as the trail to Sibley Mansion. It follows a shelf road all the way, climbing high above Copper Creek. There are panoramic views over the San Pedro River Valley to the Santa Catalinas and closer views over the Copper Creek drainage and the Galiuro Mountains.

Immediately before the mine, two cabins are passed—one adobe and one timber. The mine has concrete foundations and a large tailings pile remaining. On the hill above the mine are many stone walls constructed around the hillside. Opposite is a deep crevasse in the hill, where it looks like the miners followed a vein of ore.

Current Road Information

Bureau of Land Management
Tucson Field Office
12661 East Broadway Blvd.
Tucson, AZ 85748
(520) 258-7200

Coronado National Forest
Santa Catalina Ranger District
5700 North Sabino Canyon Rd.
Tucson, AZ 85750
(520) 749-8700

South Trail #30:
Sibley Mansion and Bluebird Mine Trail

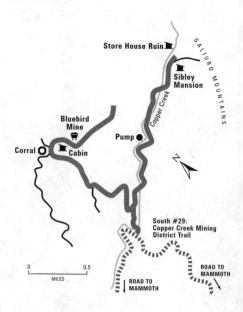

Map References

BLM   Mammoth
USGS 1:24,000   Oak Grove Canyon
          1:100,000 Mammoth
Maptech CD-ROM: Phoenix/Superstition
          Mountains
Arizona Atlas & Gazetteer, p. 67

Route Directions

▼ 0.0   From the old Copper Creek sign embedded in the rock wall, 10.5 miles from the start of South #29: Copper Creek Mining District Trail, zero trip meter and turn northeast on the trail that descends toward Copper Creek.
        GPS: N32°45.07' W110°28.62'

▼ 0.1   BR Ford Copper Creek, then switchback to the right up creek. Track on left at switchback.
        GPS: N32°45.10' W110°28.56'

▼ 0.3   SO Track on right crosses wash.
        GPS: N32°45.16' W110°28.39'

▼ 0.4 BL Trail forks at large cottonwoods. To the right is the spur to the Sibley Mansion. To the left is the spur to the Bluebird Mine. Left climbs up ridge away from Copper Creek and continues to the Bluebird Mine. Zero trip meter.
GPS: N32°45.18' W110°28.34'

Bluebird Mine Spur

▼ 0.0 At the intersection, bear left away from Copper Creek and start to climb ridge.
GPS: N32°45.18' W110°28.34'

▼ 0.1 SO Track on left.
▼ 0.7 BR Track on left on right-hand switchback.
GPS: N32°45.48' W110°28.46'

▼ 1.2 BR Track on left. Bear right and pass corral on left.
GPS: N32°45.85' W110°28.42'

▼ 1.3 SO Track on left after corral, then remains of rock and adobe cabin on right.
▼ 1.4 SO Timber cabin on right.
GPS: N32°45.89' W110°28.32'

▼ 1.5 SO Bluebird Mine.
GPS: N32°45.77' W110°28.24'

▼ 1.8 SO Track on right goes 0.1 miles to campsite.
▼ 2.1 UT Trail reaches campsite, the old road past this point is seldom-used. Turn around and retrace your steps to the intersection where you last zeroed your trip meter.
GPS: N32°45.67' W110°27.73'

Sibley Mansion Spur

▼ 0.0 BR At the intersection where the trail forks, bear right and continue up Copper Creek.
GPS: N32°45.18' W110°28.34'

▼ 0.1 BL Track on right, bear left and exit wash.
GPS: N32°45.20' W110°28.20'

▼ 0.2 SO Re-enter wash.
▼ 0.3 SO Cross rock fall; then cross through Copper Creek, start of difficult section.
GPS: N32°45.27' W110°28.08'

▼ 0.4 SO Cross through creek.
▼ 0.5 SO Cross through creek.
▼ 0.6 SO Old pump on left of trail; then cross through creek.
GPS: N32°45.29' W110°27.87'

▼ 0.7 SO Cross through creek.
▼ 0.9 SO Cross through creek.
GPS: N32°45.37' W110°27.86'

▼ 1.0 SO Cross through creek.
GPS: N32°45.40' W110°27.61'

▼ 1.1 SO Cross through creek.
GPS: N32°45.42' W110°27.54'

▼ 1.2 SO Cross through creek.
GPS: N32°45.47' W110°27.50'

▼ 1.3 SO Difficult off-camber climb up loose rock pile with pool on right; then small stone ruin on left.
GPS: N32°45.46' W110°47.39'

▼ 1.4 SO Enter picnic area under sycamores alongside Copper Creek. Sibley Mansion is on the right of the trail.
GPS: N32°45.46' W110°27.24'

▼ 1.5 UT Track on right climbs difficult, moguled hill and loops around to rejoin the trail near the start of the spur to Bluebird Mine. Bear left and cross the creek to the store house ruin. Spur trail ends. Turn around and retrace your steps to South #29: Copper Creek Mining District Trail.
GPS: N32°45.50' W110°27.13'

Redington Road

STARTING POINT	San Pedro River Road at Redington
FINISHING POINT	Tucson
TOTAL MILEAGE	23.3 miles
UNPAVED MILEAGE	23.3 miles
DRIVING TIME	2 hours
ELEVATION RANGE	2,800–4,400 feet
USUALLY OPEN	Year-round
BEST TIME TO TRAVEL	October to May
DIFFICULTY RATING	2
SCENIC RATING	8
REMOTENESS RATING	+0

Special Attractions
- Easy trail winding through the Coronado National Forest and state lands close to Tucson.
- Access to many 4WD trails and backcountry campsites.
- Panoramic views of the San Pedro River Valley, Galiuro Mountains, and Rincon Mountains.
- Many hiking trails, including a short trail to Tanque Verde Falls.

History
Today Redington is a small ranching settlement, but there are some hair-raising tales associated with its past. The area was settled in 1875 by the Redfield brothers, Henry and Lem, who initiated establishment of a post office on their ranch, some six miles south of where the present-day settlement is located. They wanted to call the site Redfield, but this was denied by the post office, so they decided upon Redington.

Over the next several years, the area around Redington attracted many outlaws who hid in the hills. In 1883 outlaws robbed a stage and murdered a man just north of the Riverside stage station. The bandits were tracked to the Redfield Ranch, and Joe Tuttle, Frank Carpenter, and Lem Redfield were caught with the money. They were taken to

the prison at Florence, where Tuttle confessed, saying that Lem Redfield was to be given a share of the profits for providing the hideout, an accusation that Lem denied.

Meanwhile Henry Redfield rounded up seven of his friends and a deputy marshal and went to Florence to try to free his brother. Incensed by what they perceived as a bypassing of justice, the citizens of Florence lynched both Lem Redfield and Joe Tuttle. To this day, no one knows for sure if Lem was guilty; in fact much of the available evidence points to his innocence.

The Redington post office was closed in December 1940.

Tanque Verde Canyon, which is near the western end of the trail, is named after water holes in the canyon that contain green algae. The name dates back to the 1860s.

Description
Redington Road is a popular exit from Tucson for backcountry travelers. Not only does the trail provide a scenic and peaceful alternative to I-10 for eastbound travelers, but it is a beautiful drive in its own right. Its proximity to Tucson means it is popular for weekend camping, four-wheeling, and hiking.

The trail travels across grasslands, dotted with mesquite and abundant prickly pear, on the edge of the Santa Catalina Mountains. The Rincon Mountains are to the south and to the east are the Galiuro Mountains and the San Pedro River Valley.

The initial part of the trail crosses a mixture of state land and private ranchlands, following alongside the wash in Youtcy Canyon for a short distance before continuing to climb toward the boundary of the Coronado National Forest. There is a good chance of seeing wildlife within the national forest. Mule deer, Gambel's quail, javelina, many birds of prey, and reptiles live in the rocky hills. It is fairly easy to find a pleasant, peaceful campsite as well. There are some spots directly on the graded road and other quieter spots down the many side trails.

The final portion of the trail runs around

a wide shelf road, with views down into Tanque Verde Canyon, before ending on the outskirts of Tucson.

The trail could be traversed by a passenger vehicle with care. It is regularly graded, but is still more suited to a high-clearance vehicle because of the lumps and rough sections.

Current Road Information

Coronado National Forest
Santa Catalina Ranger District
5700 North Sabino Canyon Rd.
Tucson, AZ 85750
(520) 749-8700

Map References

BLM   Tucson
USFS Coronado National Forest: Safford and Santa Catalina Ranger Districts
USGS 1:24,000   Redington, Buehman Canyon, Piety Hill, Agua Caliente Hills
1:100,000 Tucson
Maptech CD-ROM: Southeast Arizona/

Tucson
Arizona Atlas & Gazetteer, p. 67
Arizona Road & Recreation Atlas, pp. 54, 88
Recreational Map of Arizona

Route Directions

▼ 0.0   From San Pedro River Road, 13 miles south of San Manuel at a fork in the graded road, zero trip meter and turn southwest on graded dirt road marked Redington Road.
1.2 ▲   Trail ends at junction with San Pedro River Road. Turn left for Mammoth, turn right for Benson.
          GPS: N32°27.09′ W110°29.22′

▼ 0.4   SO Graded road on right.
0.8 ▲   SO Graded road on left.

▼ 0.5   SO Cross through Edgar Canyon Wash; then cattle guard. Track on left after cattle guard.
0.7 ▲   SO Track on right, cattle guard; then cross through Edgar Canyon Wash.

Corral beside the trail

▼ 0.6   SO   Two tracks on right along pipeline.
0.6 ▲   SO   Two tracks on left along pipeline.

▼ 1.0   SO   Track on left.
0.2 ▲   SO   Track on right.

▼ 1.1   SO   Track on right.
0.1 ▲   SO   Track on left.

▼ 1.2   SO   South #32: Buehman Canyon Trail is on the right. Zero trip meter.
0.0 ▲   Continue to the north.
    GPS: N32°26.21' W110°29.80'

▼ 0.0   Continue to the south.
7.9 ▲   SO   South #32: Buehman Canyon Trail is on the left. Zero trip meter.

▼ 0.6   SO   Cross through wide wash.
7.3 ▲   SO   Cross through wide wash.

▼ 0.7   SO   Private road on left, track on right.
7.2 ▲   SO   Private road on right, track on left.
    GPS: N32°25.57' W110°29.96'

▼ 1.4   SO   Track on left.
6.5 ▲   SO   Track on right.

▼ 1.6   SO   Track on right.
6.3 ▲   SO   Track on left.

▼ 2.0   SO   Track on right.
5.9 ▲   SO   Track on left.

▼ 2.1   SO   Cattle guard.
5.8 ▲   SO   Cattle guard.

▼ 2.5   SO   Track on right.
5.4 ▲   SO   Track on left.

▼ 3.4   SO   Track on right.
4.5 ▲   SO   Track on left.

▼ 4.0   SO   Track on left.
3.9 ▲   SO   Track on right.

▼ 4.2   SO   Track on left.
3.7 ▲   SO   Track on right.

▼ 4.5   SO   Track on right.
3.4 ▲   SO   Track on left.
    GPS: N32°22.91' W110°31.14'

▼ 4.9   SO   Track on left.
3.0 ▲   SO   Track on right.

▼ 6.2   SO   Track on left and track on right.
1.7 ▲   SO   Track on right and track on left.

▼ 6.4   BR   Track on left followed by graded ranch road on left.
1.5 ▲   BL   Graded ranch road on right; then track on right.
    GPS: N32°21.31' W110°31.08'

▼ 6.7   SO   Cross through wash.
1.2 ▲   SO   Cross through wash.

▼ 7.0   SO   Track on right.
0.9 ▲   SO   Track on left.

▼ 7.5   SO   Track on right and track on left.
0.4 ▲   SO   Track on left and track on right.

▼ 7.8   SO   Cattle guard.
0.1 ▲   SO   Cattle guard.

▼ 7.9   SO   Track on right on saddle at left-hand bend is south end of South #32: Buehman Canyon Trail. There is a campsite on the junction and an old white sign warning, "Travel at own risk." Piety Hill is to the northwest. Zero trip meter.
0.0 ▲   Continue to the northeast.
    GPS: N32°20.89' W110°32.40'

▼ 0.0   Continue to the south.
3.6 ▲   Track on left on saddle at right-hand bend is south end of South #32: Buehman Canyon Trail. There is a campsite at the intersection and an old white sign warning, "Travel at own risk." Zero trip meter. Piety Hill is to the northwest.

▼ 0.5   SO   Cross through wash; then track on right.
3.1 ▲   SO   Track on left; then cross through wash.

The trail makes a gentle climb after a creek crossing

GPS: N32°20.45' W110°32.41'

▼ 0.7 SO Cross through wash, then cattle guard.

2.9 ▲ SO Cattle guard, then cross through wash.

▼ 0.9 SO Cross through Youtcy Canyon wash, ranch buildings and well on left, then cattle guard.

2.7 ▲ SO Cattle guard, ranch buildings and well on right, then cross through Youtcy Canyon wash.

GPS: N32°20.07' W110°32.35'

▼ 1.0 SO Track on left to ranch.

2.6 ▲ SO Track on right to ranch.

▼ 1.4 SO Track on left.

2.2 ▲ SO Track on right.

▼ 2.0 SO Cross through wash.

1.6 ▲ SO Cross through wash.

▼ 2.1 SO Track on right.

1.5 ▲ SO Track on left.

▼ 2.9 BR Well-used track on left.

0.7 ▲ BL Well-used track on right.

GPS: N32°18.80' W110°32.46'

▼ 3.4 SO Cross through wash.

0.2 ▲ SO Cross through wash.

▼ 3.6 SO Entering Coronado National Forest over cattle guard. Road is now designated FR 371. No forest boundary sign, just the route marker. Zero trip meter at cattle guard.

0.0 ▲ Continue into ranch lands.

GPS: N32°18.77' W110°33.14'

▼ 0.0 Continue into the Coronado National Forest.

2.7 ▲ SO Leaving Coronado National Forest over cattle guard. Zero trip meter.

▼ 0.5 SO Track on right is FR 4429.

South Trail #31: Redington Road

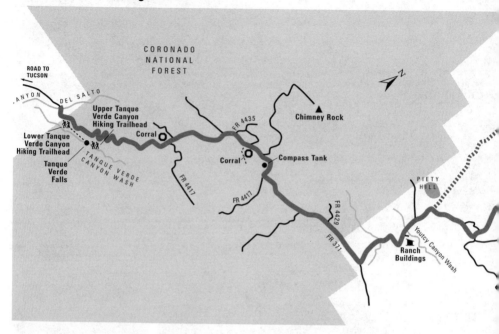

CORONADO NATIONAL FOREST		

ROAD TO TUCSON

CANYON DEL SALTO

Upper Tanque Verde Canyon Hiking Trailhead

Lower Tanque Verde Canyon Hiking Trailhead

Corral

Tanque Verde Falls

TANQUE VERDE CANYON WASH

FR 4417

FR 4435

FR 4417

Corral

Compass Tank

Chimney Rock

FR 4429

FR 311

PIETY HILL

Youtcy Canyon Wash

Ranch Buildings

2.2 ▲ SO Track on left is FR 4429.
GPS: N32°18.74' W110°33.71'

▼ 0.6 SO Track on left.
2.1 ▲ SO Track on right.

▼ 1.3 SO Track on left.
1.4 ▲ SO Track on right.

▼ 1.4 SO Track on right.
1.3 ▲ SO Track on left.
GPS: N32°18.38' W110°34.53'

▼ 1.6 SO Two tracks on left.
1.1 ▲ SO Two tracks on right.
GPS: N32°18.30' W110°34.72'

▼ 2.1 SO Campsite on left.
0.6 ▲ SO Campsite on right.

▼ 2.7 SO FR 4417 leaves over cattle guard on left immediately before a right-hand bend. Zero trip meter.
0.0 ▲ Continue to the east.
GPS: N32°18.13' W110°35.78'

▼ 0.0 Continue to the northwest.

0.8 ▲ FR 4417 leaves over cattle guard on right immediately after a left-hand bend. Zero trip meter.

▼ 0.1 SO Concrete tank on left.
0.7 ▲ SO Concrete tank on right.

▼ 0.4 SO Track on right, then cattle guard.
0.4 ▲ SO Cattle guard, then track on left.

▼ 0.8 SO Graded road on right goes to Chimney Rock. There is a small grass island in the middle of the intersection. Zero trip meter.
0.0 ▲ Continue to the east.
GPS: N32°18.41' W110°36.26'

▼ 0.0 Continue to the west.
2.7 ▲ SO Graded road on left goes to Chimney Rock. There is a small grass island in the middle of the intersection. Zero trip meter.

▼ 0.2 SO Track on right.
2.5 ▲ SO Track on left.

▼ 0.4 SO Corral on left followed by hiking and

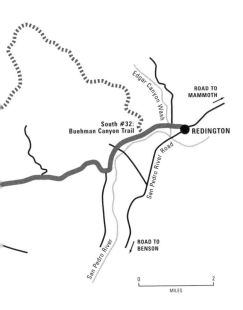

South #32:
Buehman Canyon Trail

Edgar Canyon Wash

ROAD TO
MAMMOTH

REDINGTON

San Pedro River Road

San Pedro River

ROAD TO
BENSON

0   2
MILES

pack trail through gate on left.

2.3 ▲   SO   Hiking and pack trail through gate on
right; then corral on right.
GPS: N32°18.20′ W110°36.71′

▼ 0.9   SO   Track on right is FR 4435, then cattle
guard.

1.8 ▲   SO   Cattle guard, then track on left is FR
4435.
GPS: N32°18.18′ W110°37.07′

▼ 1.2   SO   Track on right.

1.5 ▲   SO   Track on left.

▼ 2.3   SO   Track on right.

0.4 ▲   SO   Track on left.

▼ 2.7   SO   FR 4417 on left across cattle guard.
Track on right alongside corral. Zero
trip meter.

0.0 ▲   Continue to the north.
GPS: N32°16.90′ W110°37.96′

▼ 0.0   Continue to the south.

4.4 ▲   SO   Corral, then track on left alongside corral, FR 4417 on right. Zero trip meter.

▼ 0.2   SO   Cattle guard.

4.2 ▲   SO   Cattle guard.

▼ 3.0   SO   Upper Tanque Verde Canyon hiking trail
on left. Small parking areas on left and
right.

1.4 ▲   SO   Upper Tanque Verde Canyon hiking trail
on right. Small parking areas on left
and right.
GPS: N32°15.48′ W110°39.29′

▼ 3.6   SO   Lower Tanque Verde Canyon hiking
trail on left, goes 0.5 miles to Tanque
Verde Falls. Parking area on right.

0.8 ▲   SO   Lower Tanque Verde Canyon hiking
trail on right, goes 0.5 miles to Tanque
Verde Falls. Parking area on left.
GPS: N32°15.22′ W110°39.90′

▼ 3.9   SO   Leaving Coronado National Forest over
cattle guard.

0.5 ▲   SO   Entering Coronado National Forest over
cattle guard.
GPS: N32°15.20′ W110°40.10′

▼ 4.4   Trail ends at the start of the paved
road on the outskirts of Tucson, at the
crossing of Canyon del Salto. Continue
straight on along Redington Road for
Tucson.

0.0 ▲   To reach the trailhead, from the intersection of Houghton Road and Tanque
Verde Road in southeast Tucson, proceed east on Tanque Verde Road for
5.5 miles. The road changes to
Redington Road. The trail starts at the
intersection of Redington View Road
and Redington Road, immediately after
the road crosses over Canyon del
Salto. The road turns from paved to
gravel at this point.
GPS: N32°15.23′ W110°40.38′

Buehman Canyon Trail

STARTING POINT   South #31: Redington Road, 1.2 miles from the north end, 0.1 miles north of mile marker 26

FINISHING POINT   South #31: Redington Road, 0.2 miles southwest of mile marker 18

TOTAL MILEAGE	11.6 miles
UNPAVED MILEAGE	11.6 miles
Driving Time	2.5 hours
ELEVATION RANGE	3,000–4,200 feet
USUALLY OPEN	Year-round
BEST TIME TO TRAVEL	October to May
DIFFICULTY RATING	4
SCENIC RATING	8
REMOTENESS RATING	+0

Special Attractions

■ Pleasant, easy trail traversing a variety of scenery.

■ Lush and shady Buehman Canyon.

■ Steep climb out of Buehman Canyon.

Description

Buehman Canyon is one of the deep canyons that drains the east side of the Santa Catalina Mountains. The Buehman Canyon Trail leaves South #31: Redington Road and climbs up the open grassy ridge away from the San Pedro River. Initially the trail crosses private property; access is granted under the Sportsman-Landowners Respect Program. The trail is easygoing as it winds along a gravelly surface, passing stands of saguaro, prickly pear, palo verde, and the ubiquitous creosote bush. Farther along, the vegetation is open grassland studded with palmillas (soaptree yucca) and mesquite.

The trail drops gradually down toward the deep gash of Buehman Canyon, passing a large cristate saguaro near the bottom of the descent. Within the canyon the terrain is lush and shady. Large cottonwoods and sycamores provide shade, and there is water in the creek approximately six months of the year. As this is private property, access to the creek itself is restricted.

The 200 yards of bumpy river rock immediately before leaving Buehman Canyon are the lumpiest part of the trail. It then swings around and starts to climb steeply out of the canyon back toward South #31: Redington Road. The trail is steep and powdery as it climbs. Vehicles with less aggressive tires may spin wheels. It climbs quickly up a ridge giving excellent views over Buehman Canyon and the Santa Catalinas before continuing to undulate along a ridge with steep drops on either side. The trail then rejoins South #31: Redington Road near Piety Hill.

The trail is not shown in its entirety on the BLM map, but it is shown on the US Forest Service map, where it is marked as FR 654 and FR 801.

Current Road Information

Coronado National Forest
Santa Catalina Ranger District
5700 North Sabino Canyon Rd.
Tucson, AZ 85750
(520) 749-8700

Map References

BLM   Tucson
USFS   Coronado National Forest: Safford and Santa Catalina Ranger Districts
USGS   1:24,000   Redington, Buehman Canyon, Piety Hill
           1:100,000 Tucson
Maptech CD-ROM: Southeast Arizona/ Tucson
Arizona Atlas & Gazetteer, p. 67

Route Directions

▼ 0.0   Trail commences 1.2 miles from the north end of South #31: Redington Road. Zero trip meter and turn west on unmarked, well-used, formed trail. Immediately pass through a gate onto private property.

5.3 ▲   Trail ends on South #31: Redington Road, 1.2 miles from the north end of the trail. Turn left for San Manuel, turn right for Tucson via Redington Road.

GPS: N32°26.21' W110°29.80'

▼ 0.2   SO   Track on left.
5.1 ▲   SO   Track on right.

▼ 0.5   SO   Track on right.
4.8 ▲   SO   Track on left.

▼ 1.0   BR   Small track on left and small track ahead. Bear right, remaining on main trail.
4.3 ▲   BL   Small track on right and small track ahead. Bear left, remaining on main trail.

GPS: N32°26.23' W110°30.63'

▼ 1.2   SO   Cross through wash.
4.1 ▲   SO   Cross through wash.

▼ 1.3   SO   Track on right; then gate, entering state land. Permit required.
4.0 ▲   SO   Gate, entering private land; then track on left.

GPS: N32°26.42' W110°30.84'

▼ 1.7   SO   Cross through wash. Trail follows wash course, crossing it often for next 0.4 miles.
3.6 ▲   SO   Cross through wash.

▼ 2.1   SO   Leave wash course.
3.2 ▲   SO   Cross through wash. Trail follows wash course, crossing it often for the next 0.4 miles.

▼ 2.6   SO   Track on left.
2.7 ▲   SO   Track on right.

▼ 2.7   SO   Track on left.
2.6 ▲   SO   Track on right.

▼ 3.0   SO   Private road on left. Continue straight on, remaining on designated access route.
2.3 ▲   SO   Private road on right. Continue straight on, remaining on designated access route.

▼ 4.0   SO   Track on right.
1.3 ▲   SO   Track on left.

Looking down on the trail as it exits Buehman Canyon

Sycamore trees border the trail in Buehman Canyon

South Trail #32: Buehman Canyon Trail

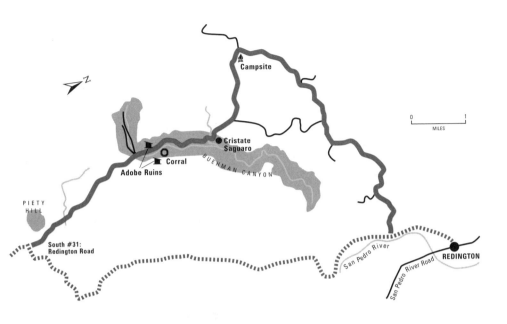

▼ 4.6   SO   Cattle guard. Entering private property on designated access route. Remain on main trail.

0.7 ▲   SO   Cattle guard. Entering state land.
         GPS: N32°25.64′ W110°33.62′

▼ 5.3   BL   Well-used track on right. Zero trip meter. Intersection is unmarked but there is a camping area just before it on the left. Trail ahead can be seen running around the hill on the left. Track on right drops down toward the canyon.

0.0 ▲   Continue to the north.
         GPS: N32°25.16′ W110°34.02′

▼ 0.0   Continue to the south.

3.5 ▲   BR   Well-used track on left. Zero trip meter. Intersection is unmarked but there is a camping area immediately after it on the right.

▼ 1.4   SO   Private road on left.

2.1 ▲   SO   Private road on right.

▼ 1.7   SO   Cattle guard.

1.8 ▲   SO   Cattle guard.

▼ 1.9   SO   Cristate saguaro on left.

1.6 ▲   SO   Cristate saguaro on right.
         GPS: N32°24.18′ W110°32.76′

▼ 2.0   SO   Cross through wash.

1.5 ▲   SO   Cross through wash.
         GPS: N32°24.19′ W110°32.95′

▼ 2.1   SO   Track on left is private. Road is now running alongside Buehman Canyon.

1.4 ▲   SO   Track on right is private.

▼ 2.6   SO   Track on right.

0.9 ▲   SO   Track on left.

▼ 2.8   SO   Track on right.

0.7 ▲   SO   Track on left.

▼ 2.9   SO   Corral on left.

0.6 ▲   SO   Corral on right.
         GPS: N32°23.38′ W110°33.05′

▼ 3.0   SO   Corner of adobe ruin on left; then pass

through gate. Old well on left. Second adobe ruin on right just off trail.

0.5 ▲   SO   Adobe ruin on left, pass through gate, well on right, followed by corner of adobe ruin on right.
GPS: N32°23.37' W110°32.99'

▼ 3.1   SO   Cross through wash; then track on right is foot access only.

0.4 ▲   SO   Track on left is foot access only; then cross through wash.

▼ 3.5   TL   Pass a small, square tank on the left, then turn sharp left past the tank onto trail leading steeply out of Buehman Canyon. There is a large tank in the trees at the intersection and a well-used track straight on and to the right. Zero trip meter.

0.0 ▲   Continue to the northeast.
GPS: N32°22.99' W110°33.08'

▼ 0.0   Continue to the south.

2.8 ▲   TR   Enter Buehman Canyon, continue straight on and pass a small, square tank on the right, then turn right down the wash. Zero trip meter. There is a large tank in the trees at the intersection and a track on the left and a track straight on.

▼ 0.8   SO   Top of climb.

2.0 ▲   SO   Start to descend toward Buehman Canyon.
GPS: N32°22.49' W110°32.98'

▼ 1.3   SO   Gate.
1.5 ▲   SO   Gate.

▼ 2.0   SO   Cross through wash.
0.8 ▲   SO   Cross through wash.

▼ 2.8   Trail ends at the junction of the graded dirt South #31: Redington Road. Turn left for Redington, turn right for Tucson.

0.0 ▲   Trail commences on the graded dirt South #31: Redington Road. Turn north on unmarked, well-used, formed trail. There is a campsite at the start and an old white sign warns, "Not a thru road." The turn is 0.2 miles southwest of mile marker 18. The track is not shown on the BLM map, but is shown as FR 801 on the forest map.
GPS: N32°20.89' W110°32.40'

Jackson Cabin Trail

STARTING POINT	Muleshoe Ranch Visitor Center
FINISHING POINT	Jackson Cabin
TOTAL MILEAGE	13.4 miles (one-way)
UNPAVED MILEAGE	13.4 miles (one-way)
DRIVING TIME	3.5 hours (one-way)
ELEVATION RANGE	4,200–4,800 feet
USUALLY OPEN	Year-round
BEST TIME TO TRAVEL	September to May
DIFFICULTY RATING	4
SCENIC RATING	9
REMOTENESS RATING	+0

Special Attractions

■ Historic cabins at Pride Ranch and Jackson Cabin.
■ Panoramic views of the Galiuro Mountains.
■ Wildlife viewing and bird watching.

History

The Muleshoe Ranch was not always the serene and peaceful desert oasis you see today. In its past were ruptured friendships, disagreements over ownership, and bloodshed.

The first owner of the ranch was supposedly Dr. Glendy King, who owned the hot springs (now known as Hooker Hot Springs) and the area immediately surrounding them. His nearest neighbors to the north were Melvin Jones and Ed Drew who ranched in the Bass Canyon area. Jones and Drew believed they were the legitimate owners of part of King's holdings. King, on the other hand, believed that Jones and Drew had simply annexed part of his ranch. In August 1884 the neighbors settled their dispute with gunfire, and Dr. King was killed.

In 1885, King's Ranch (minus the disputed section) was bought at auction by Colonel Hooker and added to his substantial Sierra Bonita holdings. Hooker was host to many visitors from the East, including Augustus Thomas, a famous American playwright, who subsequently based his leading characters of the stage play *Arizona* on Colonel Hooker and his daughter-in-law Forrestine. *Arizona* appeared on Broadway in 1889 and went on to become a novel and finally was the basis of the John Wayne movie *'Neath Arizona Skies* in 1934.

In the meantime, Ed Drew continued to ranch in Bass Canyon. His holdings were in his name alone now, because he had dissolved the partnership with Melvin Jones, feeling Jones was not living up to his side of the deal. Jones established his own ranch nearby. Ed Drew, originally from Montana, had moved to Arizona in 1873 with his parents, three brothers, and his sister, Cora, who happened to be an exceptional horsewoman. Cora's prowess later led her to be offered a place in Buffalo Bill Cody's Wild West Show, an offer her mother made her turn down, fearing it was not a suitable place for a girl of only sixteen. The Drews were active in the local area. Besides running the ranch, the youngest brother, David, ran a butcher shop in Willcox, selling meat from the family ranch. Ed was also a champion rodeo rider in Arizona for many years.

Life was hard and a little too exciting at times for the settlers of Muleshoe Ranch. Apaches were still active in the area, and they raided the settlers' cattle, on one occasion butchering them in sight of the house, and in 1886 attacking Melvin Jones's ranch close by.

In 1898 Sam and Johnny Boyett purchased the Drew Ranch and Ed Drew became the foreman of the Sierra Bonita. Later, he was elected sheriff of Graham County. He died in 1911 in a saloon gunfight.

Johnny Boyett took over as foreman of the Hot Springs Ranch in 1899, and in 1900, on

Jackson Cabin

The trail drops down into Sycamore Canyon

an Independence Day gathering in a Willcox saloon, he killed Warren Earp in a gunfight. Warren was one of the infamous Earp brothers, best known for their association with the rowdy town of Tombstone.

By 1930, the original Drew Ranch in Bass Canyon had been added to Colonel Hooker's ranch and the new expanded ranch was renamed the Muleshoe Ranch. In 1935 it was purchased by Mrs. Jessica MacMurray, who wanted the solitude that ranch life offered. She lived there with her long-time companion, Mrs. Patterson, for many years. One summer, Mrs. MacMurray toured Italy, giving her friend permission to build a small cottage on the grounds of the ranch. On her return she was horrified to find a massive stone lodge of ten rooms, a swimming pool, and private hot tubs. Mrs. Patterson was immediately ordered off the property, but to compensate for the building, she was given the deeds to the original Drew Ranch.

The Nature Conservancy now owns all the holdings of Muleshoe Ranch and the Drew Ranch. Encompassing 49,120 acres of land, the Muleshoe Ranch Cooperative Management Area is jointly owned by the Nature Conservancy, the U.S. Forest Service, and the Bureau of Land Management. Within the area are important riparian conservation areas, including seven permanently flowing streams.

Description

The historic Jackson Cabin is reached by 26 miles of graded dirt road, followed by a 14-mile, rough 4WD trail. The scenery around the beautiful Galiuro Mountains, combined with the lush riparian habitat, abundance of birds and wildlife, and many hiking trails, make the area well worth visiting. The trail crosses Muleshoe Ranch, now owned by the Arizona Nature Conservancy as well as the BLM and the U.S. Forest Service. It commences outside the gate of the Muleshoe Ranch Visitor Center. The visitor center is normally open from 9 to 5 daily and is well worth a visit to learn about the plants, birds, and wildlife of the area. There are also small casitas that can be rented by the night. Contact Muleshoe Ranch Cooperative Management Area by phone at 520-507-5229 or e-mail, muleshoe@tmc.org, for prices and bookings. The Hooker Hot Springs are available for use as well.

At the start of the trail is a trail log. All users are required to sign in and out. The trail leaves along a wash before climbing up onto a ridge. It undulates as a well-used, formed trail, with a loose, uneven surface. However, both the grades and the surface should be no trouble to any 4WD, SUV, or truck.

The section along the ridge top has one of the best views along the trail. The west face of the Galiuro Mountains rises abruptly from the valley floor. A short spur leads down to the remains of the Browning Ranch, set beside the Double R Canyon creek. A corral and a small adobe ruin remain. There are also two informal campsites with fire rings beside the creek. Other campsites, mainly for single vehicles, exist along the trail. There are other good camping places in Sycamore Canyon as well.

The Pride Ranch Cabin, which belongs to the Nature Conservancy, is a small brick, three-room cabin, with few facilities. It can also be rented in advance through the Muleshoe Ranch Cooperative Management Area for a nominal fee, but be aware that it is extremely primitive with very limited furniture and extremely basic facilities.

The latter part of the trail drops down into Sycamore Canyon and passes through a gap in the high, red walls before climbing out again and heading over a saddle for the final descent down to Jackson Cabin. The final part of the trail travels along a narrow, rough shelf road as it descends; this is possibly the trickiest part of the trail. The final 0.2 miles are slightly brushy as the trail runs along in the wash. But apart from this section there is little close brush along the trail.

The trail ends at the small stone and timber three-room Jackson Cabin sitting in a clearing in Jackson Canyon. Return to Muleshoe Ranch headquarters along the same road. Don't forget to sign out.

To reach Muleshoe Ranch from Willcox, get off I-10 at exit 340 and proceed to the south side of the highway. Immediately turn right (south) at the stop light on Bisbee Avenue and continue for 0.7 miles. Turn right (west) onto Airport Road. Continue straight on, the pavement runs out and the road is now the graded dirt Cascabel Road. Proceed for 14.1 miles and then bear right onto Muleshoe Road following the sign for Mule Shoe. Continue for 13.1 miles to the entrance to Muleshoe Ranch and then another 0.4 miles to the visitor center. The Hooker Hot Springs are for use by casita guests only. There are five casitas available for overnight stays. Pride Ranch Cabin is also available for overnight stays.

Current Road Information
Coronado National Forest
Santa Catalina Ranger District
5700 North Sabino Canyon Rd.
Tucson, AZ 85750
(520) 749-8700

Map References
BLM Tucson
USFS Coronado National Forest: Safford and Santa Catalina Ranger Districts
USGS 1:24,000 Hooker Hot Springs, Soza Mesa, Cherry Spring Peak
1:100,000 Tucson
Maptech CD-ROM: Southeast/Tucson
Arizona Atlas & Gazetteer, p. 68
Arizona Road & Recreation Atlas, pp. 54, 88

Route Directions

▼ 0.0 At the entrance to the Muleshoe Ranch HQ, zero trip meter and proceed north on formed trail, following the sign to Jackson Cabin. Immediately on the left is an information board and trail register. You must sign in and out of the area. Trail initially crosses private property.
GPS: N32°20.26′ W110°14.20′

▼ 0.5 SO Cross gas pipeline, foot access permitted on left along pipeline; then track on right.
▼ 0.8 SO Pass through fence line.
▼ 1.0 SO Cross through wash.
▼ 1.2 SO Pass through fence line.
▼ 1.4 SO Cross through wash, a tributary of Double R Canyon, then enter public land.
GPS: N32°21.35′ W110°14.28′

▼ 2.4 SO Cross through small wash.
▼ 2.9 SO Pass through fence line.
GPS: N32°22.11′ W110°15.00′

▼ 3.6 SO Track on right goes 0.2 miles to the remains of the Browning Ranch.
GPS: N32°22.74′ W110°15.09′

▼ 3.9 SO Entering private land.
GPS: N32°22.98′ W110°15.19′

▼ 5.4 SO Pass through fence line.
▼ 5.8 SO Track on right to well, track on left to Pride Ranch Cabin. Zero trip meter.
GPS: N32°24.16′ W110°16.21′

▼ 0.0 Continue to the north.
▼ 0.1 SO Second track on left to Pride Ranch Cabin.
▼ 0.2 SO Pass through fence line; then second cabin and windmill on left.
GPS: N32°24.30′ W110°16.27′

▼ 0.5 SO Entering public land.
GPS: N32°24.52′ W110°16.20′

▼ 0.7 SO Pass through fence line.
▼ 1.9 SO Cross through Swamp Springs Canyon wash, follow alongside wash.
GPS: N32°25.62′ W110°15.99′

▼ 2.0 SO Cross through wash.
▼ 2.3 SO Cross through wash, then climb away from wash.
▼ 2.4 SO Well and stone tank on right. Zero trip meter opposite well.
GPS: N32°26.00′ W110°16.16′

▼ 0.0 Continue to the northeast.

South Trail #33: Jacson Cabin Trail

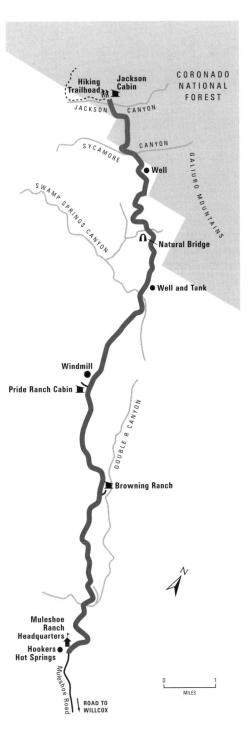

▼ 1.0 SO Natural bridge on left of trail, then pass through fence line.
GPS: N32°26.72′ W110°16.46′

▼ 1.3 SO Cross through wash.
GPS: N32°26.84′ W110°16.69′

▼ 1.8 SO Cross through wash and follow along-side it for next 0.2 miles.
▼ 2.6 SO Cross through wash.
▼ 3.0 SO Well on right; then cross through wash.
GPS: N32°27.53′ W110°17.29′

▼ 3.2 SO Cross through wash.
▼ 3.6 SO Entering Sycamore Canyon. Many campsites under the trees alongside the wash.
▼ 3.7 SO Cross through wash.
▼ 3.9 SO Cross through wash, then pass through fence line. Fence line is USFS boundary. Start to climb up to saddle.
GPS: N32°27.81′ W110°17.79′

▼ 4.5 SO Saddle. Jackson Cabin can be seen ahead down in Jackson Canyon. Trail descends shelf road down canyon.
GPS: N32°28.23′ W110°17.94′

▼ 5.1 SO End of shelf. Cross through wash; then hiking trails on left are West Divide Trail #289 and Powers Garden Trail #96.
GPS: N32°28.33′ W110°18.41′

▼ 5.2 Trail ends at Jackson Cabin. There is also a second stone shed and corrals on the left. There are some semi-shaded campsites at the end of the trail around the cabin.
GPS: N32°28.38′ W110°18.42′

Selected Further Reading

100 Desert Flowers of the Southwest. Tucson, Ariz.: Southwest Parks and Monuments Association, 1989.

Alden, Peter, and Peter Friederici. *National Audubon Society: Field Guide to the Southwestern States.* New York: Alfred A. Knopf, 1999.

Anderson, Dorothy Daniels. *Arizona Legends and Lore.* Phoenix: Golden West Publishers, 1991.

Arizona: A State Guide. New York: Hastings House, 1940.

Arizona: The Grand Canyon State. 2 vols. N.p.: Western States Historical Publishers, Inc., 1975

Ayer, Eleanor H. *Birds of Arizona.* Phoenix: Renaissance House Publishers, 1988.

Bahti, Tom, and Mark Bahti. *Southwestern Indian Tribes.* Las Vegas: KC Publications, 1997.

Barker, Scott. *Arizona off the Beaten Path.* Old Saybrook, Conn.: The Globe Pequot Press, 1996.

Barnes, Will C. *Arizona Place Names.* Tucson, Ariz.: The University of Arizona Press, 1988.

Bischoff, Mike. *Touring Arizona Hot Springs.* Helena, Mont.: Falcon Publishing, Inc., 1999.

Burke, Larry. *Arizona Boonies: The Arizona Even the Zonies Don't Know About.* Phoenix: Niche Publishing, 1998.

Chronic, Halka. *Roadside Geology of Arizona.* Missoula, Mont.: Mountain Press Publishing Company, 1983.

Cook, James E., Sam Negri, and Marshall Trimble. *Travel Arizona: The Back Roads.* 3rd ed. Edited by Dean Smith and Wesley Holden. Phoenix: Book Division of Arizona Highways Magazine, 1994.

Cowgill, Pete. *Back Roads and Beyond.* 2nd ed. Tucson, Ariz.: Broken Toe Press, 1997.

Cross, Jack L., Elizabeth H. Shaw, and Kathleen Scheifele, eds. *Arizona: Its People and Resources.* Tucson, Ariz.: the University of Arizona Press, 1960.

Crutchfield, James A. *It Happened in Arizona.* Helena, Mont.: Falcon Press Publishing Co., 1994.

Dale, Edward Everett. *The Indians of the Southwest.* London: University of Oklahoma Press, 1949.

Earle, W. Hubert *Cacti of the Southwest.* Phoenix: Arizona Cactus and Native Flora Society, Inc., 1963.

Epple, Anne Orth. *A Field Guide to the Plants of Arizona.* Helena, Mont.: Falcon, 1995.

Farrell, Robert J., and Bob Albano, eds. *Wild West Collections.* 4 vols. Phoenix: Book Division of Arizona Highways Magazine, 1997–99.

Fireman, Bert M. *Arizona: Historic Land.* New York: Alfred A. Knof, 1982.

Florin, Lambert. *Ghost Towns of the West.* New York: Promontory Press, 1993.

Granger, Byrd Howell, *Arizona's Names: X Marks the Place.* N.p.: Falconer Publishing Company, 1983.

Grubbs, Bruce. *Camping Arizona.* Helena, Mont.: Falcon Publishing, Inc., 1999.

Heatwole, Thelma. *Arizona off the Beaten Path!.* Phoenix: Golden West Publishers, 1982.

———. *Ghost Towns and Historical Haunts in Arizona.* Phoenix: Golden West Publishers, 1981.

Hernandez, Luis F. Aztlan: *The Southwest and Its Peoples.* Rochelle Park, N.J.: Hayden Book Company, Inc., 1975.

Hinton, Richard J. *The Handbook to Arizona: Its Resources, History, Towns, Mines, Ruins and*

Scenery. Tucson, Ariz.: Arizona Silhouettes, 1954.

Jaeger, Edmund C. *Desert Wildlife.* Stanford, Calif.: Stanford University Press, 1950.

Kosik, Fran. *Native Roads.* Tucson, Ariz.: Treasure Chest Books, 1996.

Lamb, Edgar, and Brian Lamb. *Pocket Encyclopedia of Cacti in Colour.* Revised ed. London: Blandford, 1969.

Lockwood, Frank C. *Pioneer Days in Arizona.* New York: The Macmillan Company, 1932.

———. *Thumbnail Sketches of Famous Arizona Desert Riders 1538–1946.* Tucson, Ariz.: University of Arizona, 1946.

Love, Frank. *Mining Camps and Ghost Towns.* N.p.: Westernlore Press, 1974.

Marks, Paula Mitchell. *And Die in the West.* New York: Simon and Schuster Inc., 1989.

Miller, Donald C. *Ghost Towns of the Southwest.* Boulder, Colo.: Pruett Publishing Company.

Mitchell, James R. *Gem Trails of Arizona.* Baldwin Park, Calif.: Gem Guides Book Co., 1995.

Morris, Eleanor, and Steve Cohen. *Adventure Guide to Arizona.* Edison, N. Jer.: Hunter Publishing, 1996.

Nash, Robert. *Encyclopedia of Western Lawmen and Outlaws.* New York: Da Capo Press, 1989.

O'Neal, Bill. *Encyclopedia of Western Gunfighters.* Norman, Okla.: University of Oklahoma Press, 1979.

Recreation Sites in Southwestern National Forests and Grasslands. N.p.: United States Department of Agriculture, n.d.

Schuler, Stanley, ed. *Simon and Schuster's guide to Cacti and Succulents.* New York: Simon and Schuster Inc., 1985.

Searchy, Paula. *Travel Arizona: The Scenic Byways.* Edited by Bob Albano, Evelyn Howell, and Laura A. Lawrie. Phoenix: Book Division of Arizona Highways Magazine, 1997.

Sheridan, Thomas E. *Arizona: A History.* London: The University of Arizona Press, 1995.

Sherman, James E., and Barbara H. Sherman.

Ghost Towns of Arizona. Norman, Okla.: University of Oklahoma Press, 1969.

Trimble, Marshall. *Arizona Adventure!.* Phoenix: Golden West Publishers, 1982.

———. *Roadside History of Arizona.* Missoula, Mont.: Mountain Press Publishing Company, 1986.

Varney, Philip. *Arizona Ghost Towns and Mining Camps.* Phoenix: Book Division of Arizona Highways Magazine, 1994.

———. *Arizona's Best Ghost Town.* Flagstaff, Ariz.: Northland Press, 1980.

Walker, Henry P., and Don Bufkin. *Historical Atlas of Arizona.* 2nd ed. London: University of Oklahoma Press, 1979.

Wagoner, Jay J. *Arizona's Heritage.* Salt Lake City: Peregrine Smith, Inc., 1977.

Wahmann, Russell. *Auto Road Log.* Cottonwood, Ariz.: Starlight Publishing, 1982.

Waldman, Carl. *Atlas of the North American Indian.* New York: Checkmark Books, 2000.

———. *Encyclopedia of Native American Tribes.* New York: Facts on File, 1988.

Ward, Geoffrey C. *The West: an Illustrated History.* Boston: Little, Brown and Company, 1996.

Warren, Scott S. *Exploring Arizona's Wild Areas.* Seattle: Mountaineers Books, 1996.

Wilderness and Primitive Areas in Southwestern National Forests. N.p.: United States Department of Agriculture, n.d.

Zauner, Phyllis. *Those Legendary Men of the Wild West.* Sacramento, Calif.: Zanel Publications, 1991.

Selected Web sources

Arizona-Sonora Desert Museum, http://www.desertmuseum.org/

Desert USA: http://www.desertusa.com

Ghosttowns.com: http://www.ghosttowns.com

GORP.com, http://gorp.away.com

National Center for Disease Control: Hantavirus Pulmonary Syndrome, http://www.cdc.gov/ncidad/diseases/hanta/hps/

The Nature Conservance, Muleshoe Ranch

Cooperative Management Area,
http://www.nature.org/wherewework/
northamerica/states/arizona/preserves/art1971
.html

U.S. Bureau of Land Management, Arizona:
http://www.blm.gov/az/

U.S. Forest Service, Southwestern Region
(Arizona): http://www.fs.fed.us/r3

Yuma, Arizona, Chamber of Commerce,
http://yumachamber.org

Yuma, Arizona, Convention and Visitors
Bureau, http://www.visityuma.com

About the Authors

Peter Massey grew up in the outback of Australia, where he acquired a life-long love of the backcountry. After retiring from a career in investment banking in 1986 at the age of thirty-five, he served as a director for a number of companies in the United States, the United Kingdom, and Australia. He moved to Colorado in 1993.

Jeanne Wilson was born and grew up in Maryland. After moving to New York City in 1980, she worked in advertising and public relations before moving to Colorado in 1993.

After traveling extensively in Australia, Europe, Asia, and Africa, the authors covered more than 80,000 miles touring the United States and the Australian outback between 1993 and 1997. This experience became the basis for creating the Backcountry Adventures and Trails guidebook series.

As the research team grew, a newcomer became a dedicated member of the Swagman team.

Angela Titus was born in Missouri and grew up in Virginia, where she attended the University of Virginia. She traveled extensively throughout the western states pursuing her interests in four-wheeling, hiking, and mountain biking. She moved to Alabama and worked for *Southern Living Magazine* traveling, photographing, and writing about the southeastern U.S. She moved to Colorado in 2002.

Since research for the Backcountry Adventures and Trails books began, Peter, Jeanne, and Angela have traveled more than 75,000 miles throughout the western states.

more
arizona trails
backroad guides

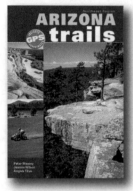

Arizona Trails–Northeast
This guidebook consists of meticulous details and directions for 47 trails located near the towns of Flagstaff, Williams, Prescott (northeast), Winslow, Fort Defiance and Window Rock.
ISBN 978-1-930193-02-4, Price $24.95

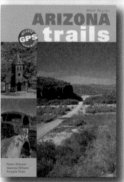

Arizona Trails–West
This volume consists of comprehensive statistics and descriptions for 33 trails located near the towns of Bullhead City, Lake Havasu City, Parker, Kingman, Prescott (west), and Quartzsite (north).
ISBN 978-1-930193-00-0, Price $24.95

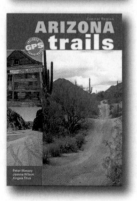

Arizona Trails–Central
This field guide includes meticulous trail details for 44 off-road routes located near the towns of Phoenix, Wickenburg, Quartzsite (south), Payson, Superior, Globe and Yuma (north). **ISBN 978-1-930193-01-7, Price $24.95**

california trails
backroad guides

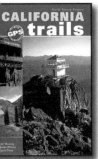
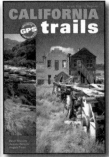

California Trails—Northern Sierra This book outlines detailed trail information for 55 off-road routes located near the towns of Sacramento (east), Red Bluff (east), Truckee, South Lake Tahoe, Sonora, Susanville, Chico, Oroville, Yuba City, Placerville, Stockton (east), Jackson, and Sonora. **ISBN 978-1-930193-23-9, Price $24.95**

California Trails—High Sierra This guidebook navigates and describes 50 trails located near the towns of Fresno (north), Oakhurst, Lone Pine, Bishop, Bridgeport, Coulterville, Mariposa, and Mammoth Lakes. **ISBN 978-1-930193-21-5, Price $24.95**

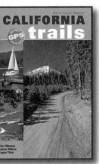
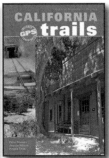

California Trails—North Coast This guide meticulously describes and rates 47 off-road routes located near the towns of Sacramento, Redding (west), Red Bluff, Clear Lake, McCloud, Mount Shasta, Yreka, Crescent City, and Fort Bidwell. **ISBN 978-1-930193-22-2, Price $24.95**

California Trails—Central Mountains This guide is comprised of painstaking detail and descriptions for 52 trails located near the towns of Big Sur, Fresno, San Luis Obispo, Santa Barbara, Bakersfield, Mojave, and Maricopa. **ISBN 978-1-930193-19-2, Price $24.95**

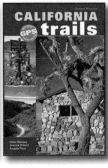

California Trails—South Coast This field guide includes meticulous trail details for 50 trails located near the towns of Los Angeles, San Bernardino, San Diego, Salton Sea, Indio, Borrego Springs, Ocotillo and Palo Verde. **ISBN 978-1-930193-24-6, Price $24.95**

California Trails—Desert This edition of our Trails series contains detailed trail information for 51 off-road routes located near the towns of Lone Pine (east), Panamint Springs, Death Valley area, Ridgecrest, Barstow, Baker and Blythe. **ISBN 978-1-930193-20-8, Price $24.95**

to order
call 800-660-5107 or
visit 4WDbooks.com

colorado trails
backroad guides

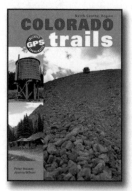

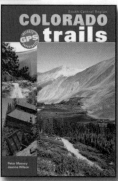

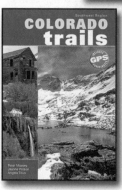

utah trails
backroad guides

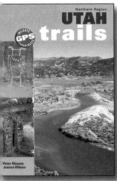

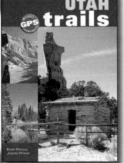

Utah Trails–Northern
This field guide includes meticulous trail details for 35 off-road routes near the towns of Vernal, Logan, Salt Lake City, Price, Wendover, Beaver, and Milford. **ISBN 978-1-930193-30-7, Price $19.95**

Utah Trails–Central
This volume is composed of comprehensive trail statistics for 34 trails near the towns of Green River, Richfield, Hanksville, Crescent Junction, and Castle Dale. **ISBN 978-1-930193-31-4, Price $19.95**

Utah Trails–Moab
This guidebook contains detailed trail information for 57 trails in and around Moab, Monticello, Canyonlands National Park, Arches National Park, Green River, Mexican Hat, Bluff, and Blanding. **ISBN 978-1-930193-09-3, Price $24.95**

Utah Trails–Southwest
This travel guide outlines detailed trail information for 49 off-road routes in the Four Corners region and around the towns of Escalante, St. George, Kanab, Boulder, Bryce Canyon, Hurricane, and Ticaboo. **ISBN 978-1-930193-10-9, Price $24.95**

backcountry adventures
guides

Each book in the award-winning *Adventures* series listed below is a beautifully crafted, high-quality, sewn, 4-color guidebook. In addition to meticulously detailed backcountry trail directions and maps of every trail and region, extensive information on the history of towns, ghost towns, and regional history is included. The guides provide wildlife information and photographs to help readers identify the great variety of native birds, plants, and animals they are likely to see. This series appeals to everyone who enjoys the backcountry: campers, anglers, four-wheelers, hikers, mountain bikers, snowmobilers, amateur prospectors, sightseers, and more...

Backcountry Adventures Northern California
Backcountry Adventures Northern California takes readers along 2,653 miles of back roads from the rugged peaks of the Sierra Nevada, through volcanic regions of the Modoc Plateau, to majestic coastal redwood forests. Trail history comes to life through accounts of outlaws like Black Bart; explorers like Ewing Young and James Beckwourth; and the biggest mass migration in America's history—the Gold Rush. Contains 152 trails, 640 pages, and 679 photos.
ISBN 978-1-930193-25-3, Price $39.95

Backcountry Adventures Southern California
Backcountry Adventures Southern California provides 2,970 miles of routes that travel through the beautiful mountain regions of Big Sur, across the arid Mojave Desert, and straight into the heart of the aptly named Death Valley. Trail history comes alive through the accounts of Spanish missionaries; eager prospectors looking to cash in during California's gold rush; and legends of lost mines. Contains 153 trails, 640 pages, and 645 photos.
ISBN 978-1-930193-26-0, Price $39.95

backcountry adventures
guides

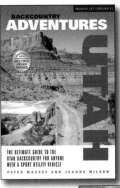

Backcountry Adventures Utah

Backcountry Adventures Utah navigates 3,721 miles through the spectacular Canyonlands region, to the top of the Uinta Range, across vast salt flats, and along trails unchanged since the riders of the Pony Express sped from station to station and daring young outlaws wreaked havoc on newly established stage lines, railroads, and frontier towns. Trail history comes to life through the accounts of outlaws like Butch Cassidy; explorers and mountain men; and early Mormon settlers. Contains 175 trails, 544 pages, and 532 photos.
ISBN 978-1-930193-27-7, Price $39.95

Backcountry Adventures Arizona

Backcountry Adventures Arizona guides readers along 2,671 miles of the state's most remote and scenic back roads, from the lowlands of the Yuma Desert to the high plains of the Kaibab Plateau. Trail history is colorized through the accounts of Indian warriors like Cochise and Geronimo; trailblazers; and the famous lawman Wyatt Earp. Contains 157 trails, 576 pages, and 524 photos.
ISBN 978-1-930193-28-4, Price, $39.95

4WD Adventures Colorado

4WD Adventures Colorado takes readers to the Crystal River or over America's highest pass road, Mosquito Pass. This book identifies numerous lost ghost towns that speckle Colorado's mountains. Trail history is brought to life through the accounts of sheriffs and gunslingers like Bat Masterson and Doc Holliday; millionaires like Horace Tabor; and American Indian warriors like Chief Ouray. ains 71 trails, 232 pages, and 209 photos.
ISBN 978-0-9665675-5-7, Price $29.95